AF478010

ANARCHISM TODAY

ANARCHISM TODAY

RANDALL AMSTER

Foreword by John Clark

PRAEGER

AN IMPRINT OF ABC-CLIO, LLC
Santa Barbara, California • Denver, Colorado • Oxford, England

Library of Congress Cataloging-in-Publication Data

Amster, Randall.
   Anarchism today / Randall Amster ; foreword by John Clark.
     p. cm.
   Includes bibliographical references and index.
   ISBN 978–0–313–39872–8 (cloth : alk. paper) — ISBN 978–0–313–39873–5 (ebook)
1. Anarchism. I. Title.
HX833.A47   2012
335′.83—dc23   2011046778

ISBN: 978–0–313–39872–8
EISBN: 978–0–313–39873–5

16 15 14 13 12   1 2 3 4 5

This book is also available on the World Wide Web as an eBook.
Visit www.abc-clio.com for details.

Praeger
An Imprint of ABC-CLIO, LLC

ABC-CLIO, LLC
130 Cremona Drive, P.O. Box 1911
Santa Barbara, California 93116-1911

This book is printed on acid-free paper ∞

Manufactured in the United States of America

For Arlo, a shining star, and Zeno, a natural-born anarchist . . .

Contents

Foreword

The best political works are those that are rooted most deeply in the truths of experience, maintaining their connection with the demands of the real lives of people and communities. Randall Amster's *Anarchism Today* is one of those works.

I first met Randall in September of 2005, shortly after Hurricane Katrina. My friend Leenie Halbert had just opened up her house as a center for relief activities. Volunteers—a spirited collection of anarchists, greens, friends, and neighbors—had spontaneously gathered, inspired in part by the anarchist-influenced Common Ground Collective that had organized a week before. Randall and a group of wonderful student volunteers from Prescott College appeared, and they immediately became an integral part of our small community.

Sometimes, in a period of severe crisis and great trauma, the desire for a better world is vividly awakened. Sometimes, it impels people to begin to create that better world, here and now, in the midst of the crisis. This is what Rebecca Solnit writes about beautifully in her excellent book *A Paradise Built in Hell*.[1] It seems to me that this was very much what occurred in our little solidarity community. I think that we had the good fortune, in those difficult times, to experience vividly some of the most basic things that anarchist community is all about.

A reporter from the New York daily *Newsday* wrote an article entitled "On a Street Named Desire" about our work.[2] He described our group as "people who believe in do-it-yourself action within small groups," who wanted to "feed the hungry and bring water to the thirsty, to fix the broken homes of the neighbors and to offer a sense of community in their deserted streets." As Leenie explained it, "I just wanted to bring love back to my neighborhood."

To me, all this expresses perfectly the spirit of anarchism, a spirit that is also conveyed eloquently in Randall Amster's book. He says, at one point, in a wonderfully revealing passage, "I truly love anarchism in the same way that I love humankind." I find this to be very moving and inspiring. What is our political practice really about? We are fortunate, indeed, if we can say that it is above all a way of loving people, and loving the earth. Ideally, this is what our life's work should be about. This is the meaning of "right livelihood," and it also describes the goal of an anarchist community.

Certain transformative experiences have the potential to become the models by which to judge the rest of our lives. We can come to learn that an anarchist life means, at least in part, overcoming the devastating and demoralizing instrumentalization of our lives by the system of domination. One of our great musical geniuses, Dr. John, wrote a famous song entitled "Right Place, Wrong Time." We all know the experience. To live an anarchist life means that, at least part of the time, as in our experience "On A Street Named Desire," we can have a sense of being in exactly the right place, doing exactly the right thing, at exactly the right time. And it means looking forward to, and striving for, a day when this is what everyone's everyday life will be like.

Strangely, many discussions of anarchism, including some of the most technically competent ones, fail to focus on what is most basic, most meaningful, and most compelling about anarchism. A great strength of Randall's book is that he continually brings us back to these basics. He reminds the reader that anarchism is not a collection of abstract hypotheses about the state or other theoretical questions, but rather "a sensibility, a way of being in the world, an ethos, a vision, a cosmology." It's an all-encompassing mode of thought and practice. It's a way of experiencing the world and living in the world, and specifically, a way of being-together in the world and being-together with the world.

Randall gets exactly to the point in proclaiming that anarchism is about "reclaiming our essential humanity" and "our innate conviviality." Anarchism is not, contrary to a common criticism, a naive belief in the "essential goodness" of everyone. However, it is a belief that as malleable as human beings may be, there are certain realities rooted deeply in our evolutionary heritage and our social history upon which we can draw in our pursuit of a world of mutual aid and solidarity. Tibetans call this reservoir of goodness *Lha*, the beneficent spirit within each person. Many other traditions have similar concepts. But contemporary researchers such as Michael Tomasello have also demonstrated, in experiments showing that infants and young children exhibit spontaneous altruism, that these realities are empirically verifiable.[3] There is a material basis for solidarity!

It has been popular recently to describe anarchist projects as "prefigurative," a term that is often explained by using the Gandhian injunction (perhaps never actually uttered by Gandhi) to "be the change you want to see." But despite all the talk about pre-figuring, for anarchists the "be" is always more important than the "pre." As Randall stresses again and again in this book, anarchism is above all about realizing the free community *here and now*. As he notes, "Anarchy is everywhere." This has always been a major theme in anarchist thought, from Reclus's and Kropotkin's classic works on the ubiquity of mutual aid in human history and nature to Colin Ward's recent accounts of "anarchy in action."

In *Anarchism Today*, we find several long lists of a multitude of forms of anarchist organization that are going on right now. These lists convey an idea of the vast scope of anarchist activity, as well as of the very specific ways in which a new world really is being created within the shell of the old. There is no need to repeat the lists, since you are about to read the book. The important thing to note is that they depict the development of a many-sided project of social transformation. Randall shows that contemporary anarchism is a very practical effort that takes on (to summarize briefly a vast project) the creation of a new ethos, a new counter-ideology, a new social imaginary, and new forms of organization, all of which add up a new world of free, cooperative communities.

This relates to another of Randall's pervasive themes. He rightly places enormous emphasis on the importance of *direct action* in anarchism. A major issue in contemporary left theory has been the "Problem of the Act." This preoccupation is a reaction to the decline of truly radical and revolutionary left movements across the globe, as well as to the seeming lack of any will to fundamentally challenge the system of domination. In the context of a demoralized and immobilized left, we can only conclude, as this book attests to, that contemporary anarchism is where the action is—where the potential for "the Act" really lies—today. Randall conveys very well the fact that the contemporary anarchist milieu is unusual in being to a great degree the locus of "spaces of hope." We might say more anarchistically that it generates very vital, concrete, and localized *places of hope*. It is a community that still has a sense of the possible and is in the process of making the possible actual.

Finally, Randall signals something absolutely crucial about anarchism when he notes that "both our fulfillment and our salvation" depend on our creating the new world of free community and solidarity. In an age of disastrously disruptive climate change and of the looming catastrophe of the Sixth Great Mass Extinction in the history of life on earth, talk of survival is not misplaced. The almost unthinkable tragedy today is that at the same time that we have the means for abundance and for the flourishing of persons and communities across the planet, we are faced with the specter of global collapse. In an age that is dominated by cynicism and resignation, anarchism is almost alone among contemporary political ideologies in reminding us that we humans are extraordinary beings who are still capable of great things. We can not only survive but thrive! For anarchism, "our fulfillment and our salvation" are integral to one another.

Anarchism Today is, on one level, a miniencyclopedia of recent anarchist thought and practice, and it will be highly useful in filling in any of the reader's anarchological gaps. But even more significantly, this work is a testimony to the enduring spirit of anarchism and an expression of its living reality today.

John Clark
Loyola University, New Orleans

Preface

How exactly does one approach a topic as vast and diverse as *anarchism today*? Perhaps the starting point should be anarchism's resurgence in the academy as a topic of cutting-edge scholarship and dynamic pedagogy. Or maybe the framing should devolve upon radical street-level activism and its penchant for "smashing" the symbols of empire and oppression. Still further on, the focus might be on the shadowy and multifarious "liberation"-type movements that broach the edge of "terrorism" through acts of spectacular sabotage. Or we could swing the pendulum entirely in the other direction and frame the subject around the pacific adherents practicing non-violent organizing, community empowerment, and back-to-the-earth ethics.

In each case, we would likely find as many people alienated by the formulation as those applauding it. With a subject as broad and inherently pluralistic as anarchism, any of these entry points would reflect something of an accurate rendering yet would likewise skew the ensuing discussion in ways that could delimit the scope of inquiry. Anarchism is, after all, a set of tenets linked by the basic premise of "no gods and no masters," meaning that none should dominate another and that social structures built upon hierarchies are necessarily unjust. This ethos extends to the mapping of anarchism itself, and thus on a practical level no one can properly claim priority in determining precisely what anarchism is or what makes someone an anarchist.

This may well be a virtue for dynamic organizing and theorizing, but it makes any attempt to deliver an authoritative work on the subject highly problematic if not outright untenable. This opening disclaimer, then, is not of the usual sort where the author merely defines the terms of engagement and nobly accepts blame for any shortcomings or deficiencies. The tack here is even more basic and is conditioned by the nature of the topic itself. Anarchism simply is not susceptible to any unitary definition that would make it truly possible to depict and analyze fully how it functions and what it means in a contemporary context. All that can be presented here is one person's take on anarchism, and no claim is made to speak for or on behalf of any other constituency beyond the impressions of a single individual—namely, me.

This too might be problematic, except that it comports with anarchism's foundational values of autonomy and self-realization. While taking its initial inspiration from the rejection of external rule (*anarchy* is literally "not *archy*" from the Greek, meaning "no rule" or "no government"), anarchism has tenuously come to discover that this also implies a number of proactive corollaries. If there is to be no hierarchical rule, then does that mean no rule at all? If power in its dominator sense is rejected, are all forms of power likewise to be forsworn? If centralized modes of organizing are seen as unworkable and illegitimate, does this imply that anarchists are thus inherently disorganized? In grappling with these basic questions of human interaction and exchange, the contemporary anarchist milieu (if it can be said to cohere around any set of principles at all) might plausibly be taken as the collective and sometimes fragmented attempt to define what an anarchistic version of *society* (viz., governance, power, and organization) looks like beyond the mere rejection of the dominant forms in place today.

This notion will serve as the primary point of departure for this work. There are myriad texts available on what anarchists have stood against, but less so focusing on what anarchists are actually *for*. Anarchists today still by necessity struggle against oppression and injustice, but they are equally if not more concerned with what alternative models might look like in actual practice. In this manner, anarchism can be seen both as a set of tactics for challenging authority and as a working vision of a better world that is always in the offing. Anarchism is, in short, both a means *and* an end, and it is uniquely comfortable engaging at levels ranging from the intensely pragmatic (e.g., deciding how the dishes are to get done) to the quixotically utopian (e.g., modeling what life might be like "after the revolution"). Viewed through this lens, anarchism is more than merely a political theory: it is a sensibility, a way of being in the world, an ethos, a vision, a cosmology. It is, at the end of the day, a doctrine with only one rule: *no rules*.

Having said this, I do not plan here to hedge and vacillate throughout the course of this text. I will tell you what I think anarchism is—informed by the views and practices of others, to be sure—and no more nor less than that. I do consider myself an anarchist, although as in all cases the moniker is surely self-ascribed, and I readily acknowledge at the outset that there are myriad ways in which my actual life falls short of being truly anarchistic. Still, it has been an active identity construction and intellectual driving force in my life for nearly two decades. While I came to anarchism a bit later in life, having traversed a circuitous path to get there, I nonetheless have found in its discovery some sense of the ideological and practical home that I had spent many years seeking. I suppose you might say that I am something of a "true believer"—which of course is the worst sort, and yet it has served me well over the years.

Even more to the point, you might say that I truly love anarchism in the same way that I love humankind—and likewise struggle with the reality that anarchists in particular (much like people in general) frequently leave much to be desired. For instance, oftentimes there is great infighting over location in the larger movement, with some factions being denigrated as mere "lifestyle anarchists" and others dismissed as detached "anarchist academics." Some of this tension is subsumed by the supposed distinction between *anarchy* (i.e., the lived practice or condition of existence) and *anarchism* (i.e., the study and/or production of a political philosophy), as if the two spheres were not always already interrelated. Similarly, great internal rifts often develop over tactics and strategies for resisting oppression and promoting change, with certain sectors claiming the mantle of being "authentic" anarchists either due to their professed militancy or their adherence to non-violence, as the case may be. Other key schisms to be explored in the milieu include those centered on geography (e.g., the global north versus the global south), temporality (e.g., longing for a bygone "golden age" versus prefiguring the future society), and spirituality (e.g., a "no gods" atheism versus a "god is everything" pantheism).

In each case, the banner of anarchism can be claimed with sound historical and contemporary support. What I intend here is a synthetic view that highlights the common ground among these varying strands of anarchism as they exist today, embracing a perspective that is sometimes referred to as "anarchism without adjectives" to indicate its integrative spirit. I begin with an introduction to anarchism and an exploration of its unlikely resurgence in recent years. Next, in Chapter One, I analyze anarchism as a viable and cohesive political theory that has been steadily gaining traction in academia and beyond. In Chapter Two, I consider the concomitant rise of anarchism as an action-oriented set of principles that has figured prominently in recent social and environmental movements. Chapter Three reflects on the complex (and sometimes litmus-test) question of anarchism's association with the use of *violence* as a tactic for change, and in Chapter Four I turn specifically to anarchism's relationship to ecology and its direct engagement with the pressing environmental issues of our time.

In Chapter Five, I explore the challenge of resolving individual liberty and social organization, looking at some of the unique ways that anarchists have navigated this profound sociopolitical question. Extending this analysis, the issue of how to reconcile highly localized efforts with global consciousness and praxis is explored in Chapter Six. One of the pieces of the puzzle that is often omitted in analyzing radical political theories or underground sub-cultures is an actual assessment of their efficacy and utility, which I undertake here in Chapter Seven. Does anarchism work in theory or practice? What would an anarchist society look like in actuality, and how do anarchists manage the major issues of our time, from war and climate change to crime and the economy? Does anarchism require at the outset that we alter our view of human nature, or would people living in anarchist societies simply change for the better over time? Embracing these queries, I will assess anarchism's successes and failures, its triumphs and pitfalls, in an effort to promote more of the former by realistically engaging the latter.

These culminating insights will inform the concluding chapter on "future visions," and they will in turn raise additional questions in the process. Exploring anarchism's potential as a tool for navigating social and environmental issues promises to convey a sense of its singular status—it is a set of theoretical and pragmatic principles seeking to connect the past, present, and future, while simultaneously striving to synthesize conceptions of the self, society, and nature. In so doing, we will highlight anarchism's mutualistic spirit of process and result, means and ends, action and vision—finding at every turn an emergent contemporary anarchism that is at once critical and affirmative, equal parts contestation and construction. While this integrative spirit in itself is noteworthy among sociopolitical theories, more to the point is anarchism's inherent capacity to point us unflinchingly toward the pervasive sense of crisis and opportunity that defines the modern world. In the end, this may well be our essential human task—regardless of whether we identify as anarchists—as we meet the challenges rapidly unfolding in our collective midst.

Acknowledgments

This book could not have been written without the support of my family, first and foremost. Only those who live with the author truly share in the full dimensions of the "labor of love" that it takes to complete a project such as this. The combination of empathy, stimulation, and forbearance evidenced by those closest to us makes the work possible as a technical matter but even more broadly provides the *raison d'être* for doing it in the first place.

Over the years that I have been studying and (hopefully) practicing anarchism, innumerable colleagues and friends have engaged in mutual dialogue, scholarship, and activism that have greatly informed my understanding of the subject. From my earliest proto-anarchistic musings to contemporary pursuits, these bright lights have figured prominently in my development not only as an anarchist but as a human being. Listing any of them only increases the likelihood that some will be omitted, yet I wish to express particular thanks to Pat Lauderdale, Luis Fernandez, Gabriel Kuhn, Pancho Ramos Stierle, Joel Olson, Emily Gaarder, Jeff Ferrell, Geoff Boyce, Sarah Launius, Matt Meyer, Uri Gordon, Vikki Law, John Clark, and especially Leenie Halbert (without whom this project would not have been possible) for their insights, encouragements, and provocations over the years.

Gabriel Kuhn in particular has been a valued colleague and friend, and his incisive reading of the manuscript as it was being produced yielded many critical points of reflection and positive amendments, for which I am beyond grateful. Luis Fernandez has likewise been a dear friend and fellow agitator, and he has served as an essential sounding board for many of the key concepts developed in this text. I also want to convey my profound appreciation to John Clark, for his pioneering and prolific work in the field, and for graciously agreeing to write the Foreword to this volume. A debt of gratitude is owed to the Interlibrary Loan department at Prescott College, which helped me to secure access to many of the foundational texts cited in this volume. As well, the editors at Praeger/ABC-CLIO were enormously helpful at every turn and provided gentle guidance throughout the entire process.

Many of the central arguments presented here have been incubated over nearly two decades, including the seeds of concepts that have appeared in journals including *Anarchist Studies*, *Peace Review*, and *Contemporary Justice Review*. Additionally, a number of these foundational ideas were presented (and refined) in workshops at venues including the Mondragon Bookstore and Coffeehouse (Winnipeg, Manitoba), the Metta Center for Nonviolence (Berkeley, California), and the Local to Global Justice Teach-In (Tempe, Arizona). As always, any errata, misconceptions, or inconsistencies are solely the author's doing—except those that are the unconscious products of living in a dehumanizing and rapidly degrading world. It is to confront and alter these dominant trends that I gladly share this work with you.

Randall Amster
Oikos Homestead, Arizona
September 2011

The Resurgence of Anarchism

In recent years, anarchism has enjoyed a resurgence among activists and academics alike, influencing many of the major social movements of the last generation. It is by now taken as indisputable that the world has witnessed "the re-emergence of anarchism as a political movement with a corresponding outpouring of academic and movement literature."[1] At the same time, anarchism has become increasingly caricatured as naively incoherent in mainstream depictions and as violently terroristic by law enforcement entities. Whatever view one takes, the present reinvigoration of anarchist theory and practice is undeniable, and thus it merits the attention of anyone interested in the pursuit of social and environmental justice.

Roots and Rekindling

In arguing that anarchism is resurgent, it is necessarily implied that it has previously surged in other eras. Indeed, the history of anarchism is a rich one filled with myriad ebbs and flows, with the earliest underpinnings of the philosophy often attributed to schools of thought as diverse as Lao-Tzu's Taoism in China (circa sixth century BCE) and Zeno of Citium's founding of Stoicism in ancient Greece (circa 300 BCE). Anarchism's more recognizable roots are generally fixed with the publication of William Godwin's two-volume treatise *Enquiry Concerning Political Justice and Its Influence on Morals and Happiness* in 1793, which "may be considered the starting point of modern anarchist thought."[2] By arguing against the privations of government and religion and for cooperation and the public good, "Godwin's status in anarchist thought is similar to that of Beethoven's in music—he summed up all that had come before him and foreshadowed all that was to come after."[3] Yet Godwin never used the word *anarchy* except in pejorative terms as synonymous with *disorder*, leaving it to Pierre-Joseph Proudhon to coin the term in its modern sense as a non-governmental state of social order in his famous 1840 essay, "What is Property?"

The ensuing decades represented something of a heyday for anarchism and comprise what is today known as its "classical" period. The work of writers including Max Stirner, Josiah Warren, Michael Bakunin, Elisée Reclus, Peter Kropotkin, Errico Malatesta, Voltairine de Cleyre, and Emma Goldman, among many others, not only helped to develop an emerging anarchist canon but also fostered an action-oriented perspective that made anarchism one of the most influential strands of social movement culture in the decades immediately before and after the turn of the twentieth century. There are many outstanding histories of anarchism available, and I will not recapitulate the narrative here since my focus is on the present anarchist milieu.[4] Two formulations from the classical era, however, stand out as particularly relevant to understanding anarchism today. The first is Kropotkin's entry on "Anarchism" for the 1910 edition of *The Encyclopedia Britannica*, in which he described

> harmony in such a society being obtained, not by submission to law, or by obedience to any authority, but by free agreements. . . . In a society developed on these lines, the voluntary associations which already now begin to cover all the fields of human activity would take a still greater extension so as to substitute themselves for the state in all its functions. They would represent an interwoven network, composed of an infinite variety of groups and federations of all sizes and degrees, local, regional, national and international—temporary or more or less permanent—for all possible purposes: production, consumption and exchange, communications, sanitary arrangements, education, mutual protection, defense of the territory. . . . Such a society would represent nothing immutable. On the contrary—as is seen in organic life at large—harmony would (it is contended) result from an ever-changing adjustment and readjustment of equilibrium between the multitudes of forces and influences, and this adjustment would be the easier to obtain as none of the forces would enjoy a special protection from the state.[5]

In this early vision, Kropotkin anticipates a networked globe, the decline of influence of nation-states, and an organic quality of human existence that mirrors patterns in nature as depicted by modern ecology.

As he prophetically concluded, "the anarchists recognize that, like all evolution in nature, the slow evolution of society is followed from time to time by periods of accelerated evolution which are called revolutions; and they think that the era of revolutions is not yet closed."[6] In a similar spirit that speaks directly to many of the sensibilities maintained by contemporary anarchists, Emma Goldman observed in 1927 that anarchism

> really stands for the liberation of the human mind from the dominion of religion; the liberation of the human body from the dominion of property; liberation from the shackles and restraint of government. Anarchism stands for a social order based on the free grouping of individuals for the purpose of producing real social wealth; an order that will guarantee to every human being free access to the earth and full enjoyment of the necessities of life, according to individual desires, tastes, and inclinations. . . . It is a living force in the affairs of our life, constantly creating new conditions. The methods of Anarchism therefore do not comprise an iron-clad program to be carried out under all circumstances. Methods must grow out of the economic needs of each place and clime, and of the intellectual and temperamental requirements of the individual. . . . Anarchism does not stand for military drill and uniformity; it does, however, stand for the spirit of revolt, in whatever form, against everything that hinders human growth. . . . Anarchism therefore stands for direct action, the open defiance of, and resistance to, all laws and restrictions, economic, social, and moral. . . . In short, it calls for free, independent spirits.[7]

Here again we see the seeds of a dynamic, localized, individualized, and comprehensive definition of anarchism that resonates deeply with the succeeding versions that have been developed by contemporary theorists and practitioners alike.

The classical era likewise was defined not only by theoretical evolutions but also by a number of pragmatic successes, including the anarchist-influenced workers' rights movements that sought to establish labor equity and at least a semblance of economic justice at the dawn of the industrial age. Yet despite this—or perhaps due to it—the era was also characterized by harsh repression oftentimes openly aimed at radicals in general and anarchists in particular, such as the execution of anarchist immigrants Sacco and Vanzetti and the wholesale deportation from the United States of ostensible anarchists, including Goldman herself. These patterns of repression continued into the Red Scare years of the 1950s and were at least partly responsible for the waning influence of anarchism both in America and worldwide. The social movements of the 1960s rekindled the anarchist sensibility to an extent, although they did so at times more implicitly than explicitly, and the subsequent decades yielded another downturn in overt anarchist organizing.[8]

Anarchy Ascending

And then all of this changed, seemingly overnight, with the prominent role played by anarchists in the late-1999 protests against the World Trade Organization (WTO) in Seattle. To be sure, there were many anarchist antecedents to this uprising, including the Zapatistas in Chiapas, Mexico and various autonomist actions in Europe in which anarchists played a key part.[9] There had even been a systematic treatment of *African Anarchism*, documenting its pervasiveness as a "way of life" across the continent, published two years prior to Seattle.[10] But the announcement to the world—through the graphic and sensationalized smashing of a few corporate windows that was replayed in the media after the demonstrations—of the presence of mysterious, black-clad, street-fighting anarchists was undeniably a watershed moment in the history of anarchism, and it ushered in the era of contemporary activism and theorizing.

As would soon be discovered, the presence of anarchists in what came to be termed the "anti-globalization movement" was far more extensive than just a small number of individuals engaged in property destruction. Anarchist organizing techniques and critiques of capital and the state had seemingly infused the entire ethos of the movement—from affinity groups and participatory decision-making processes to expressions of global solidarity in the face of corporate hegemony. As Luis Fernandez has discerned, "anarchism is a basic common philosophy of the movement," a notion affirmed by Süreyyya Evren in the observation that "anarchism is widely accepted as 'the' movement behind the main organizational principles of the radical social movements in the twenty-first century."[11] As such, Uri Gordon likewise describes a "full-blown anarchist revival [that] reached critical mass around the turn of the Millennium," leading Crispin Sartwell to conclude that "anarchism is more vital now than at any time since the early twentieth century."[12]

Thus, if we are to believe the press clippings, a dynamic quasi-revolution was born in late 1999. "Seattle was a once-in-a-lifetime, world-changing event. It energized a whole new movement, radicalized thousands of new activists, and opened a whole new chapter in the history of resistance to corporate globalization."[13] "WTO week in Seattle was a global tailspin at the end of the century, a fly in the face of the new millennium, an elephant in the ointment. It was an unruly uprising of the masses, a divine intervention, a traffic nightmare, a human rights activist's dream."[14] Yet even sympathetic observers were concerned that "what the media reflected back to us was a culture of hatred and stupidity in which none of us could recognize ourselves.... The answers all came down to a televised continuous cartoon loop of property damage. A broken window became more profound, more telling, more compelling, more valuable than all of us put together."[15] Nevertheless, these nascent critiques still acknowledged the double-edged nature of spectacular episodes of property destruction, wondering: "Would the WTO protests have received as much worldwide attention if anarchists hadn't done their thing in Seattle and if the media hadn't focused on it?"[16] As Teoman Gee more bluntly surmised: "If the image of the dangerous, masked, black-clad, and violent anarchist had been completely absent from the corporate media, Seattle might never have born any new anarchism."[17]

Further defending the role of anarchists and their millennial pronouncement of "Hello, we exist!" David Graeber noted in 2002 that

> after two years of increasingly militant direct action, it is still impossible to produce a single example of anyone to whom a US activist has caused physical injury.... [Anarchists have been] attempting to invent a "new language" of civil disobedience, combining elements of street theatre, festival and what can only be called non-violent warfare—non-violent in the sense adopted by, say, Black Bloc anarchists, in that it eschews any direct physical harm to human beings.[18]

As Starhawk explained in her 2002 first-person chronicle, the Black Bloc "have perfected the art of looking like archetypal Anarchists ... but in reality, they have clear principles [and] consider themselves to be acting protectively toward other demonstrators."[19] Jeff Ferrell, writing in 2001, likewise evidenced an empathetic perspective on these matters. Affirming Bakunin's dictum that "the destructive urge is a creative urge, too," Ferrell maintained that

> the destruction launched by these groups aims directly at restoring humanity, human relations, and human communities, not at destroying them. It suggests that one way to disentangle the dehumanizing conflation of property and people, to confront the

confusion of consumption with community, to dismantle the hierarchy of commodification by which law and property stand above
people and places, is to assiduously destroy the former while affirming the latter.[20]

Ferrell specifically sought to cast the sudden tangible presence of anarchists in American political life in terms of the history that enabled it:

In confronting authority in all of its manifestations, anarchists have
for centuries fought not just the attempts by outside authorities to
control shared public space, but also the insidious encoding of
authoritarian arrangements in public life itself. In embracing instead
autonomy, spontaneity, and playful uncertainty, anarchists have
long sought to unleash these unregulated dynamics in the spaces of
everyday life, and to build emergent communities out of their
confluence.[21]

In his exposition, Ferrell took pains to develop a synchronous vision of
historical and contemporary anarchist attributes including a "do-it-
yourself" ethic and spontaneous "cultural self-invention," and in so
doing demonstrated that modern anarchism was not merely confined to
large-scale demonstrations—exemplified by his invocation of homeless
advocates, graffiti artists, skate punks, anarchist biker gangs, pirate radio
stations, BASE jumpers, Critical Mass bicyclists, and "buskers" as exemplars of the practice.[22]

Taken together, these real-time analyses depicted a burgeoning global
movement grounded in local struggles for which "anarchism is the
heart . . . its soul; the source of most of what's new and hopeful about
it."[23] Despite critics' allegations of a contemporary anarchist movement
lacking ideological coherence and moral centering, the movement "is
not opposed to organization. It is about creating new forms of organization. It is not lacking in ideology. Those new forms of organization are
its ideology. It is about creating and enacting horizontal networks instead
of top-down structures like states, parties or corporations; networks
based on principles of decentralized, non-hierarchical consensus democracy."[24] Following the initial momentum coming out of Seattle, the task
before anarchists was seemingly to elaborate upon this vision of what a
decentralized network of autonomous communities might look like in
actual practice. Then again, anarchists historically have avoided specific
blueprints on the theory that such are likely to become new regimes of
authoritarian control, instead favoring emerging designs in which the

means of struggle are already ends in themselves. As Ferrell concluded, "Anarchism offers no clear avenue ... only the conviction that the spirit of revolt remains always a pleasure, that the revolution is in some ways won as soon as you begin to fight it."[25]

Success, and Successors

In the new millennium, anarchism has undergone a perceptible transformation in terms of its stature as a political and social theory. As such, a new set of problems for the anarchist movement have arisen, often taking the form of an "anarchist chic" that has reinvigorated black t-shirt sales and moved the "circle-A" symbol from the recesses of history onto teenage backpacks everywhere by constructing the "new anarchist [as] a pop-cultural hero."[26] As one critic has observed, the resurgence of "protest culture" was typified by "feel-good anarchists" who generally have "little patience for theory" and are "too frenzied to worry much about serious alternatives," representing "a revolt of the affluent" by way of a "connection to youth culture" that has kept anarchism "hip and current."[27] In a sense, this resurgent anarchism became a victim of its own success, as its "subcultural codes of dress [and] its sometimes-tired protest tactics can make it seem like a parody of itself."[28] Mainstream publications have even issued feel-good proclamations that "there is an anarchist in all of us. Deep inside we yearn to be free."[29]

Those concerned with the direction and ultimate fate of the movement after Seattle thus would face a new set of challenges that are as concerned with co-optation and commodification as they are with perceptions of violence and associated forms of repression. The unique cultural climate of the United States in particular "allows for near all-encompassing capitalist commodification of, well, just about anything," as Gee writes, and "the concept of turning a political radical into a pop-cultural hero simply works much better in the US-American socio-economic model" than it does elsewhere.[30] At the same time, dominant motifs of danger and demonization are equally palpable in the contemporary landscape. As Fernandez describes in his investigation of the control of social movements, the ready-made "anarchists are coming" trope has become a significant law enforcement strategy to promote fear, create divisions, caricature the movement, and ultimately justify the rise of militarized policing and the security state.[31] A recent media portrayal of the "elusive face of anarchism" captures in quintessential fashion this dualistic sense of deification and denigration that has taken hold, and is worth exploring at some length:

Portrait of an anarchist: Daniel Kyle Wilson, age 20. In a news photo taken May 1, 2008, he looks like a thrift-store ninja, ski-masked. … Wilson stands in profile. His arm is cocked. His fist clutches a rock. He aims it at the window of the U.S. Bank [that] represents everything he opposes: corporate power, hierarchy, an unjust pecking order, financial backing of "ecocide." …

Protests and vandalism tied to anarchists have risen. On the website pugetsoundanarchists.org, anonymous writers have claimed credit for 18 incidents of vandalism in Tacoma and Olympia since December [2010], along with similar acts in Seattle, Portland and Vancouver, B.C. Banks and police facilities are the most common targets. Broken windows, banged-up cars, spray paint and ATM machines clotted with super glue are typical features. …

July 6, 2011: Daniel Wilson, now 23, sits outside an Olympia cafe, talking in long sentences and reeling off strings of injustice and inequity—the sorry state of the world.

"There are more sweatshops now than there were last year. More oil's being taken out of the ground than last year," he says. "There are mountains that are literally being cut down by Massey Energy, which is funded by Bank of America, which is why I (expletive) broke their (expletive) windows out, because I hate them. I hate them for their overdraft fees, I hate them for giving money to capitalists. I hate them for being a bank, for the bailouts. There's numerous reasons for this class hatred. I can distinguish that from—I have loving relationships. And I'm really a nice person if you get to know me. Not a dangerous anarchist who's going to screw you up."

"I am a dangerous anarchist, I guess," he says finally. "If ideas are dangerous."[32]

In this light, along with new challenges have come myriad opportunities as well. A spate of cutting-edge and in-depth treatments of anarchism have appeared in print and other media, and "anarchism has become a respected field of study within academia."[33] Beyond the academy, as Cindy Milstein observes, a thoroughgoing anarchist movement has arisen:

On the ground, the first decade of the twenty-first century has provided a remarkable opening for anarchism, thereby swelling the numbers of those who identify as anarchists. This has led to a flowering of anarchist infrastructure, from a dramatic increase worldwide in social centers and infoshops, to an upsurge in collectively run projects meeting needs like legal support, food, and art. We've developed informal though articulated global networks of exchange as well as solidarity, facilitated by everything from savvy uses of communication technologies and indie media to material aid.[34]

In celebrating this eventuality, it has further been asserted that "the global revolutionary movement in the twenty first century will be one that traces its origins [to] anarchism" and likewise that "everywhere from Eastern Europe to Argentina, from Seattle to Bombay, anarchist ideals and principles are generating new radical dreams and visions."[35] Confirming this sentiment, Gordon writes that "today the anarchist movement is a mature global network of activist collectives, involved in any number of struggles and constructive projects. ... The number of anarchist publications, bookfairs and websites is rising every year, as is the geographical, cultural and age diversity among anarchists themselves."[36]

While it is largely the case that the sense of a "new anarchism" was "mainly a US-American invention" in the aftermath of Seattle,[37] the movement has steadily approached this horizon of a "global network" as the forces of corporate globalization have convened subsequent meetings in locales across Europe, North America, Latin America, Asia, and elsewhere—only to be met with large-scale demonstrations in which anarchists have played a prominent role.[38] In addition to the evidence of increasing immiseration brought on by globalization, the U.S.-led wars in Iraq and Afghanistan have sparked "global movements of resistance" and contributed to the revival of anarchist activism in the process.[39] The global financial crisis and concomitant austerity measures imposed from Argentina to Australasia have galvanized radical organizing. Across Europe in recent years, the United Kingdom, Spain, Italy, and perhaps most notably Greece have seen a spike in dramatic anti-austerity actions, simultaneously giving rise to allegations of "anarcho-terrorism" and the grudging recognition of "the new appeal of anarchism."[40] At the same time, cyber attacks on corporate and governmental entities have been launched by shadowy, anarchistic associations like "Anonymous," in professed defense of WikiLeaks in particular and as a statement against global "tyrannies and injustices" in general.[41]

Tapping into this sense of growing global unrest, the Occupy Wall Street (OWS) demonstrations emerged as a leaderless, decentralized movement across North America and around the world in the fall of 2011. The dynamic and emergent nature of OWS, as well as its penchant for consensus-based governance by way of General Assemblies, suggests strong anarchist undercurrents to the movement—and indeed Graeber is widely known as one of the originators of the initial group that organized in New York. As he described the OWS vision,

> it's pre-figurative, so to speak. You're creating a vision of the sort of society you want to have in miniature. And it's a way of juxtaposing yourself against these powerful, undemocratic forces you're protesting. If you make demands, you're saying, in a way, that you're asking the people in power and the existing institutions to do something different. And one reason people have been hesitant to do that is they see these institutions as the problem.[42]

As one commentator has observed, "ideas born out of anarchist ideology exercise an influence far beyond their numbers within the movement."[43] Graeber has likewise characterized OWS as "a movement based on fundamentally anarchist principles—direct action, direct democracy, a rejection of existing political institutions and [an] attempt to create alternative ones," even as it is apparent that few Americans "are actual anarchists" and as it further remains unclear "how many would ultimately wish to discard the state and capitalism entirely."[44] Thus, while it would be an overstatement to call OWS an anarchist movement *per se*, it is also the case that its presence is indicative of anarchism's increasing political influence.

When considering the contours of anarchism's resurgence, the legacy of history (both remote and proximate) is palpable; as Colin Ward notes, "anarchism has, in fact, an enduring resilience."[45] Today, it frequently appears that "the anarchist" archetypically represents something approximating "the new prototype of a political radical."[46] Specific indicators of an expanding post-Seattle permeation of this rediscovered anarchist identity range from the playful, in-your-face, and widely distributed anarchism of the CrimethInc. Ex-Workers' Collective (a self-described "memberless underground pledged to the total transformation of Western civilization and life itself") to Gabriel Kuhn's broad-ranging compilation (and translation into German) of over a dozen foundational texts that define the scope of "New Anarchism in the U.S." following Seattle and its aftereffects.[47] Still, beyond the undeniable resurgence of anarchism as a viable political identity, critical questions remain as to exactly what contemporary anarchists stand for and how far they have come in developing a cohesive theoretical framework that subsumes the past, guides the present, and looks to the future. These queries comprise the basis for the next chapter.

CHAPTER 1

Contemporary Anarchist Thought

What is anarchism? Perhaps the most misunderstood of the major political theories, anarchism actually derives from a rich intellectual tradition dating back at least two centuries—and perhaps far longer depending upon how we determine exactly who qualifies as an anarchist. In the contemporary milieu, a new crop of anarchist theorists has added much to our understanding of the common threads that generally are taken as comprising modern anarchism. Yet the roots of this endeavor run deep, and in order to understand where we are and where we might be going, it is crucial to develop a sense of where we have been.

As a starting point, consider the proposition that *anarchy is everywhere*—that "it is always in existence," and that "it is probably the oldest type of polity and one which has characterized most of human history."[1] It might not seem that way, since its antitheses (i.e., capitalism and the state) occupy the greater portion of our lives, increasingly so in this era of pervasive technologies, expanding social control, and escalating global crises. Yet we might consider how many decisions we face each day across a broad range of persons and situations, and inquire as to the nature of our own behavior. Are our social interactions by and large pacific or aggressive? Are the choices we make conditioned by the threat of punishment, or do they flow from a different logic? How many voluntary social and cultural associations are we involved with? I do not mean to suggest that people are always good or that they behave exclusively in socially useful ways; in fact, from a macrocosmic perspective, it is apparent that casual violence and routine force are woven into the fabric of modern life at nearly every level, rendering many of us (at best) as unconscious purveyors of myriad non-anarchistic behaviors.

What I am asserting, however, is that people often demonstrate great resiliency and forbearance in coping with life's ever-changing variables, and they do not rely upon someone else to tell them how or why to do it. As the CrimethInc. pamphlet "Fighting for Our Lives" opines, *you may already be an anarchist* if "your idea of healthy human relations is a dinner with friends, where . . . responsibilities are divided up voluntarily and informally," and likewise "whenever you act without waiting for instructions or official permission."[2] Despite the incessant impetus of various mechanisms of social control through both hardware (e.g., security and surveillance) and software (e.g., ideology and law), a large portion of everyday life remains within the domain of individual choice. What we consume, how we earn a living, what we believe, who we associate with, and how we define our communities all present moments where a range of options are present—albeit in rapidly narrowing fashion. The salient point is that at every juncture, we make numerous decisions that are still due primarily to personal volition more so than the overt imposition of central authority upon our moral centers.

Anarchism is at root a philosophy and set of practices based on the premise that people can and should act from a place of freedom from domination and coercive force. This does not mean that "anything goes," since many of our behaviors will remain constrained by good sense and social necessity alike. "What's good for others is good for us, since our relationships with them make up the world in which we live."[3] In this view, we are also free to choose our own constraints, creating a world where the only acceptable limits are those that are self-imposed. The saving grace—which has permeated human societies since their inception—is that we come to see almost immediately that our self-interest is wholly bound up with the interests of everyone else, making anarchism in its full dimensions a theory of radical egalitarianism as much as one of individual autonomy. In this sense, we might say that in addition to the anarchist mantra of "do it yourself," there is a concomitant practice that balances the equation by asking us to "do it together." Indeed, many anarchists practice forms of *community* that demonstrate precisely this inherent sense of organic connectedness—and when extended beyond purely human terms this sensibility offers a vision of anarchism that is radically ecological as well.

Suspending Our Disbelief

I present this nascent framework here for two related purposes. First, I want to clearly indicate and openly disclose my unique bias when it comes to how I understand anarchy: as equal parts resistance to domination in all of its multifarious forms and as the practice of manifesting the world we desire to live in at every opportunity before us. Viewed in this light, anarchism is both critical and constructive, confrontational and compassionate, pragmatic and utopian, destructive and creative. It is, arguably, reflective of an inherent duality contained in all things, as divined by various strands of physics and metaphysics alike. Perhaps it is a crude approximation in some ways, given the limited range of human perception, but anarchism in this sense is potentially the closest of our political and social theories to the patterns that might be observed in *nature*. This raises the sort of incipient spiritual questions that are likely to get one in trouble with many anarchists and non-anarchists alike—yet it should be noted that even the most ardent nihilist at least proclaims an abiding faith that *nothing* has meaning after all.

In fact, although far from axiomatic, it can be argued plausibly that "anarchism has a spiritual or quasi-religious quality to it."[4] As David Graeber and Andrej Grubacic note, "on one level it is a kind of faith," which Cindy Milstein affirms in her observation that, "at its core, anarchism is indeed a spirit."[5] In fact, supportive strands can be found among prominent anarchists throughout history. Errico Malatesta expressly invoked an "anarchist spirit" that was based on a "deeply human sentiment, which aims at the good of all, freedom and justice for all, solidarity and love among the people."[6] Emma Goldman celebrated "the spiritual light of Anarchism" and described it as "a living force in the affairs of our life."[7] Leo Tolstoy professed a "spiritual anarchism" that was derived explicitly from his abiding Christianity.[8] Dorothy Day, Ammon Hennacy, and many other Catholic Workers have expressly identified as anarchists. And as a general matter, it has been observed that "many religious teachings—including those that lie at the very core of faith— support anarchy," and likewise that "anarchists also borrow from many spiritual traditions including paganism, Buddhism and various New Age and Native American spiritualities."[9]

Notwithstanding his identity as a scientist, Peter Kropotkin himself deployed lofty rhetoric in exhorting readers to "keep the spirit alive" and in his observation that "it is always hope ... which makes revolutions."[10] "Overflow with emotional and intellectual energy," he wrote in arguing for an anarchist morality, "and you will spread your intelligence, your love, your energy of action."[11] Kropotkin further located his foundational concept of "mutual aid" as an "instinct in Nature" that was confirmed by his "pantheistic views."[12] In charting the terrain of his "ontological anarchy" as reflected in the call for creating "temporary autonomous zones," Hakim Bey playfully invoked a paganism that "has not yet invented laws—only virtues. No priestcraft, no theology or metaphysics or morality—but a universal shamanism in which no one attains real humanity without a vision."[13] And in their edited collection of the works of anarchist geographer Elisée Reclus, John P. Clark and Camille Martin refer to "his recognition of the continuity and underlying unity of all being, and the awe with which he contemplated nature," characterizing this as a form of "infinite pantheism" and as "nature mysticism."[14]

More recently, Murray Bookchin described his *social ecology* in similarly naturalistic terms (even as he rejected religiosity): "In social ecology, a truly *natural* spirituality centers on the ability of an awakened humanity to function as moral agents in diminishing needless suffering, engaging in ecological restoration, and fostering an aesthetic appreciation of natural evolution in all its fecundity and diversity."[15] Todd May likewise contends that "from its inception, anarchism has founded itself on a faith in the individual to realize his or her decision-making power morally and effectually."[16] Even in formulations that do not use the language of faith or spirituality, there is a nascent moralistic tendency evident in many cases: "Anarchism is naturally present in every healthy human being."[17] Colin Ward grounds his "anarchy in action" perspective in an explicit reliance upon "the natural and spontaneous tendency of humans to associate together for their mutual benefit."[18] And Teoman Gee emphasizes that "flow, change, and transformation characterize a free society of diversity—and therefore what I'd call an anarchist life."[19] Aside from these implicit invocations, in the contemporary milieu Starhawk is perhaps the most prominent example of an anarchist who explicitly frames it in spiritual terms:

> It's the faith that there is a great, creative power that works through the living world toward life, diversity, healing, and regeneration. That power works in us, in our human love, in our work for justice, in our courage and our visions. We don't need priests or ministers or even Witches to contact that power for us—we each have our own direct line. It exists within us, infinite, unlimited. Ultimately, it is stronger than fear, stronger than violence, stronger than hate.[20]

This spiritual digression is offered merely as a reminder that anarchism, like most -isms, is at root a *belief* system. As such, it relies primarily upon the force of persuasion and example to communicate its basic tenets, although at times it may resort to the use of more conventional forms of force as well. But unlike other theories, anarchism generally is not concerned with attracting adherents through conversion or indoctrination, since this would (in principle at least, if not practice) contravene the virtues of autonomy, self-realization, and freedom from coercion that undergird the philosophy. In fact, one of the leading objections made against anarchism is that it is naive and unrealistic in its foundational view that humans can associate freely and fairly for positive purposes without being forced to do so. Anarchists themselves often take the premises of "voluntary association" and "mutual aid" as articles of faith, even as figures such as Kropotkin and Harold Barclay have attempted to root these values in biology and anthropology, respectively.

In any event, anarchists are certainly asking people to suspend their disbelief and take a leap of faith in "smashing the state" and other repressive artifacts on the theory that an egalitarian and sustainable social order will emerge with sufficient rigor to subsume all of life's necessities. Even if the dominant system today is showing clear signs of instability and potential (even imminent) collapse, it is still difficult for many people to abandon what they know for a theory that is widely perceived as ill-informed at best and terroristic at worst. Thus, one of the central aims of contemporary anarchist thought has been to articulate a cohesive set of values and principles that can begin to foster a new narrative capable of competing with the one relentlessly plied by capital and the state. The task is further complicated by the fact that anarchism eschews doctrinaire ideologies and immutable precepts, preferring instead a model in which people think and act autonomously. Anarchism, in short, refuses easy systematization and instinctively rebels against even its own core principles when they are in danger of being imposed. "Nothing is sacred, least of all the fetishized, reified shibboleths of anarchism," as John Moore reminds us.[21] This caveat will inform the quest to render a version of what contemporary anarchism has come to stand for in constructing itself as a viable theory in today's landscape.

Toward an Anarchist Canon

Here, then, is my attempt at setting forth (with the proper provisos in place) a working model of contemporary anarchist thought. What I strive for is a synthesis that weaves together past and present incarnations of anarchism, with an eye toward laying the foundation for an alternative future to the one being increasingly marketed and imposed as we speak. For each of these points there is likely to be contestation (if not consternation), and surely not every anarchist will agree with all of them or with how they are rendered here. That said, it is my belief that this list represents the best of anarchism's potential for promoting a new vision that can help guide action as well. While I refer to it sardonically as a *canon*—fully aware that anarchism embodies an intriguing tendency to "turn against its own foundations"—this framework at least possesses the virtue of not requiring a *cannon* in order for it to become widely adopted.[22] As it turns out, anarchism as a system of thought is really the combination of a number of smaller -isms, some of which overlap and others that can appear contradictory. Indeed, this is as it should be, given anarchism's propensity for embracing tensions and fostering interconnections all at once.

Anti-authoritarianism

> An anarchist society, a society which organizes itself without authority, is always in existence.
>
> —Colin Ward (1973)[23]

The rejection of authority is the sine qua non of anarchism. In this view, the imposition of power through force, coercion, domination, and oppression is both unconscionable and untenable. This is equally the case whether the system doing the imposing is fascistic or representative in nature. Anarchism challenges claims to authority that are vested with the enforcement power of the state, no matter its underpinnings, as well as the claims advanced by subsidiaries and/or partners of the state such as corporations and religious institutions. The intertwining of these various authoritarian forces is observed in innumerable ways, from the kindred "black robes" of priests and judges to the inscription of "In God We Trust" on currency. More broadly, the imperialistic powers that unite militarism and corporatism to impose regimes of resource exploitation and human subjugation are taken as global manifestations of authoritarianism writ large.

Anarchists see these same forces of control being disseminated in the media, in schools, through medicalization, and in most of the appurtenances of modern culture as a whole. Sometimes these expressions of authority are inscribed on bodies through processes including criminal justice, pharmacology, and security systems; other times they appear through more subtle but equally destructive devices such as standardized testing, consumer identity, and popular culture. While anarchists are not alone in pointing out the expanding Orwellianism in our modern midst, they do offer the most comprehensive and thoroughgoing critique of the intersecting forces that work to undermine human dignity and individual liberty. Whereas other doctrines may be content to abolish one sphere of control in favor of another or to merely democratize structures that are inherently authoritarian, anarchism remains unflinching in its wholesale rejection of any system that seeks to impose its will on people and communities.

This naturally makes anarchism anti-government and anti-capitalist. It also raises the question of how an anarchist society would function without anyone in charge. As it turns out, contemporary anarchism is nuanced enough in its values to narrow its anti-authoritarianism to those exercises of power that are rigid, reified, and imposed, but not necessarily to those that are present in healthy communities grounded in equality and respect. In an anarchist society, someone with expertise may well represent an *authority* in a certain sphere, without then asserting his or her power in other matters. For instance, we can defer to another's proficiency in matters of health care or food production without creating socioeconomic structures that allow them to convert that expertise into wider forms of coercive authority, as we generally find in even a representative political system. The critical factor for anarchists is that "the advice of an expert should only be accepted on the basis of voluntary consent," meaning that the acceptance of authority in any particular matter rests with the recipient and not the person or group asserting it.[24] Absent the state and its various apparatuses, power in an anarchist society finds itself ebbing and flowing as various needs arise and are addressed, but at no time does it become centralized in a manner that allows it to be turned back on the very people in whom it inheres.

Anarchists have unearthed examples of anti-authoritarian societies throughout the course of human history and across every continent. As such, the appearance of authoritarian control and political coercion are actually relatively recent phenomena, representing an aberration from the norm of human relations established over the eons. Anarchists today draw inspiration from many of these models, sometimes explicitly adopting a *primitivist* or "back to the earth" stance that seeks to tap into this basic spirit of statelessness and diffuse power. It also manifests in many forms of anarchist organizing, from consensus decision-making models to anonymous attacks on symbols of authoritarian oppression. Some of these tactics have compelled anarchists to self-reflect on their own deployment of potentially coercive practices, including the use of physical force against property or persons as well as tacit forms of vanguardism and claims to authenticity or superiority within the milieu. Indeed, just because anarchists reject authority does not mean they have entirely abolished it from within their own midst. Still, it is the reflexive nature of anarchism as a constantly negotiated theory that offers promise as a tool for undoing the myriad forces of authority in society and promoting a vision of genuine human liberation.

Voluntarism

> There is no fixed and constant authority, but a continual exchange of mutual, temporary, and, above all, voluntary authority and subordination.
>
> —Michael Bakunin (1871)[25]

It might be said that voluntarism is the proactive, positive counterpart to anti-authoritarianism. When we lift the veil of top-down control and the sort of legal compulsion that typifies modern societies, we find that people will oftentimes act from below in socially useful ways. Voluntarism not only results from throwing off the shackles of moral and physical coercion, but it likewise calls forth a spirit of societal engagement that is readily altruistic. This simultaneous quality of being coercion-free and other-centered embodies the sense of voluntary association that has long been a cornerstone of anarchist theory and practice. And intriguingly, it derives equally from anarchism's intense individualism and its collectivist tendencies alike.

From a self-actualization perspective, people ought to be allowed to decide for themselves how to behave and what to do with the course of their lives. Freed from pervasive forces of domination and authoritarianism, it would necessarily become the case that human interactions flow from a place of voluntarism, since no one would be made to do anything apart from their own volition. In this sense, all activities and engagements in an anarchist society would be voluntary, and any ensuing limits on behavior would be purely self-imposed. Over time, people living under such a condition would reclaim lost powers of morality and utility sufficient to hold together a community of individuals. In this view, the individual retains primacy even as an instinct toward voluntary participation in society is cultivated.

From a communal perspective, voluntarism contains an ethic of compassion and reciprocity that makes human associations not only inevitable but desirable. People have always lived in community and have maintained bonds of affinity and affiliation that serve to promote positive behaviors. The critical factor for anarchism is that when conduct is prescribed and obedience enforced, people lose the capacity to act for the right reasons and in fact become susceptible of being made to do so for all the wrong reasons. This is not a moral statement as much as it is an empirical one; it cannot logically be argued that human behavior is improved by dehumanizing processes of social control, just as it is the case that one cannot be forced to be free. For anarchists, voluntary association is at once a rejection of imposed morality (being oxymoronic in any event) and a call instead for manifesting a cooperative "volunteer spirit" in our social and political engagements. Contemporary anarchism readily embraces both the individualistic and communitarian impulses contained in the basic premise that voluntarism is preferable to authoritarianism as an organizing principle for the guidance of human affairs.

Mutualism

> Anarchism [is] the consciousness of an overriding human solidarity.
> —Herbert Read (1954)[26]

This leads straightforwardly to the next foundational piece of both the classical and contemporary anarchist lexicons. Since the time of Kropotkin, anarchism has taken the concept of *mutual aid* as something of a fait accompli. Even in the most cynical and/or militant wings of its confines, anarchism accepts the premise that humans are social animals who have always found ways to live, work, and play together. This sense of mutualism is sometimes expressed as solidarity, affinity, or community; in all cases, there is a fundamental recognition that people need each other to survive and flourish. This can be manifested by large-scale action in common such as that found at a mass demonstration; through smaller band-level affinity groups engaging in forms of direct action; in community-based efforts and shared spaces like infoshops; by common movement practices of legal support and jail solidarity; through the workings of a *free economy* centered on gift-giving and shared bounty; and in the more specifically personal gestures of friendship and camaraderie found in anarchist networks around the world.

In this manner, mutualism is essentially the glue that holds the anarchist vision together and that keeps it from degenerating into barbarism or nihilism. As reflective of a broadly mutualist spirit found in nature and throughout human history alike, contemporary expressions weave together both instinctivist and normative impulses in the deployment of mutual aid. Freed from compulsion, people learn to act at least in part for the common good, since there exists an undeniable recognition of the necessity of human community and sociality. Further, it turns out that in this formulation others are likewise no longer forced to do anything in particular for one another, meaning that if we desire equitable treatment it becomes incumbent upon us to both offer it and learn how to encourage it in others. This sense of basic reciprocity is both behavioral and moralistic, representing the essence of practices such as barter and exchange as well as teachings akin to the "golden rule" of "do unto others" that is found in nearly every society. Following Gustav Landauer, anarchists oftentimes maintain that the forces of social control exist principally at the levels of motivation and conduct, and that the surest path toward overcoming them is to behave differently and for different reasons. In this view, the aim is to cultivate alternative arrangements and relationships, as Landauer opined: "The entire system would vanish without a trace if the people began *to constitute themselves as a people apart from the state.*"[27] Mutualism, as a cooperative and constitutive practice, is the highest expression of this aim.

Anarchism today has evolved a sophisticated understanding of the workings of power and domination. The patterns of corporate hegemony and statecraft are evident everywhere, and the concomitant values of consumption and compulsion that they inculcate are equally widespread. Against this, anarchists propose—and struggle to model—a social order in which people largely behave in socially responsible and life-affirming ways because (a) it is advantageous to do so and/or (b) it is the right thing to do. Anarchism grasps the interlocking and reinforcing nature of repressive tendencies in society, including the profound synergies between capital and the state, and it argues instead for a bottom-up version of mutualism that enables collective action while forestalling authoritarianism. It is a delicate balance, yet among the sociopolitical theories, anarchism is perhaps alone in its eagerness to embrace the tensions as a source of productive energy. It is precisely the kinetic energy found in the messiness and constant negotiation underlying human relationships that anarchists thrive upon, as well as that comprises the basis for wider forms of networking and federation that link both individuals and communities in an inescapable web of mutuality (to borrow a phrase from Martin Luther King, Jr.).

Autonomism

> By "ruling from below," anarchists believe, at the level of localized, self-governing communities, society will be able to transform itself into a self-managed, directly democratic and ecologically sustainable system.
>
> —James Horrox (2009)[28]

Autonomy is the capacity to make decisions and manifest them upon one's own volition. It is closely related to anti-authoritarianism but goes further in prioritizing self-governance at both the individual and societal levels. As a basic proposition, autonomism is akin to what Gandhi called "swaraj," namely, the practice of self-rule. Without this as the bedrock, we can find ourselves on a path—widely seen today—toward self-possession and even self-destruction. Autonomy as self-rule asserts not only the freedom to govern ourselves but also the *requirement* that we do so; in this sense, it is equal parts liberty and responsibility. Absent the state and other coercive apparatuses, human communities will still require levels of coordination beyond the purview of any particular individual. In order to accomplish this without merely replicating current practices of stratification and domination, anarchists start with a conception of the individual rooted in the virtue of freedom as well as the capacity to exercise it responsibly.

When contemporary anarchists talk about autonomy, they often refer to this personal imperative of self-management as a precondition for wider forms of association that exist in opposition to the state. Autonomous spaces are those liberated from the forces of regulation and control that are typified by private property regimes; they can include a building occupied during a demonstration, a vacant lot that is reclaimed as a community garden, or an abandoned dwelling that is inhabited by squatters. Autonomism in this context represents the capacity for people to self-organize in opposition to dominant modes of exchange, and it often includes a strong component of simultaneous resistance to legal and commercial norms imposed by society.

As a response to corporate globalization in particular, an autonomist movement has arisen that prioritizes local and regional actions as a strategy of both resistance and self-realization. The impetus to live and work at a smaller scale, to reduce the collective footprint of human impacts on the environment, and to reclaim a sense of power in the decisions that directly impact our lives are all expressions of autonomy. These various autonomous efforts—ranging from free schools and foraged foods to alternative economies and cooperative workplaces—have shown a capacity to link together through various media of exchange, forming a burgeoning loose federation of small-scale nodes that make up what is today a global anarchist network. Yet again, this is a precarious balance to strike, that between autonomy and federation. But anarchists are keenly aware that without autonomy, federation can become fascism; and without federation, autonomy often results in isolationism and, ultimately, eradication. Autonomy thus serves as a personal hedge against the potential totalitarianism of the community and likewise as a collective hedge against ready incorporation into the globalized neoliberal economy. It is, in short, a radical reclaiming of the desire to determine the conditions of our own lives at all levels.

Egalitarianism

> Anarchism is aristocratic—anarchists just insist that the elite should consist of *everyone*.
>
> —CrimethInc. (circa 2010)[29]

In order for autonomy to work, it must be balanced by equality. Anarchism's version is neither the watered-down premise of "equal opportunity" that is often given lip service in liberal-capitalist societies, nor the rigid austerity of an "equal outcomes" approach frequently proffered by exponents of state socialism. Anarchists instead strive for a radical egalitarianism conditioned by the foregoing application of anti-authoritarian, voluntarist, mutualist, and autonomist principles. On some level, all of these attributes are different ways of expressing the core anarchist premise of freedom from (and active resistance to) imposed rule. Yet each also possesses unique qualities that are reflexively and dynamically engaged with the others. An anarchist social order that eliminates coercion and domination promises to cultivate self-governing individuals who exhibit voluntary behaviors that are often mutually beneficial, ideally creating a horizontal network of productive enterprises and self-managing communities that could subsume the material and emotional necessities of life. Far from a blueprint, this is more so a guide to decision making without dictating outcomes—and the key to achieving it is equality.

At the outset, anarchism's egalitarianism is a function of political economy. It applies to decision making and governance through a predilection for processes of consensus and participation that vest power in every individual and all constituencies potentially impacted. It argues for a system of production anchored in values of common dignity, shared labor, and equal entitlement to the collective wealth of humankind. In striving for this, it is also by necessity a sociocultural phenomenon, calling upon us to actively confront patterns and practices of racism, sexism, heterosexism, ageism, ableism, classism, and the like—including our own participation in promulgating these invidious systems and the ways in which we have internalized them. Anarchism promotes such a vision of egalitarianism not out of moralism, guilt, or political correctness but in order to foster the dual sense of self-rule and collective responsibility—of voluntarism and mutualism—that underscores the theory. Equal treatment works as an organizing principle because, by definition, it is either realized universally or not at all; you cannot have an unequal distribution of equality, after all. This makes it a lofty aim indeed, but one that if attained promises to revolutionize all aspects of society.

At an even larger scale, anarchism's radical egalitarianism is also a viable instrument for resistance to colonialism, imperialism, and globalization. Such processes depend upon the differential maintenance of power relations and are intertwined with structural hierarchies that assign worth based on factors of race, gender, and so on. Just as the "equal rights" rhetoric of the state is, in practice, largely a misnomer for the protection of wealth and privilege, the equal opportunity promise of capitalism is likewise a palliative for profound stratification both within and among nations. Anarchism rejects these hierarchies in the name of an active equality that empowers individuals, communities, and nations (as distinct from states) to simultaneously take ownership of their lives and refuse to be owned in the process. As such, it also requires the rejection of hierarchies that set person against person and nation against nation, offering a potential pathway to peaceful relations in a world where no one gets their needs met unless everyone does. To accomplish this strong sense of "revolutionary egalitarianism," anarchists oftentimes will apply its basic teachings not only within human communities but toward the balance of the biosphere as a whole.

Naturalism

> The "children of mother earth" claiming their right to live—what else could it be about?
>
> —P. M. (1995)[30]

Not every anarchist is an environmentalist, but anarchism itself is inherently ecological. The sense of immutable change and open-endedness that frames the anarchist project is likewise found in human interpretations of nature itself. Anarchism, like ecology, strives to understand the complex relationship between humans and the environment, and it patterns key aspects of its social ideology (e.g., mutual aid) explicitly on processes observed within and among biotic and animal communities. As Emma Goldman once wrote: "A natural law is that factor in man which asserts itself freely and spontaneously without any external force, in harmony with the requirements of nature."[31] While contemporary anarchists may not be as consumed as in the past with questions of *human nature* (even in Goldman's time there was a developing sense that, "with human nature caged in a narrow space, whipped daily into submission, how can we speak of its potentialities?"), there remains a firm recognition that we are embedded within the larger workings of the biosphere, as well as that our very existence is conditioned by the primary relationship between human communities and the larger environment.[32] This insight has become even more pronounced in recent years, as anarchists have increasingly engaged issues including climate change, food justice, resource wars, animal rights, and popular struggles to preserve biodiversity—sometimes to an extent that includes the more militant strands of the movement and their penchant for confrontational, nonlinear tactics in the name of "liberation."

Unsurprisingly, then, *diversity* is "today a core anarchist value," as Uri Gordon observes.[33] Just as biological diversity is essential to the health of ecosystems, so too is cultural diversity fundamental to the continued existence of healthy societies. From an ecological perspective, no aspect of the complex web of life has primacy, meaning that diversity is at root an expression of mutual interdependence—and thus of anarchism as well. In social terms, diversity is inclusive of all of the identity attributes that impel the struggle for equality. Anarchists recognize that qualities defined as "normal" at a given historical moment are often associated with the trappings of power and privilege. In creating self-fulfilling norms around the major characteristics of identity construction, dominant power is able to perpetuate itself as a set of political and economic relations and, perhaps even more insidiously, as a form of consciousness. Over time, members of less-favored identities will suffer widening gaps in health, wealth, and opportunity—even as they may slowly internalize the dominant norms to such a degree that their oppression and liberation alike can become bound up with the master narrative, either by struggling against it or in striving to attain its blessings. Anarchists work to overcome these challenges by deconstructing privilege, abolishing hierarchy, democratizing decision making, and deploying a "diversity of tactics" in the quest to surmount oppression.

The shared cultural heritage of humankind is at risk proportionally to how the biosphere is being rapidly degraded. Languages, which are strong indicators of unique cultures, are disappearing at a rate comparable to forests and species. The present geological era, which is sometimes referred to as the "Anthropocene" to signify its human-driven qualities, has as its hallmark the creation of monolithic biological and socioeconomic systems premised on a hierarchy of interests and the control of resources. Against this totalizing quality, subaltern voices around the planet strive to reassert themselves as potential guardians of biological and cultural diversity, and in so doing they often manifest a sense of political diversification that brings to the fore a crucial indigenous perspective that is widely embraced among contemporary anarchists. Perhaps partly due to this perception of effective empowerment, there can also be a concomitant tendency to fetishize and/or commodify diverse identities. In the anarchist milieu, dialogues and practices are thus often fostered to deepen the notion of diversity as a tool for unpacking critical issues of power and privilege and likewise as a fundament of healthy systems at all levels. All of this points to an inherently naturalistic sensibility in anarchism and serves as an important component of its staunch opposition to the forces of global capitalism.

Anti-capitalism

> Anarchism is necessarily anti-capitalist. . . . A consistent anarchist must oppose private ownership of the means of production and the wage slavery which is a component of this system.
> —Noam Chomsky (1970)[34]

A cornerstone of anarchism throughout history has been the abolition of private property; anarchism today extends the critique to include processes of privatization and commodification that are part and parcel of corporate globalization. Anarchists assert the interests of "people, not profits" and challenge the prevailing Western mythos of human superiority vis-à-vis nature. Capitalism is seen as a system of exploitation, domination, and coercion—simultaneously dehumanizing and denaturalizing in its quest to control people and conquer nature. Anarchists have figured prominently in the myriad anti-capitalist demonstrations held around the world in recent years, and they have likewise been a driving force in uprisings against austerity measures and other tools utilized by capital and the state to maintain their joint seat of power. Anarchists have also been part of solidarity efforts aimed at promoting economic justice for immigrants, the homeless, refugees, displaced communities, and working-class people around the world.

In addition to an unquestionably anti-capitalist penchant, contemporary anarchism further strives to promote alternative economic arrangements. These new visions are often explicitly framed as a rejection of capitalism, typified by the "really, really free market" concept that originated at mass demonstrations against the corporatists' version of "free trade." Anarchists embrace the egalitarian and voluntaristic values of the *gift economy* and regularly manifest the virtues of a free-economy perspective through efforts including "dumpster diving" and the decentralized global movement Food Not Bombs. Anarchism does not entirely reject the enterprising or entrepreneurial spirit—indeed, modern anarchists are nothing if not resilient and resourceful—but refuses to deploy it in the service of ruling others or allowing oneself to be ruled. Anarchism stands in opposition to wage slavery, conspicuous consumption, and wealth maldistribution, sometimes embodied in purposefully provocative slogans such as "Eat the Rich."

By taking on capitalism in its systemic dimensions, including its inherent intertwining with the workings of the state, anarchism propounds a civilizational critique that marks it as the most radical of contemporary sociopolitical theories. The roots of oppression and authoritarianism run deep for many anarchists—quite literally down into the earth itself, as a result of the modern tendency to privatize the essentials of life and control their distribution:

> The first man who, having enclosed a piece of ground, bethought himself of saying "This is mine," and found some people simple enough to believe him, was the real founder of civil society. From how many crimes, wars, and murders, from how many horrors and misfortunes might not any one have saved mankind, by pulling up the stakes, or filling up the ditch, and crying to his fellows: "Beware of listening to this impostor; you are undone if you once forget that the fruits of the earth belong to us all, and the earth itself to nobody."[35]

While these words were written by Rousseau over two centuries ago, many contemporary anarchists are at least implicitly cognizant of the call to "pull up the stakes and fill up the ditch" in defiance of corporate capitalism. Indeed, some of anarchism's most spectacular interventions, from breaking windows to burning buildings, have been undertaken specifically in response to perceived injustices committed by the ostensible forces of privatization and exploitation.

Dynamism

> Anarchism can be described first and foremost as a visceral revolt.
> —Daniel Guérin (1970)[36]

Beyond mere theorizing, anarchists have long held a preference for "propaganda by the deed." The theory behind this is simply that actions are often more dramatic and galvanizing than words, at least in a social movement context. The exhortation contained in the aphorism is one intended to foment a revolutionary consciousness, and it is sometimes offered as a justification for highly confrontational acts that possess a potentially terroristic quality. On the other hand, today the phrase has come to mean more generally any activity that communicates an intended message or that models the central tenets of anarchism—including not just spectacular violence but more accepted forms of organizing as well. Thus, while anarchism clearly embraces a posture of dynamic action, there is much debate about precisely what message is being conveyed by a given act and whether it actually serves productive purposes.

Still, whatever course of conduct one opts for, it remains the case that anarchism in all of its incarnations is inherently revolutionary. It propounds a critique of capital and the state that calls into question the most basic assumptions of civilization, and it carries the mantle of "freedom and equality" to an extent that promises to remake the workings of modern society in its entirety. It is perhaps for this reason above all that anarchism has been (and continues to be) demonized and used as a convenient touchstone of public fear by entrenched interests. As a coherent system of thought, anarchism is in fact "dangerous" in terms of its uncompromising critique of domination and oppression in all its multifarious forms; moreover, its idyllic example of an egalitarian, dynamic social order is likewise threatening to the "powers that be." Frequently lost in the hysteria over the "violent anarchist" trope, however, is a more pertinent discussion about the innate violence and pervasive danger presented by militarization, maldistribution, dehumanization, and environmental degradation—all of which are prominent features of capitalism and the state.

One of the primary ways that anarchism distinguishes itself is through creative, spontaneous, and playful actions. For many contemporary anarchists, the state is little more than a "killing machine," and capitalist society is merely an elaborate "death cult." Against the stagnant, mechanistic, and routinized qualities of modern life, anarchism counterposes an air of excitement and unpredictability in its open-endedness and fluidity. Anarchism is often taken as a "theory of spontaneous order," as Ward describes it, and "it is only in revolutions, emergencies, and 'happenings'" that this key principle emerges.[37] In this sense, anarchy is not disorganization but is more accurately a form of *self-organization*. It is revolutionary but not irresponsible, visionary but not didactic, creative but not scripted. In the end, anarchism is not an amoral philosophy of "anything goes"—it is, rather, a perspective that goes with anything and that infuses all aspects of everyday life.

Pragmatism

> Anarchism always "demands the impossible" even as it tries to also "realize the impossible." Its idealism is thoroughly pragmatic.
>
> —Cindy Milstein (2010)[38]

The theory of spontaneous order pervades human existence at every level. It applies equally in the domains of the personal and interpersonal as it does to societal and global concerns. Whether it is a matter of individual lifestyle preference, small group decision making, or global solidarity networking, the practices of anarchy are always at hand. Anarchism is a belief system, a political perspective, a state of being, a form of consciousness—and it is also an ongoing, ever-changing lived experience. The mutability and even ambiguity associated with anarchism can make it seem impracticable, but in actuality these qualities foster a sense of flexibility and permeability that allows anarchism to slip the bonds of meta-theory in favor of engaged pragmatism. As Cindy Milstein observes, "anarchism's laboratory is the whole of life," and thus the opportunity to apply its core values is present in each moment.[39]

As a revolutionary theory, anarchism bears the burden of addressing the multitude of challenges facing humankind not in piecemeal or reformist fashion but in toto. Anarchism's practical revolution is not won when some governmental program or corporate concession is announced; it is not complete upon a platform being adopted or a candidate being elected. Anarchism is a condition of permanent revolution and eternal vigilance against the creeping authoritarianism that is always with us; it is there when we consume, communicate, transact, travel, labor, and love. Contemporary activists have infused every sphere of life with anarchist values and tenets: free schools, anarchist parenting, dumpster diving, pirate radio, infoshops, hackers, bike co-ops, cohabitation, libertinism, urban farms, free stores, reading groups, sports, street theater, and more. Not every project of this ilk necessarily refers to itself as anarchist, but many do. Taken together, these endeavors convey the lived sense of anarchism, moving it from theory to practice and highlighting its potential for offering a comprehensive vision of social order absent domination and hierarchy.

Utopianism

> That we are Utopians is well known.
>
> —Peter Kropotkin (1906)[40]

Notwithstanding Kropotkin's enthusiasm, many anarchists eschew utopianism for a variety of related reasons. Interestingly, much as with the notion of anarchy itself, the concept of *utopia* suffers from frequent mischaracterization. Historically it invokes a quasi-religious, unattainable perfected state of humanity, a "good place" that can never actually be located. It is often associated with a simplistic and static lifestyle that presupposes a benign human nature and an idealized order in which needs are satisfied magically and without conflict. On the other hand, this utopia is also viewed as over-organized, anti-individualistic, and potentially authoritarian in its benevolent regimentation. From another perspective, utopia dangerously promises future salvation and thereby deflects critical attention from the urgent needs of the present. It is, in short, frequently seen as both too idealistic and too cynical, airy yet oppressive. Interestingly, some of these very same critiques are delivered against anarchism itself.

Even as future-oriented utopianism remains controversial, there exists a tendency among some anarchists to exalt examples from history as "anarchist utopias" of a bygone day: indigenous cultures, the Diggers, the Paris Commune, the Spanish Revolution. In practice today, there are intentional communities around the world operating on anarchist principles, some self-consciously. In literature, a rich and growing sub-genre of anarcho-utopianism has solidified in recent years, and academic treatments have likewise proliferated. We can surmise that this trend is influenced at least in part by anarchism's expansive engagement with the pragmatic aspects of life in addition to its wholesale critique of, and revolutionary posture toward, civilization itself. Like anarchism, utopianism is equal parts critical and constructive, and perhaps that shared duality is responsible for the affinity and hostility alike.[41]

Contemporary anarchism has tenuously resolved some of these issues by recasting them in terms of *prefiguring*. The essential notion is that present-day anarchist endeavors are also harbingers of a potential future that remains indeterminate. Anarchist organizing today, as to both the means employed and the ends imagined, provides us with a glimpse of what an alternative social order might look like. What differentiates this from old-school notions of utopia is the fragmentary open-endedness of its future vision; anarchism is always a work in progress and is not susceptible of a unitary definition—thus any attempt to do more than allude to a "better world" is rejected in the name of the freedom of those who inhabit the future to determine it for themselves. Unfortunately, as Noam Chomsky notes, we are rapidly asserting "our control over the fate of future generations" through oppressive social structures and concomitant environmental impacts; thus we are all futurists whether we want to be or not.[42] Still, anarchists seek to exercise this responsibility in a manner that is firmly committed to revolutionizing the present without foreclosing the future; as Chomsky counsels, "whatever social structures and arrangements are developed, they ought to maximize the possibilities for people to pursue their own creative potential, and you can't make a formula for that."[43]

Decentralism

> Things fall apart; the center cannot hold; Mere anarchy is loosed upon the world . . .
>
> —William Butler Yeats, *The Second Coming* (1920)

If "you can't make a formula," then it is difficult to convince people of the soundness and solidity of one's ideas. Anarchism is unique in that it rarely proselytizes, at least in terms of seeking unquestioning converts, and it rejects attempts at grand theorizing that are intended to create universalistic morals and models alike. What keeps the anarchist vision of an organic, spontaneous, and egalitarian social order from becoming a repressive meta-narrative is its concomitant impulse toward decentralization as a formative value. As noted above, anarchists rebel against even their own core principles, not necessarily in an attempt to abolish or undermine them so much as to keep them vibrant and ensure that they are always negotiated by the people and communities to whom they are intended to apply. In other words, contemporary anarchism strives to deconstruct its own center, and in so doing it posits a theory of radical "decentering" that extends beyond sheer politics into the realms of language and thought as well.

Sometimes referred to as "post-anarchism"—to indicate simultaneously its willingness to transcend classical anarchism as well as its affinity for "post-structuralist" critiques of power and hegemony—this cutting-edge tenet of anarchism actually fits quite well within the larger historical tradition and its penchant for decentralization. Rudolf Rocker, for instance, decried centralism as "a curse which weakens its power of decision and systematically represses every spontaneous initiative."[44] "The anarchist alternative," as Ward asserts, "is that of fragmentation, fission rather than fusion, diversity rather than unity, a mass of societies rather than a mass society."[45] Anarchism's longstanding prioritization of autonomy and spontaneity as the bases for effective organizing encapsulates some of the post-anarchist sensibility, yet out beyond this is a further tendency to deconstruct power relations at their most basic (and often more subtle) levels. The radical decentering urged by post-anarchism outstrips mere political economy in favor of a penetrating analysis of language, knowledge, culture, and even desire in exploring the ways in which social control is imposed and how best to resist it without replicating hierarchical and representational forms of association in the process.[46]

While some anarchists embrace the potential of this perspective and its inherent capacity to foster "a systematic deconstruction of the claims to legitimacy of any institutional authority," others raise concerns about whether this line of reasoning overemphasizes anarchism's deconstructive aspects without acknowledging its constitutive tendencies as a counterbalance.[47] As May wonders, "can there be critique without representation?"[48] On what basis do anarchists oppose dominant forms of militarization, criminalization, and capitalization and seek to posit against them a vision of voluntary association, mutual aid, autonomous action, and pragmatic utopianism? Anarchism is right to check its own potential authoritarianism and to deconstruct its central values and aims (as Rocker summarizes, "it rejects all absolute schemes and concepts"),[49] yet it is also vital to articulate what the theory stands *for* rather than merely what it is *against*. Moreover, as I wrote over a decade ago, "it is important to believe that what we do and how we live matters; to fail to do so can only invite cataclysm and perhaps even extinction."[50] Fortunately, anarchism's explicit embrace of decentralism as a core value encourages precisely the kind of inquiry that enables healthy foundations—namely those that appear as tenuous planks in a nascent floor but never as finished ceilings above our heads.

In Conclusion

I have sought here to present a working version of contemporary anarchism as a cohesive school of thought. By necessity, this has included reference to action as well, since anarchism rejects the false dichotomies of means/ends and theory/practice. Anarchism is a way of looking at the world *and* a way of living in it; it is deeply engaged with the minutia of the present as well as suggestive of a broader vision for the future. Anarchism prioritizes the individual and the community at the same time, including nature itself in its conceptions of equality and diversity. Each of the hesitant tenets specified here could serve as a definition of anarchism by itself, since every part is reflective of the ethos of the whole. Taken together, these various strands of anarchism begin to trace the contours of a complete theory that is comfortable with its own ambiguity and that revels in the productive possibilities of its inherent tensions. And nowhere are these themes of unity and diversity, of cohesion and dissension, more prevalent than in the realm of anarchist action, which I consider in the following chapter.

CHAPTER 2

Anarchism in Action

In addition to its theoretical resurgence, anarchism has been intimately involved with the evolution of strategies for societal transformation. The presence of anarchists and anarchist tenets in movements focusing on issues including global justice, environmentalism, racial equality, and economic alternatives to capitalism has been a force for enhancing movement dynamism and at the same time leading to internal tensions and official repression. Anarchists often bear the distinction of being misunderstood (or even demonized) by both the mainstream culture and their own apparent allies alike. In practice, the range of actions associated with anarchism is incredibly broad, from compassionate acts like sending books to prisoners and finding food for the hungry to more confrontational tactics such as property destruction and skirmishing with police at demonstrations. The image of "the anarchist" today might not conjure quite the same trepidation as it did around the turn of the twentieth century—during the brief heyday of ostensibly anarchist-inspired political violence—but it still provides ample fodder for suppression and further raises many pointed questions for movement culture itself.

Anarchism has infused today's activism with numerous essential values, practices, and terminologies. Contemporary social and environmental movements often speak in terms of autonomy, solidarity, and community, and specific innovations such as the affinity group and the preference for a "diversity of tactics" are by now part of the parlance. Anarchists have brought with them a strong preference for horizontal forms of organizing, in which decisions are rendered from a place of equal power, and where individuals themselves are empowered to act from their consciences in opposing structures of repression and exploitation. Perhaps the key contribution of anarchism to today's movements is the notion of *direct action*, which contains within it the dual sense of contestation and construction that lies at the very heart of anarchism. Related to this is the notion of *prefiguring*, sometimes translated simply as the apocryphal Gandhian exhortation to "be the change" we wish to see in the world. Thus, while anarchists might sometimes throw bricks, they are equally likely to build something with them.

One of the signs of anarchism's flexibility and pervasiveness is the hyphenation it has come to enjoy with a number of other political theories and identities. For instance, the adjectival prefix "anarcho-" has found itself attached over the years to persuasions including socialist, communist, syndicalist, primitivist, libertarian, pacifist, feminist, and even capitalist. One can be a Green Anarchist, run with the Black Bloc, or be a punk and hippie all at once with the milieu. Anarchists hack, jam, graffiti, bike, dumpster dive, and set ablaze; they also educate, cooperate, feed, communicate, and garden. An intriguing array of anarchist movement tactics is presented in the 2004 CrimethInc. tome *Recipes for Disaster: An Anarchist Cookbook*, from banner drops and hitchhiking to shoplifting and sabotage—but this is not your father's incendiary *Anarchist Cookbook* from the 1960s, which has been disavowed even by its original author as "misguided and potentially dangerous."[1] Like contemporary anarchism overall, this widely distributed CrimethInc. text possesses a whimsical yet sophisticated sensibility, advocating personal empowerment and community engagement as foundations for effective action. Above all, it serves to affirm the reflexive notion that practice does not simply flow from theory; rather, it shapes it, reinforces it, and creates it. In this sense, the "anarchist revolution" is much more than a statement of principles—it is a living exercise.

Something in the Air

Anarchism carries with it an inherent, and oftentimes urgent, sense of revolution. Once the gaze has been fixed on differential power relations and organized oppression, it is difficult not to see it wherever one looks in modern society. Much as philosophers like Michel Foucault have discerned the workings of discipline throughout nearly every human institution, so too do anarchists generally see "the emperor's new clothes" of subjugation, distraction, and impending ruination draped across the global system. Anarchists decry perpetual war, the ravages of climate change, privatization of the commons, the commodification of life, and the widening gap between the rich and the poor both within and among nation-states. Anarchists generally recognize the interlocking challenges presented by the modern world, likewise the paradox of confronting a system to which one belongs and contributes on multiple levels. Many anarchists intrinsically understand how high the stakes are and how deep the roots go, and, like Starhawk, "want a revolution that changes the very nature of how power is structured and perceived, that challenges *all* systems of domination and control"—arguing in the final analysis that "we need nothing less than a global economic, social, political, and spiritual revolution."[2]

This is obviously a daunting task, and it sets a high bar for action. The undertaking is further complicated by the experimental nature of any revolt, as expressed by Subcomandante Marcos of the Zapatistas in 1994: "We hope you understand that this is the first time that we have tried to carry out a revolution, and we are still learning."[3] Should anarchists bother engaging in small-scale activities in local communities or expending energy working for piecemeal reform on a given issue? Should they forge alliances with individuals or groups whose aims are less than total revolution? When it appears that a global "crash" is in the offing, should anarchists help it along or work to prevent it? Are there any ethical limits to the tactics that might be employed in the service of promoting a global revolution under present conditions where the urgency is so great? In particular, what sorts of actions are likely to be effective in fomenting a sociopolitical revolution that supplants authoritarianism and exploitation? What is being proposed by anarchists as an alternative model for a complex society, and how can it be constructed in a hostile environment? Who decides what is to be done in the name of revolution?

While it is clear that anarchists do not have the answers to all of these questions, they have served to bring these issues to the fore of contemporary movement culture, and in so doing they have helped to keep alive a revolutionary impulse that has been part of anarchism since its earliest days. As Howard Zinn wrote in the introduction to Herbert Read's book *Anarchy and Order*: "Anarchism arose in the most splendid days of Western 'civilization' because the promises of that civilization were almost immediately broken."[4] Zinn argues that an anarchist revolution in its full dimensions cannot be achieved by "force of arms" but that it must arise in the "minds and behavior" of people before institutions themselves will change.[5] Encapsulating a rich history of thinking about (and acting for) a comprehensive social revolution, Zinn provides a template for anarchist organizing that still resonates today:

> The anarchist sees revolutionary change as something immediate, something we must do now, where we are, where we live, where

we work. It means starting this moment to do away with authoritarian, cruel relationships—between men and women, between parents and children, between one kind of worker and another. Such revolutionary action cannot be crushed like an armed uprising. It takes place in everyday life, in the tiny crannies where the powerful but clumsy hands of state power cannot easily reach. It is not centralized and isolated, so that it can be wiped out by the rich, the police, the military. It takes place in a hundred thousand places at once, in families, on streets, in neighborhoods, in places of work. It is a revolution of the whole culture. Squelched in one place, it springs up in another, until it is everywhere. Such a revolution is an art.[6]

As Starhawk concurs, "we don't have to wait for [the revolution], we can be it, live it now."[7]

In addition to the expansive scope of its aims, another distinguishing feature of anarchist revolutionary praxis is that it does not seek control of existing power structures, but instead it strives to replace them altogether with an egalitarian, anti-authoritarian social order. "It would obviously be a mistake to create the kind of machinery which, at the successful end of a revolution, would merely be taken over by the leaders, who then assume the functions of government," as Read observes.[8] Anarchists have long perceived the reactionary nature of prior revolutions in which a new government was formed, and through that government how the interests of a new privileged class (sometimes including members of the old one as well) steadily eroded the movement's gains and took back as much power as it could from the people. In a contemporary context, for example, such processes of revolutionary retrenchment have been observed in relation to the "Arab Spring" uprisings across the Middle East during the first part of 2011: "The historic revolutions that have rippled through the Arab world this year were in danger of eclipse . . . as protesters returned to the streets to profess their disgust at how the movement is being stymied by regimes old and new. . . . The scenes served as a reminder that following the euphoria of the Arab spring, little concrete progress towards reform has been made."[9]

For Errico Malatesta, to take but one powerful voice from history, an anarchist revolution represents "the destruction of all coercive ties," and thus "we must avoid replacing one state of coercion by another."[10] Alexander Berkman likewise understood the anarchist's conception of revolution to be "not any more a mere change of rulers, of government, not a political revolution, but one that seeks to alter the whole character of society."[11] As such, for Berkman and Malatesta alike, there was a recognition that this effort obviously would meet with great resistance—not only from entrenched power but from "popular ignorance and prejudice" (as Berkman termed it) among those who blithely profit from it. Among contemporary theorists, David Graeber echoes these concerns and adds new ones particular to this era in his essay, "Revolution in Reverse":

> Our customary conception of revolution is insurrectionary: the idea is to brush aside existing realities of violence by overthrowing the state, then, to unleash the powers of popular imagination and creativity to overcome the structures that create alienation. Over the twentieth century it eventually became apparent that the real problem was how to institutionalize such creativity without creating new, often even more violent and alienating structures. As a result, the insurrectionary model no longer seems completely viable, but it's not clear what will replace it. . . . In retrospect, what seems strikingly naïve is the old assumption that a single uprising or successful civil war could, as it were, neutralize the entire apparatus of structural violence.[12]

In the end, Graeber advocates "the revival of direct action" as a means of meeting these challenges of retrenchment, fragmentation, and co-optation.

Direct Action and Dual Power

It has been said that direct action is "the core of practical anarchist politics."[13] The concept is historically rooted, with Emma Goldman asserting its primacy: "Anarchism therefore stands for direct action, the direct defiance of, and resistance to, all laws and restrictions, economic, social, and moral."[14] Voltairine de Cleyre, who Goldman described as "the most gifted and brilliant anarchist woman America ever produced," offered a historical rendering of direct action that included the Quakers' refusal to pay church taxes, bear arms, or swear allegiance to any government; episodes from the colonial era including tax resistance and the Boston Tea Party; the anti-slavery movement; and the working-class organizing that began at the dawn of industrialization.[15] De Cleyre observed that "direct action has always been used" and took an expansive view of its locus of operation: "Every person who ever had a plan to do anything, and went and did it, or who laid his plan before others, and won their co-operation to do it with him, without going to external authorities to please do the thing for them, was a direct actionist."[16] She concluded that

> political action is never taken, nor even contemplated, until slumbering minds have first been aroused by direct acts of protest against existing conditions. ... It is by and because of the direct acts of the forerunners of social change, whether they be of peaceful or warlike nature, that the Human Conscience, the conscience of the mass, becomes aroused to the need for change. ... Direct action is always the clamorer, the initiator, through which the great sum of indifferentists become aware that oppression is getting intolerable.[17]

The operative premise is that by acting in direct fashion, "rather than appealing to an external agent," an individual or group becomes empowered by "taking social change into one's own hands."[18] For Graeber, who has extensively chronicled its use in contemporary movements, direct action "is the insistence, when faced with structures of unjust authority, on acting as if one is already free."[19] While it can cover "an enormous range" of activities and overlaps with tactics of civil disobedience, it is also the case that in recent years "the term has become synonymous with a certain degree of militancy."[20] As Luis Fernandez observes, direct action "disrupts and confronts rather than negotiates, [although] contrary to common perception, it is not inherently violent."[21] The obvious example would be the breaking of corporate windows, but direct action can also include "a rent strike, a consumer boycott, or a blockade; it may involve sit-ins, squatting, tree living, or the occupation of target buildings."[22] Despite its historical legacy and the array of activities that it subsumes, direct action is still at times disparaged as being too confrontational and ultimately counter-productive, even by those who have benefited from it; as de Cleyre lamented, it has had "the historical sanction of the very people now reprobating it."[23]

In addition to this spirit of open defiance to injustice, direct action in the modern lexicon has also come to include a constructive element that is equally crucial to its efficacy. For Starhawk, "it's anything that directly confronts oppressive power, prevents a wrong or interferes with an unjust institution, or that directly provides for a need or offers an alternative."[24] In this sense, beyond contesting repressive invocations of authority through unmediated (and often militant) forms, direct action possesses the quality of "being the change we wish to see in the world" by simultaneously redressing a wrong and providing "a living alternative to the existing structure of authority," thereby "setting an example others can imitate."[25] For many anarchists, direct action has come to embody the notion of "dual power," namely that it unites means and ends by "actively engaging with the world to bring about change, in which the form of the action—or at least, the organization of the action—is itself a model for the change one wishes to bring about."[26] Rob Sparrow has attempted to detail the contours of this dual power approach:

> Examples of direct action include blockades, pickets, sabotage, squatting, tree spiking, lockouts, occupations, rolling strikes, slowdowns, the revolutionary general strike. In the community it involves, amongst other things, establishing our own organizations such as food co-ops and community access radio and TV to provide for our social needs, blocking the freeway developments which divide and poison our communities and taking and squatting the houses that we need to live in. In the forests, direct action interposes our bodies, our will and our ingenuity between wilderness and those who would destroy it and acts against the profits of the organizations which direct the exploitation of nature. ... Direct action is not only a method of protest but also a way of "building the future now."[27]

We will consider in more detail below the "building the future" aspect of anarchism, but for now it is worth recalling that direct action possesses this same quality of modeling the global justice slogan "Another World Is Possible." The critical point, perhaps at times obscured by glass shards or bravado, is that this is true of both the constitutive *and* contestational spheres of direct action. For an anarchist society to remain so, an ongoing vigilance and even militancy toward emerging structures of authoritarianism will be necessary. It will also entail cultivating a populace that is capable and desirous of taking a broad range of political matters and lifestyle essentials into their own hands to a large extent. As a mode of conduct that frequently includes working in concert with others, direct action fosters a spirit of cooperative, voluntary association among participants, and it sets an exemplar of effective organizing that facilitates coordinated decision making without sacrificing individual initiative in the process. By embracing a wide view of direct action as resistance to injustice *or* the creation of any positive alternative, direct action comes to be infused in everyday life and thus moves beyond its better-known association with protest-oriented activism.

One of the conundrums of direct action in the context of mass demonstrations is that most actions undertaken in that sphere are more symbolic than substantive, due to the nature of political protest. By "locking down" and blocking a street, or dropping a series of banners from buildings and overpasses, or even smashing the windows of corporate chain stores, activists are plainly behaving in a direct manner—but the degree to which the purveyors of injustice and oppression are impacted is debatable. Moreover, even if the intent is to inflict a modicum of economic damage or prevent a tool of global capitalism from convening its ministerial meetings, it can be argued that this still recognizes the power holders' authority and constitutes "an appeal to the powers-that-be to change their behavior."[28] This critique raises some important questions about the nature of tactics and how they fit into an overall strategy, but it misses the larger point that any open defiance of "law and order" is a potentially subversive act; further, it sets an example for others to be empowered by in confronting injustices in their communities. Direct action works by being bold in its display of "anarchy breaking out," conveying a sense that the future is not yet decided despite official pretenses to the contrary. And nowhere is this duality more apparent—and equally controversial—than in its manifestation as the Black Bloc.

Back in Black

The image of black-clad, street-fighting anarchists has, for good or bad, become the face of contemporary anarchism for many observers. In reality, the "Black Bloc" is more mythical than tangible, and it constitutes a relatively small—though often quite spectacular—part of contemporary anarchism. It has been critiqued as vanguardist, irresponsible, and intolerant, while others lionize its capacity for promoting personal empowerment and developing a "credible threat" to entrenched power. Often misunderstood as an organized group, the Black Bloc is actually a *tactic*, "an approach to action that stresses group unity, mobility, and confrontation."[29] It is equal parts analysis and adrenaline, with a penchant for both solidarity and anonymity, a walking anachronism yet at the edge of innovation. Some have already declared that "the Black Bloc is dead," while others see it as part of a growing global movement that has found relevance "in various parts of North America, Europe, Mexico, Turkey, and Brazil," among other locales.[30] Whatever its legacy, it is clear that the Black Bloc has served to spark imperative movement debates about what is meant by *violence* and how it fits within contemporary anarchism.

I will consider the specific subject of violence in greater depth in the following chapter. For now, at the outset, we can take the Black Bloc as an outgrowth of the direct action tradition, embodying the dual power ethos in its militancy and egalitarianism alike. In a comprehensive study titled "The Black Blocs Ten Years after Seattle," Francis Dupuis-Déri recounts many of the specific actions attributed to the Bloc in recent years, including skirmishes with the police; attempting to spark a riot in a gentrified neighborhood; drawing the attention of the police away from other demonstrators; setting a puppet afire; protecting puppets from the police; blocking streets; setting fire to a McDonald's and trashing three banks; breaking store windows; protecting a police vehicle making its way through a rally; engaging in a peaceful march; attacking a prison; harassing a police security perimeter; and protecting non-violent demonstrators against police assaults.[31] In this compendium, the seeming contradictions are resolved through the application of dual power: contestation *and* construction.

A notable example comes from the lone Black Bloc action described by Dupuis-Déri that was not specifically connected to a mass demonstration, in Buffalo, New York, in the spring of 2001: "A Black Bloc enters a poor neighborhood to collect the garbage. Responding to bewildered reporters asking them what they were doing, some activists tell them, 'You wrote that we would trash the town, [so] we decided to pick up the trash!' "[32] Still, most Black Bloc actions do take place within the context of larger mobilizations, and for anarchists in particular, "the major economic summits are perfect symbols of the state's illegitimacy and violence, its fundamentally authoritarian and hierarchical nature, and its collusion with capital."[33] Interestingly, most Black Bloc participants do not consider themselves violent by any means, and some even actively embrace nonviolence in their activism. Observers in the milieu such as Graeber offer the proposition that the Bloc has developed "what might be considered the most aggressive possible version of nonviolence," while Dupuis-Déri notes that "theirs is a low-intensity, nonlethal violence whose aim is primarily symbolic."[34]

Sometimes the Black Bloc is considered an affinity group, which is simply any small activist unit bonded together by "mutual trust and common feelings about the kinds of action they wish to take."[35] In the context of demonstrations, the affinity group model enables coordination both within and across groups, while still preserving individual and group autonomy in the process. Activists with shared interests, identities, and aims can loosely cohere just for the purpose of a particular protest, or they can constitute longer-term collectives working on various mutual endeavors. At a mass mobilization, the decision-making model of choice has come to be the *spokescouncil*, which meets in a *convergence center* and is comprised of delegates from the various affinity groups. These delegates, called *spokes*, possess no authority and instead serve as conduits of information and the conveyance of intentions between the groups and the whole. Graeber refers to affinity groups, including the Black

Bloc, as "the elementary particles of voluntary association" and assesses this model as one that facilitates the achievement of *consensus* by enabling mutual agreements in a shared decision-making process.[36]

Despite these collective "consensual deliberations," the Black Bloc often maintains that "the decision whether or not to resort to force during a demonstration must not be exempted from th[e] principle of autonomy."[37] In this sense, it strives to uphold a central tenet of anarchism, and "for those who have taken part in such actions, the really critical thing is the sense of autonomy created by an emphasis on solidarity and mutual defense."[38] As Graeber concludes, the Black Bloc is "a way to create one, fleeting moment when autonomy is real and immediate, a space of liberated territory, in which the laws and arbitrary power of the state no longer apply, in which we draw the lines of force ourselves."[39] Dupuis-Déri sees the Black Bloc's emergence as an important part of the effort "to organize along horizontal, egalitarian, consensual lines" and as reflective of an overall "anti-authoritarian tendency repudiating all forms of authority, hierarchy, or power, even those that proliferate within theoretically egalitarian social movements."[40] These complex representations led Starhawk to simply conclude that, "I like the Black Bloc," despite the fact that "in general I think breaking windows and fighting cops in a mass action is counterproductive."[41] In the end, Starhawk recalls that "they're my comrades and allies in this struggle and . . . we need room in this movement for rage, for impatience, for militant fervor."[42]

Still, there remain key points of contention about the Black Bloc. One is the double-edged nature of the sensationalized provocations that the Bloc represents, oftentimes generating media coverage that might otherwise be absent but seeing that coverage limited merely to the ostensible "violent protests" and lacking the context of the movement's larger aims. Critics complain that "the Bloc co-opts the movement and drowns out our message," yet simultaneously grasp the self-reflective dilemma posed by the Black Bloc as a challenge to more established movement norms that are "too often rooted in habit, comfort, or even fear."[43] A more problematic concern about the Bloc comes through the realization that "today the police anticipate it and have even borrowed its aesthetic to infiltrate and manipulate rallies," such as in Geneva in 2003 where "about fifteen police officers disguised as Black Blockers" infiltrated the convergence center and "proceeded to make a number of violent arrests."[44] As Starhawk concurs, "the police [have] used the Black Bloc . . . very effectively," citing reasons including "the anonymity, the masks and easily identifiable dress code, the willingness to engage in more confrontational tactics and in property damage" as points of entry for "police provocateurs."[45]

Two additional contentious issues involve ritualization and provocation. With the latter, it has been argued that the presence of the Black Bloc or other militant actors within a movement places everyone at risk of official reprisals, sometimes including physical brutalization and unjust arrests. Acknowledging that this is a distinct possibility, and not one to be taken lightly, Teoman Gee encourages the critical gaze to remain on the state and capital as the purveyors of violence and, further, that if peaceful protesters are attacked, "it's still the cop who swings the club, not the comrade who threw the rock."[46] Indeed, the Black Bloc has even been known to actively protect other demonstrators by erecting barricades or intentionally drawing off police attention; still, the criticism remains pertinent. Furthermore, there is a growing sense that "ritualizing property destruction or street battles with the cops threatens to empty their significance" and likewise that the ingenuity necessary for effective protest is lost through the repetition of a given action.[47] Sympathetic treatments such as Gee's ask us to view movement militants through a lens of "historical-political context,"[48] which is critical for understanding the meaning of any event—yet reliance upon the same "overused tactics" across multiple contexts can have a diminishing return that undermines movement dynamism and creativity.[49]

Further consideration of these issues, including tactical and ethical inquiries, is presented in the next chapter. As anarchist movements stand today, the tenuous resolution of these debates over actions—especially militant ones—has essentially devolved upon the almost-talismanic invocation of the preference for a "diversity of tactics." The salient points in this widely-held view are that "people should be free to make their own choices; that a nonauthoritarian movement doesn't tell people what to do; and that we should stand in solidarity even with people whose choices we disagree with."[50] This process-oriented acceptance does not fully resolve the underlying concerns—for instance, some critics argue that diversity of tactics is merely a "euphemism for violence"[51]—but it can help to preserve pluralism while averting fragmentation.

A Movement of Movements

Anarchism is inherently pluralistic, and thus any attempt to characterize it as a single "anarchist movement" is doomed at the outset (even as we at times adopt the convention for the sake of analysis). This sense of multiplicity—whether it involves tactics, strategies, theories, or visions— is actually part of anarchism's strength and also perhaps its greatest challenge. On the one hand, we have Goldman's expansive view of an anarchism that "stand[s] for the spirit of revolt, in whatever form, against everything that hinders human growth," coupled with her admonition that "the methods of Anarchism therefore do not comprise an iron-clad program to be carried out under all circumstances."[52] On the other is the position staked more recently by Michael Schmidt and Lucien van der Walt in the provocative book *Black Flame*, where they assert that " 'class struggle' anarchism, sometimes called revolutionary or communist anarchism, is not a type of anarchism; in our view it is the *only* anarchism."[53] Despite repeatedly casting their arguments in terms of constituting the "broad anarchist tradition," Schmidt and van der Walt offer a narrower version of anarchism and revolution than is generally found in the milieu, and in so doing they explicitly exclude key historical figures (for example, Godwin and Tolstoy) from the canon, contending instead that "struggle by the working class and the peasantry . . . can alone fundamentally change society" since these groups are the only ones with the interest "as well as the basic power to do so."[54]

While some may find this to be a welcomed reinvention of anarchism and a reinvigoration of important syndicalist strands within it, certain aspects require a strained historical revisionism that raises some troubling issues, including whether we are still in fact talking about anarchism at all. For instance, the authors express a preference for "large-scale organization" and the development of "political programs," defining their anarcho-syndicalist position as one in which "reforms and immediate gains" are positive and where "unions could take the lead in the struggle for revolution and form the nucleus of the new society."[55] Critiquing the post-Seattle anti-globalization protests as lacking a "systematic project to replace neoliberalism," Schmidt and van der Walt—notwithstanding their prodigious research and meticulous argumentation—swim against the current of anarchist theory and practice that generally eschews invocations of leadership, reformist projects, and the development of pat programs that could lead to new forms of domination and control. Still, the anarchist tent has room for such views, properly cast within its inherently pluralistic framework.

Indeed, I believe that this is precisely what Edward Abbey was suggesting when he said, "Anarchy is democracy taken seriously."[56] Anarchism contains its communitarian impulses, to be sure, but it is firmly rooted in the autonomy of individuals to exercise conscience and express their diverse instincts toward revolution in ways that cohere with the conditions and circumstances of their lives. No one can claim revolutionary primacy, and no single movement can encapsulate the divergent forms of political engagement that individuals and communities will seek to manifest. Working in concert is a desirable and effective way to promote transformation, but it need not limit creativity and multiplicity in the process. The overarching aim is not the promotion of a "systematic project" or a "political program," as *Black Flame* represents, but more aptly it is about "exposing, delegitimizing and dismantling mechanisms of rule while winning ever-larger spaces of autonomy and participatory management within it," as Graeber and Grubacic have articulated.[57] This harmonizes with the basic notion that, when freed from repressive institutions and ideological impositions, people are perfectly capable of fashioning egalitarian and mutualist solutions to the myriad challenges before them.

Citing examples of contemporary anarchist action—including Reclaim the Streets, which throws parties in intersections and "takes back urban space" in the process, and the Living River of blue-clad demonstrators that snakes through the streets as an expression of fluidity—Starhawk observes that "they favor mobility, surprise, and creativity" and likewise that "they are only the beginning of the experiment."[58] Jeff Ferrell highlights similar anarchist tactics, including Critical Mass bicycle actions ("We aren't blocking traffic; we are traffic") that embrace the notion that "the revolution will not be motorized," as well as pirate radio as a form of "sonic subversion" that devolves upon an ethos of "cultural reinvention, anarchic do-it-yourself media, progressive politics, and solidarity with marginalized groups."[59] And in the preface to its compendium on in-your-face anarchist movement tactics—including billboard alteration, guerrilla theater, pie throwing, and wheatpasting posters—the CrimethInc. collective states the premise in clear terms:

> The raw awareness that you have the power to change the world is more important than any other resource. . . . Self-determination . . . must be established on a daily basis, by acting back on the world that acts upon you—whether that means calling in sick to work on a sunny day, starting a neighborhood garden with your friends, or toppling a government. You cannot make a revolution that distributes power equally except by learning firsthand how to exercise and share power—and that exercising and sharing, on any scale, is itself the ongoing, never-concluded project of revolution. What you do today is itself the extent of that revolution, its limits and its triumph.[60]

In this light, it can be said that the ideology of the new movement "is embedded in its practice," and thus for many anarchists it is clear that "the democratic practice they've developed *is* their ideology."[61] In similarly advocating the "politics of the act" as against the "politics of demand" as it relates to the "newest social movements," Richard J. F. Day observes that the latter "is by necessity limited in scope: it can change the content of structures of domination and exploitation, but it cannot change their form."[62] This deep-seated and historically rooted preference for direct action recalls Gustav Landauer's prescient remarks about where movements ought to focus their efforts: "The state is a social relationship; a certain way of people relating to one another. It can be destroyed by creating new social relationships; i.e., by people relating to one another differently."[63]

Such an expansive, behavioral view finds expression in contemporary assertions that "whenever people take initiative and address social problems directly, that is a form of anarchism" and "whenever you act without waiting for instructions or official permission, you are an anarchist."[64] While critics may contend that this elevation of action as constitutive of ideology demonstrates anarchism's lack of a larger strategy or program, it is actually the case that this stance represents one of the key ways that anarchists hedge against simply replicating forms of oppression both before and after the revolution. Indeed, it might be said—just as it seeks to cultivate theory through practice—that anarchism likewise works out its ultimate vision in the lived experiences of resistance that "prefigure" tomorrow by contesting conditions today.

Prefiguring the Future

Much as it takes an expansive view of what constitutes revolutionary action, contemporary anarchism likewise sees the locus of engagement in equally broad terms, as Graeber suggests with the insight that "revolutionary change is going on constantly and everywhere—and everyone plays a part in it, consciously or not."[65] In describing "resistance as a way of life," Howard J. Ehrlich similarly asserts: "The potential for resistance—for honest, courageous, stand-up-and-be-counted resistance—is everywhere in everyday life. Power is exercised everywhere, so it can be resisted everywhere."[66] In the era of globalization, this sense of power being exercised ubiquitously is even more pronounced, exacerbating the ongoing totalization of every aspect of life yet also opening up possibilities for resistance to oppression and injustice at all points of contact—thus defying the ever-increasing authoritarianism found in structures of corporate and military domination. Cindy Milstein views this as a "qualitative retaking of the every day" and concludes that "anarchist experiments expose the cracks in this edifice. They allow people to personally feel what it could be like if life was of their own making."[67] And Jeff Shantz likewise chronicles the development of a contemporary "constructive anarchism" that strives to create "alternative futures in the present."[68] By inciting imaginations and cultivating key skills, these everyday-life moments of "anarchy breaking out" animate the self-organizing vision of what an anarchist society portends.

For Uri Gordon, *prefiguring* is a form of "constructive direct action" and further "represents a broadening of the idea of direct action, resulting in a commitment to define and realize anarchist social relations within the activities and collective structures of the revolutionary movement itself."[69] From this view, it becomes clear that "prefigurative politics is an inseparable aspect of the anarchist project in that the collectives, communes and networks of today are themselves the groundwork for the realities that will replace the present society."[70] This contemporary trend was anticipated by Malatesta, who pointed out nearly a century ago that in order to abolish "all the harmful social institutions we must know what to put in their place, not in a more or less distant future but immediately.... One only destroys, effectively and permanently, that which one replaces by something else."[71] In this light, it becomes incumbent upon anarchism to foster the creation in the present of "positive institutional alternatives" to existing structures, without merely replicating their inherent oppressiveness in the process.[72]

Contemporary methods of building these alternatives, and thus of laying a working (and non-prescribed) foundation for an anarchist society, are thematically varied and widely distributed. Graeber highlights initiatives including cooperatives, infoshops, prisoner support networks, pirate radio, squats, independent media, community gardens, bicycle collectives, cooperative bookstores, Copwatch programs, homeless and immigrant rights campaigns, and Food Not Bombs chapters as part of a "major manifestation of anarchist organizing."[73] In his pragmatic visualization of a coherent anarchist order, Ward considers alternative systems taking hold around families and parenting, education, housing, work, and social welfare, illustrating his vision with examples that constitute a "microcosm of anarchy, spontaneous, self-directed activity replacing the power structure by a network of autonomous groups and individuals."[74] My own writings have similarly expressed a preference for "anarcho-utopian visions ... premised upon inclusive and non-hierarchical social processes, including new visions of economics, gender relations, education, and self-governance."[75]

In today's anarchist milieu, there are innumerable examples of "anarchy in action" that serve to contest current power arrangements while simultaneously prefiguring a new society. As suggested above, anarchism reconciles the ponderous weight of the past with the liberatory possibilities of the future by focusing on the present as a site of both resistance and re-visioning. The anarchist think tank known as the Curious George Brigade argues that the cornerstones of prefiguring are affinity and decentralization, and that it is principally through small-scale organizing that anarchism flourishes without becoming the very thing that it is struggling against: "We should take to heart the thousands of anarchist DIY ["Do It Yourself"] projects being done around the world outside super structures."[76] The open-source Web site Wikipedia—itself a manifestation of decentralized, do-it-yourself anarchism—maintains a "list of anarchist organizations" around the world from 1827 to the present.[77] Among the 125-plus entries, a dozen or so could be considered of the overtly insurrectionist variety, and of these only a handful are still in existence today. The list also includes independent publishers, radical labor unions, anarchist libraries, guerrilla theater troupes, anti-poverty networks, feminist collectives, culture jammers, and numerous local initiatives, many of which are currently in operation.

I would like to highlight a few of these prefigurative examples to illustrate the larger points that frame this analysis of anarchism in action, which, as we have seen, includes an incredibly broad range of contemporary organizing and a longstanding penchant for exercises in *dual power* that contest and construct all at once. In Chapter Four, focusing on "Anarchist Ecologies," I will consider specifically environmental manifestations of anarchy in action; here, the emphasis is on the sociopolitical aspects of anarchist movements and how they play out today—always with an eye on tomorrow. It should also be noted that the prefigurative enterprises highlighted here have a distinctly international reach, a point that will be further considered in the discussion of local and global interconnections undertaken in Chapter Six.

Food Not Bombs

Food Not Bombs (FNB) began in 1980 as part of a protest against the Seabrook nuclear power plant in New England, soon turning its focus to the intersections between poverty, warfare, and degradation of the environment. As a decentralized movement with chapters in scores of countries and hundreds of cities in the United States, according to its Web site, FNB strives to demonstrate "by example that we can work co-operatively without leaders through volunteer effort to provide essential needs like, food, housing, education and healthcare."[78] Each FNB chapter is autonomous, and a consensus process is often used for collective decision making. In addition to providing "free, healthy vegan and vegetarian food," FNB seeks to "provide an opportunity for everyone to participate in solving the most important problems facing our world. We are empowering the public to take action and resist corporate domination and exploitation."[79] As a "loose-knit group of independent collectives," FNB maintains that "anyone who wants to cook may cook, and anyone who wants to eat may eat."[80]

The basic ideology behind the effort is that "myriad corporate and government priorities are skewed to allow hunger to persist in the midst of abundance" and that "if people really want to help the homeless, they may as well feed them directly."[81] FNB serves meals in public places, made largely from donated and recovered foods that would otherwise be discarded. Because of the public nature of its actions, as well as its radical anti-capitalist and anti-state critique, FNB has been investigated by the U.S. government for alleged "terrorist connections," and individual participants have been arrested on numerous occasions—notably in Orlando, Florida, in mid-2011, where dozens of FNB activists were arrested for violating a citywide ban on feeding people in a public place. "Special hostility on the part of authorities has been reserved for Food Not Bombs," according to Ferrell, likely due to its identity as "an anarchistic, direct action group" and its frequent presence in "highly visible or politically symbolic public settings."[82]

FNB is part of the anarchist tradition in its anti-authoritarianism, decentralism, voluntarism, and open defiance of unjust laws. As Graeber notes, it is "not an organization. There is no overarching structure, no membership or annual meetings. It's just an idea—that food should go to those that need it, and in a way that those fed can themselves become part of the process if they want to—plus [it is] a shared commitment to egalitarian decision-making and do-it-yourself (DIY) spirit."[83] In this manner, FNB combines direct action, radical critique, and a prefigurative "vision of an egalitarian, leaderless 'new society' in which people organize spontaneously and in a self-sufficient manner" in striving to provide life's essentials equitably.[84]

CrimethInc.

The CrimethInc. Ex-Workers' Collective formed in the mid-1990s and has published numerous books, pamphlets, and "zines" with explicitly anarchist themes. It is a "decentralized anarchist collective of autonomous cells" to which anyone can belong "who sees a part of herself reflected within our actions."[85] CrimethInc.'s nascent cosmology, as described on its Web site, is that it "has no platform or ideology except that which could be generalized from the similarities between the beliefs and goals of the individuals who choose to be involved—and that is constantly in flux."[86] Its published works are "communalized" and freely available under a "copyleft" perspective that seeks to place the information "at the disposal of those who, in good faith, might read, circulate, plagiarize, revise, and otherwise make use of [it] in the course of making the world a better place."[87] Among CrimethInc.'s publications are the books *Days of War, Nights of Love* (2000), *Evasion* (2003), *Recipes for Disaster: An Anarchist Cookbook* (2004), and *Expect Resistance* (2007), as well as the pamphlet "Fighting for Our Lives," of which over 600,000 copies have been freely distributed. According to Wikipedia, the name "CrimethInc." is an "anonymous tag, a means of constructing dynamic networks of support and communication within the anarchist movement, and as such anyone can publish under the name or create a poster using the logo; each agent or group of agents operate autonomously."[88]

Clearly constituting an anarchist project as to both its open-ended process and its substantive message, CrimethInc. has been called "the greatest propagandists of contemporary American anarchism" by Graeber and Andrej Grubacic, as well as "one of the more important anarchist projects happening in North America over the past decade" by Infoshop.org founder Chuck Munson.[89] While some have criticized its publications as "inchoate" and "lifestylist" in nature, the name CrimethInc. itself—derived from the notion of "thoughtcrime" as developed in George Orwell's book *1984*—conveys "a satirical self-criticism about the hypocrisy of revolutionary propaganda" that mitigates against viewing the project too heavy-handedly.[90] In the end, Graeber concludes that CrimethInc.'s basic perspective represents "an elegant statement of the logic of direct action: the defiant insistence on acting as if one is already free"—a notion further reflected in "Fighting for Our Lives," where the essence of freedom is taken as "forging new realities which will, in turn, fashion us."[91] In combination with its decentralized network and anti-copyright ethos, CrimethInc. prefigures an emergent anarchism that is at once playful and revolutionary in its process and substance alike.

Indymedia

The Independent Media Center (IMC, or simply "Indymedia") was established by various independent and alternative media organizations and activists in late 1999 to provide grassroots coverage of the World Trade

Organization protests in Seattle. The Indymedia Web site uses a democratic open-publishing system in which anyone can upload stories, articles, and accounts of events. IMC is a decentralized, autonomous global network, with centers on every continent. According to its mission statement, "the Independent Media Center is a network of collectively run media outlets for the creation of radical, accurate, and passionate tellings of the truth. We work out of a love and inspiration for people who continue to work for a better world, despite corporate media's distortions and unwillingness to cover the efforts to free humanity."[92] Since its founding, the IMC "remains closely associated with the global justice movement, which criticizes neo-liberalism and its associated institutions."[93] As with Food Not Bombs, Indymedia activists have faced official harassment, including having their servers seized and being served with grand jury subpoenas. In covering anti-globalization summit demonstrations, IMC journalists have been wounded by police on multiple occasions.[94]

From its inception, Indymedia has run on "essentially anarchist principles," as Graeber reports. "Everything was done collectively; people edited each other's stories; there was no hierarchy of editors and reporters; all decisions were made by consensus."[95] Under the decentralized auspices of the IMC, the contemporary era has been defined by a "radical web journalism that has completely transformed the possibilities of information flow about actions and events."[96] The evolution of the IMC reflects a deep distrust for corporate-owned media, but rather than simply railing against it, Indymedia activists have operated under the well-known slogan "Don't Hate Media. Become the Media!"[97] In this sense, the IMC prefigures a new society grounded in anarchist values of empowerment, participation, and self-organization.

These examples of anarchism in action are but a few of the contemporary manifestations of a longstanding preference for autonomous yet collective endeavors. These efforts directly confront existing power arrangements and also point toward a possible future that is "always already" in the offing in the present. While the broad aims of today's anarchist organizing are largely shared by a preponderance of individuals and groups in the milieu, ongoing debates about tactics and strategies pervade the field. Perhaps nowhere is this discussion more heated than around the question of *violence* and its role in anarchist thought and practice. The navigation of this ostensible rift is the subject of the next chapter.

CHAPTER 3

The Violence Question

Perhaps the dominant mainstream perception of anarchism is its equation with violence, disorder, "bomb throwing," and—even more odiously, in today's parlance—*terrorism*. This stereotype is sometimes reinforced by anarchists to an extent, particularly in the context of mass demonstrations where street battles with law enforcement and the destruction of property can occur. Still, a significant portion of anarchists embrace non-violence as well (ironically, some militantly so), leading to a vibrant dialogue with the milieu. The negotiation of the "violence versus non-violence" terrain is one of the many dichotomies presented by anarchist praxis, and it further represents something of a political litmus test for activists in ascertaining where they most readily fit within the panoply of movement culture. Although some of the deep-seated antipathies around these issues have waned a bit in recent years, as familiar ground and mutual agreements are increasingly established in a maturing movement, the debate reignites each time anarchists are alleged to have done something "violent" during the course of a given struggle.

Against this backdrop, one of the many pleasures of self-identifying as an anarchist comes from being asked the "violence question" in all its multifarious forms, from the obvious ("Doesn't anarchy mean bombing and rioting?") to the sublime ("That's easy for you to say, because anarchists don't really believe in anything, do they?"). One gets used to this sort of thing and, indeed, really should come to embrace these instances as "teachable moments" that pervade daily life. When asked about anarchism's association with violence, I often reply by inquiring whether one would ask the same thing of a retail clerk, a stockbroker, a lawyer, a priest, an engineer, a taxpayer, a consumer, a liberal, a conservative—or any other identity attribute associated with mainstream society. Most assuredly, the scale of violence perpetrated by the day-to-day operations of capital and the state is grossly disproportionate to anything in the anarchist lexicon, with upwards of 100 million deaths from wars alone during the twentieth century.[1] I daresay that the sum total of people killed or physically injured by anarchists throughout all of recorded history amounts to little more than a good weekend for the empire.

So when we talk about violence, let us keep the larger frame firmly in mind. Are anarchists violent? Sometimes, but more so when they are participating in the casual, invisible, structural violence of modern life than when they are smashing its symbols of oppression. Is it violent when slaves crush their shackles in an attempt to escape captivity? Is it violent to dismantle a tool of genocide? Is it violent to protect oneself and/or others from an ongoing (not merely imminent) assault? These sorts of queries lead naturally to broader issues about the efficacy of tactics and strategies, what messages are being communicated, where ethics and aesthetics matter, who represents a movement, and why we are struggling in the first place. As a tool for galvanizing energy around these self-reflective and essential movement questions, the trope of *violence*—both as a set of concrete actions and as a metaphysical crucible—represents a unique opportunity to investigate the nature of society, what one stands for personally, and how best to move from where we are to a world no longer plagued by domination and degradation. These are among the most pressing questions before us, not only for activists but for anyone concerned about the future of human existence.

Culture of Violence

Debates over the use of force can be productive and potentially conducive to deeper forms of solidarity, as activists come to grasp the complexities involved and the cultural frame in which they exist. To a great extent, the use of violence in a social movement context—especially when it directly targets obvious symbols of the dominant culture—is like a mirror being held back up to society. We swim in a sea of violence to such a degree that we hardly notice it; it is the medium of our existence, like water to a fish, and thus largely invisible. At the personal level, the acquisition of life's essentials—food, water, shelter—is thoroughly imbricated within the workings of a military-industrial complex that increasingly ensnares the globe. Our very identities are bound up with an inherently violent system, and through our utter dependence on it we become purveyors of violence ourselves—sometimes coerced, sometimes ignorant, sometimes willing. Interpersonally, we exercise privilege and power over others as part and parcel of "business as usual," which Alexander Berkman perceived decades ago:

> And as you are invaded and violated, so you subconsciously revenge yourself by invading and violating others over whom you have authority or can exercise compulsion, physical or moral. In this way all life has become a crazy quilt of authority, of domination and submission, of command and obedience, of coercion and subjection, of rulers and ruled, of violence and force in a thousand and one forms.[2]

On the national and international levels, the news is not much more encouraging. Foreign policy for many countries, following the lead of the United States, has by now devolved primarily upon the deployment of brute strength to secure resources and advance national interests. On a daily basis around the world, the structural violence of homelessness, poverty, racism, and more continues to proliferate. Youth are everywhere bombarded with violent imagery, and schools look more and more like pipelines to prison or proving grounds for military recruitment. An even-handed assessment of Western culture (which is relentlessly expanding its terrain) indicates that the use of force in both words and deeds is not limited to one subset, cadre, or party but is woven into the fabric of life for the majority of the planet's inhabitants—either on the perpetuating or receiving end. Martin Luther King, Jr., recognized this, and thus he was not content to condemn merely the surface appearance of violence on an issue-by-issue basis but rather understood that this was the unspoken backdrop of the entire operation. As King pointedly said in 1967, exactly one year to the day before his assassination, "I could never again raise my voice against the violence of the oppressed in the ghettos without having first spoken clearly to the greatest purveyor of violence in the world today—my own government."[3]

The use of force, both subtle and overt, is in many ways today the political rule, whereas the practice of democratic discourse has become the exception. Cultural appurtenances feed back into this narrative by constructing the "bring it on" ethos as strong-willed, bold, and part of the hero's stock-in-trade, whereas discursive displays of reasonableness, outreach, and a willingness to seek understanding are coded as forms of weakness, naïveté, and even appeasement. Yet as Berkman counsels, the reverse is actually true: "Violence is the method of ignorance, the weapon of the weak. The strong of heart and brain need no violence."[4] In this view, anarchism represents the ideal of a "society without force and compulsion, where all men shall be equals, and live in freedom, peace, and harmony."[5] Berkman concludes that "all government, all law and authority finally rest on force and violence,"[6] a point echoed in the contemporary era by David Graeber in his statement that "the coercive force of the state is everywhere."[7]

Implicit in this analysis is that the use of force can become a slippery slope to authoritarianism, in which the use of "superior force" becomes the operative principle both for those holding entrenched power and those seeking to dismantle it.[8] As Starhawk advises, however, "this is a violent system [and] I don't think it can be defeated by violence"; thus, activists tempted to "pick up a rock" have "accepted the terms dictated by a system that is always telling us that force is the only solution."[9] This is the conundrum posed by the "culture of violence," namely that it co-opts the use of force and tempts us to use it at the same time. The state represents a monopoly of violence, legitimizing its own use of it and criminalizing its deployment by others. Yet simultaneously, we are imbued with heroic images—both real and contrived—in which the use of force is lauded, and we are further given the mythos of *res publica* that renders us all custodians of the monopoly. We learn that force "is all these people understand," that it is the only "realistic" solution to a pervasive problem, that those upon whom it is inflicted are "evil" and thus deserving, that "justice" is served through its application, that "tough love" is unfortunate but necessary, that "people have always been this way," and more. We get it, and our conditioning to it is hard to overcome—yet sometimes we break free.

Change of Heart

Throughout history, "many Anarchists who at one time believed in violence as a means of propaganda have changed their opinion about it and do not favor such methods anymore," as Berkman observed back in 1929.[10] Berkman may know something of which he speaks: in 1892, he attempted to assassinate businessman Henry Clay Frick as an act of "propaganda by the deed" and served 14 years in prison as a result. Chief among these examples of anarchists reversing course on the tactical use of violence in social movements is Berkman's running mate and lifelong friend Emma Goldman, who dabbled in the use of revolutionary violence in her younger days but came to reject it in her later years. Following the co-optation of the Russian Revolution, she wrote to Berkman that "violence in whatever form never has and probably never will bring constructive results,"[11] and she further elucidated her emerging position that "methods and means cannot be separated from the ultimate aim. The means employed become, through individual habit and social practice, part and parcel of the final purpose."[12]

In the end, Goldman came to see non-violence and revolution as intertwined, famously concluding that "no revolution can ever succeed as a factor of liberation unless the means used to further it be identical in spirit and tendency with the purposes to be achieved."[13] In 1923, she articulated a position that reflected her deep moral and tactical commitment to non-violence:

> It is one thing to employ violence in combat as a means of defense. It is quite another thing to make a principle of terrorism, to institutionalize it, to assign it the most vital place in the social struggle. Such terrorism begets counter-revolution and in turn itself becomes counter-revolutionary. . . . If we can undergo changes in every other method of dealing with the social issues we will also have to learn to change in the methods of revolution. I think it can be done. If not, I shall relinquish my belief in revolution.[14]

Ira Chernus, in his book *American Nonviolence*, further assessed Goldman's remarkable and painstaking transition: "It is not surprising that Goldman eventually endorsed nonviolence. Her anarchist views embraced the fundamental premises of the nonviolent abolitionists. She believed that all people should be treated as equals because no one should have authority over another."[15]

For me, following Goldman, anarchism is a condition of being free from violence, force, and coercion. In its ideal embodiment, it is the highest expression of non-violence, and vice versa. As Berkman opined, anarchism is at root a state of "peace without violence," which was affirmed by Herbert Read in plain terms: "Peace is anarchy."[16] Even Errico Malatesta, himself a proponent of revolutionary violence as "an unpleasant necessity," acknowledged in no uncertain terms that "anarchists are opposed to every kind of violence. . . . The main plank of Anarchism is the removal of violence from human relations."[17] This, however, by no means ends the debate, since the space from action to ideal must be traversed—even if we hope to find agreement in the end that actions and ideals, means and ends, tactics and visions, are inextricably linked.

Mindful Destruction

The question of how best to move from today's conditions to a healthier world is the core of social movements of all stripes. Differences in tactical choices sometimes emerge when goals are divergent, either as to the rate of change desired (incremental or immediate), the scope of engagement (piecemeal or total), or the intended outcome (reform or revolution). In addition, individual activists and movement organizations will embrace varying tactics at times due to personal temperament, moral sensibilities, available options, or anticipation of repercussions. Likewise, movements in differing locales will have their choices conditioned by the exigencies at hand and the lessons of their own histories. For instance, what is taken to be "radical" or "violent" in a Eurocentric or North American context often appears very different to activists in the global south, a point that will be explored more in Chapter Six. Yet despite these variances, there is a basic point of agreement that social movement activists behave *intentionally* in their endeavors; that is, they act from a place of purpose. We can debate over intentions, but the starting point should be a recognition that the overwhelming majority of acts are purposeful.

This may seem self-evident, except that its antithesis is regularly invoked in phrases often applied to anarchists—by mainstream culture and fellow activists alike—such as "senseless violence" or "mindless destruction." Certainly, there are occasional sociopaths to be found in any human community, but assuredly it is the case that anarchists as a whole are neither senseless nor mindless. Discourse of this sort is intended to obscure deeper societal issues and misdirect attention from further inquiry into the motivations and claims of movement actors. When a rupture is presented through a dramatic episode such as sabotage or vandalism, the perpetrators are often coded as "thugs" or "hoodlums" as a means of preempting any discussion into *why* someone might be motivated to take such drastic action in the first place.

For example, following a student demonstration in London in November 2010, where some property destruction ensued that was attributed to anarchists, a sampling of media headlines from the coverage included the following: "brainless," "masked morons," "infantile behavior," "thuggish and disgraceful," and "no semblance of serious politics."[18] Similarly, after a demonstration in Santa Cruz, California, in early 2011, where a few windows were broken, a former mayor argued that "the actions of a few infantile thugs or self-centered sociopaths came somehow to epitomize anarchism."[19] Nevertheless, as even a grudging critic acknowledges, "it is a mistake to dismiss them as simply kids out for a riot. Many of them are as committed to the issues as anyone else in the movement."[20] Thus, despite popular perceptions, in actuality "anarchism is mindful destruction," as Crispin Sartwell succinctly observes.[21]

And as with proponents of non-violence, activists engaging in high-confrontational struggle also possess a set of principles, including, as Starhawk notes,

> that a high level of confrontation is appropriate in the situations we now face; that people have the right and responsibility to defend themselves against police violence; that many people are already angry and mostly not saintly and a political movement needs room to express that rage; that active self-defense can be empowering and may also win people to our cause; and that in order to bring down an economic and political system that worships property, property must be attacked.[22]

Moreover, even in the ways that anarchists define violence, we can find seeds of ethicality and core principles. Beyond the standard meaning of violence as the "intentional commitment of physical harm to another person," anarchists often extend the definition to include that it "not injure living creatures"[23]; likewise they widen it beyond mere physical incursions to include other forms of oppressive and dominating behavior, such as restricting freedom, limiting choices, withholding vital resources, inflicting emotional damage, or shaming and humiliating.[24] Uri Gordon offers an intriguing statement along these lines, namely that "an act is violent if its recipient experiences it as an attack or as deliberate endangerment."[25] In this formulation, the judgment about whether something is violent rests with the recipient and not the initiator, reflecting anarchism's spirit of autonomy and self-determination.

This incipient ethical engagement with the use of violence raises a host of additional questions, including most centrally whether the fundamental premises of anarchism can be read to preclude the use of force or coercion altogether. It can be argued, as April Carter has noted, "that anarchist values are inherently and necessarily incompatible with use of violence, given anarchist respect for the sovereignty of the individual."[26] Pursuing this line of inquiry, in 2010 I facilitated a series of workshops on "Anarchism and Nonviolence" in the United States and Canada. As one might expect, spirited conversations ensued in which some people felt challenged by the notion of being non-violent in a world that appears as unremittingly violent, whereas others expressed a commitment to "breaking the cycle of violence" as much as possible in their own lives. One of the exercises in these workshops was to create a working definition of anarchism and then one of non-violence. Comparing the two lists, many overlapping values emerged: self-governance, rejection of domination, respect and mutual aid, anti-war and anti-oppression practices, solidarity, radical egalitarianism, and prefiguring the future society.

It is not my intention here to argue that anarchism and non-violence are strictly unitary. Moreover, I have no interest in further reifying the tiresome (and largely false) dichotomy of violence/non-violence in social movements, including the person/property distinction that is sometimes made when confrontational tactics are deployed. The contextual, pluralistic, and individualistic aspects of anarchism make any final conclusion on these points practically impossible and frankly even undesirable. Historical debates within the milieu over insurrection (i.e., direct physical confrontation with authority) and revolution (i.e., mass organizing to undermine authority) still persist, depending upon one's point of departure. Malatesta, for instance, argued for a "transitional, revolutionary violence" as constituting "the only way to put an end to the far greater, and permanent, violence which keeps the majority of mankind in servitude," while Goldman urged that "revolution is in vain unless inspired by its ultimate ideal. ... The ethical values which the revolution is to establish in the new society must be initiated with the revolutionary activities of the so-called transitional period."[27] In this spirit, as Bart de Ligt wrote in 1937, "the greater the violence, the weaker the revolution."[28]

These differing perspectives are often the result of how one frames the issues. Anarchists reject the top-down violence of the state and corporations, leading some to argue that people have the right to defend themselves against this violence, while others contend that "violence begets violence" no matter who is utilizing it. Some assert that an inherently violent system can only be taken down by force, whereas others point out that force is the one thing the state is actually good at and that no revolution can be won that way. While anarchism is a revolutionary theory, some anarchists work from a more *evolutionary* model, rejecting both the old-school insurrectionary notion of *propaganda by the deed* and the quasi-Marxist sense of a widespread "workers' struggle"—seeking instead to construct alternative societal arrangements to replace the pervasive violence of the present system, as Gustav Landauer counseled a century ago:

> A table can be overturned and a window can be smashed. However, those who believe that the state is also a thing or a fetish that can be overturned or smashed are sophists and believers in the Word. The state is a social relationship; a certain way of people relating to one another. It can be destroyed by creating new social relationships;

i.e., by people relating to one another differently. … We, who we have imprisoned ourselves in the absolute state, must realize the truth: *we* are the state! And we will be the state as long as … we have not yet created the institutions necessary for a true community and a true society of human beings.[29]

Whatever path one chooses, a critical feature is that people must remain free to determine the conditions of their own lives, including their values and identities. Unfortunately, due in part to an ongoing association with violence, anarchists are often prevented from doing precisely that.

The Frame Game

Following the conclusion of the G20 protests in Canada in June 2010, where vandalism against storefronts and police cars occurred, the inevitable post-mortem dissection included the usual litany: activists prepared to file lawsuits, organizers vowed to do things differently next time, police pledged to investigate further, the media highlighted the "destruction" but not the issues, and world leaders promised to continue their efforts unhampered by misguided protesters. And, as is par for the post-protest course, critics cast blame on "the anarchists."[30] The following month, in the aftermath of the Oscar Grant verdict in Oakland, California— where a white police officer who killed an unarmed black youth was acquitted of the most serious charges—police blamed acts of window-breaking and looting on "outside agitators" and "anarchists," who, according to the police chief, "get into good crowds and cause issues."[31] Six months later, a reporter obtained Oakland Police Department records showing that federal authorities had an interest in "Black Bloc anarchists" days after the shooting in January 2009 and that local police had been keeping tabs on potential protesters months before the verdict.[32] "Law enforcement around the world tends to view anarchism as a terrorist threat," noted the reporter, and "the FBI even has a primer about them on their website, under the domestic terrorism section."[33]

These are but two recent examples among many where anarchists have been publicly blamed for destructive acts and even referred to in the context of terrorism. Indeed, by now this is bordering on standard operating procedure for law enforcement and the media whenever vandalism of any sort occurs in the context of political protest. In the post-9/11 era, the invocation of *terrorism* in particular taps into a carefully cultivated sense of public fear, opening a Pandora's box of security and surveillance systems that harks back to historical examples, such as the Palmer Raids of

1919–1920 that targeted U.S. anarchists for arrest and deportation. Scholars refer to this as "frame bridging," where multiple discourses—in this case, small-scale political vandalism and post-9/11 terrorism fears—are spuriously linked together, leading Luis Fernandez to conclude in *Policing Dissent* that "activists in the movement have interacted with a public that perceives them as violent and a possible national security threat."[34]

As Fernandez observes, "before each protest, the media reports that violent anarchists are coming to town, representing them as individuals likely to trash cities," and in nearly every case the framing process delivers: "It no longer matters if the violence originates with police or with anarchists. The framework is already in place; and once something happens, the public interprets the violence as an anarchist act."[35] As a consequence, deeper rifts often develop among activists, with the event's lasting images being those that depict anarchists acting in seemingly unproductive ways that put the interests and safety of others in jeopardy, and anarchists frequently stand accused of "hijacking" and/or "co-opting" the movement.[36] For the larger public, the perception of the "violent anarchist" is further cemented, and the cycle begins anew the next time a public demonstration is held and authorities need someone to blame for whatever ensues—including violence initiated by the state.

This raises the dual sense of *framing*, including both the ways in which behaviors are labeled and how the pretext of "anarchist violence" can be used to affect mass arrests, erode civil liberties, and lead to the further repression of movements.[37] As noted in the previous chapter regarding the Black Bloc, officials are able to utilize the presence of militant activists in a movement in numerous ways, from fanning the flames of public discord to actively infiltrating groups and sometimes provoking the ostensible "violence" in the process. Due to their historical associations with violence—arguably more mythical than tangible, and largely renounced in today's milieu—anarchists are easy targets for such demonization, as reflected in the July 2011 announcement that the Montreal police department had set up an "organized crime" unit specifically targeting "anarchist leaders" who have caused "otherwise peaceful protests [to turn] violent."[38] Later the same month, British officials issued a "counter-terrorist task force" order to members of the public: "Any information relating to anarchists should be reported to your local police."[39] Militant propaganda of the sort that urges people to "attack the financial centers of the country ... large scale urban rioting ... spread the battle to the individuals responsible ... strike hard and fast and retreat in anonymity" adds fuel to the fire.[40] Still, among activists there remains a sense that the "blame and frame" cycle will take place regardless of what they do, and sometimes this realization in itself can contribute to even greater militancy as a result.

Despite the pressures brought to bear, many activists have resisted this "divide and conquer" strategy, refusing to "denounce anarchist violence" in the name of respecting "solidarity."[41] In the aftermath of the London student demonstrations where a modicum of property destruction was in evidence, a group of scholar-activists in the United Kingdom issued a public statement to address the "media's assumption that there's a generalized relationship between anarchism and violence."[42] This open letter, which was published in *The Guardian* newspaper as an op-ed piece, defended the use of *direct action* as "a means for self-empowerment," noted that "this sometimes includes property damage," and concluded that "the threat to a livable world comes not from anarchists, but from governments and capitalism."[43]

A month later, following an episode involving letter bombs in Italy, allegations were leveled that European anarchists were "becoming more violent and coordinated" and were working "in solidarity" with others to organize a "global 'revolutionary war.' "[44] A note claiming credit for the attacks was signed by the Informal Federation of Anarchy and was quoted in *Time*: "We've decided to make our voices heard once again, with words and with deeds. ... We will destroy the system of domination."[45] A member of another Italian anarchist group downplayed the possibility of this episode leading to "highly coordinated and organized anarchist offensives in the future," pointing out that "anarchism by its own nature is not a hierarchical organization."[46] More pointedly, a Swiss anarchist group issued a statement declaring "no solidarity with the 'anarchist' letter bombers" based on doubts about whether there was actually "any anarchist link to these incidents." The statement concluded in no uncertain terms that such acts were irresponsible and that anarchism's basic tenets "prohibit us to injure or even kill functionaries within capitalism as part of a libertarian praxis simply for the role they play. We think this should be obvious to anybody with an anarchist understanding."[47] Unfortunately, it is not.

We Have Met the Enemy

In recent years a strand of literature has emerged, popular in some anarchist circles, scathingly rejecting non-violence and agitating for "armed struggle" as a means of revolution. Principal among these works have been Ward Churchill's *Pacifism as Pathology* and Peter Gelderloos's *How Nonviolence Protects the State*.[48] In addition, Derrick Jensen's writings have broached the subject of instituting "a well-targeted program of assassinations," even as he ostensibly rejects the notion as ultimately futile on strategic (if not moral) grounds.[49] Numerous critiques of these lines of reasoning have been propounded, and I will not rehash them here—except to note that is has often been argued that these works present a contrived version of non-violence to serve as a straw person for argumentation, and that their talismanic invocation of "violent struggle" as foundational to social movements is under-theorized and potentially irresponsible. This is not to suggest that a movement, especially one with anarchism's history, should offhandedly reject such statements; to the contrary, these provocations can provide important moments for dialogue and an evolution of tactical and strategic considerations. We can dispute the thesis, but in so doing it becomes incumbent upon us to offer an alternative formulation for bringing about the changes necessary for human survival.

As I have been asserting throughout this text, I believe that anarchism in its dualistic sense of contestation and construction represents precisely such an alternative. What keeps anarchism from degenerating into perpetual violence or nihilism is its longstanding penchant for connecting means and ends. This can be read as requiring that all means utilized in a movement context must be thoroughly peaceful, since that is the future end envisioned. On the other hand, anarchism represents a position of "eternal vigilance" against creeping authoritarianism, and thus principled protest will be part of the end vision as well. The key for anarchist organizing is that the methods of contestation should strive to prefigure the better society even as they confront current challenges and crises. While this framework opens up the possibility for myriad actions and interventions, I do not accept that it extends to the taking of human life (either targeted or indiscriminate) as posited by the proponents of armed struggle.

While anarchists generally reject a bright line of acceptable tactics, preferring instead a multiplicity of methods based on context and circumstances, the leap from vandalism or sabotage to an armed uprising is problematic, not in the least because it threatens to turn us into the very thing we are struggling against. As Harold Barclay observed, "violence is the technique of the state and the ultimate form of coercion. Those who adopt it as a means cannot help but be tainted by its use."[50] This line of reasoning led Emma Goldman to renounce it altogether: "The one thing I am convinced of as I have never been in my life is that the gun decides nothing at all. Even if it accomplishes what it sets out to do— which it rarely does—it brings so many evils in its wake as to defeat its original aim."[51]

Consider that one of anarchism's central tenets is that the state is inherently violent, indeed representing a monopoly of violence that works at cross purposes to the values of freedom, autonomy, and self-organization. Anarchists throughout history have recognized that the aim of revolution is not to seize that power but rather to dismantle it, by removing its bases of private property and militarism. In the anarchist society, the seeds of violence are addressed in large measure through cooperative systems and participatory processes (anarchist tools for redressing residual conflicts will be considered in Chapter Five). The notion is not to defeat the state through superior force or to turn its monopolization into a democratization of violence, but more so to strive toward eliminating it as a dominant currency in the conduct of human affairs. As de Ligt observed, this must be borne in mind, lest we find that our putative revolution "brings about a tyranny of means" that merely delivers us from one form of subjugation to another:[52]

> Right up to the present minute no righteous cause in the world has ever had the tenth chance of conquering by violence. And nowadays would it even have a hundredth chance? It would have none at all, for, as we have shown, the methods of modern warfare make even the justest cause unjust, since those who allowed themselves to be dragged into it cannot do other than descend to the same level of brutality as those they fight. Even were they to triumph, they would be doomed to safeguard the fruits of victory by a system of force which would always be developing and therefore growing less human, and to sink ever more deeply and inescapably into the mire of destruction.[53]

The argument for armed insurrection is largely rejected in the contemporary milieu; as Graeber notes, "very few North American anarchists would themselves go far beyond breaking a window; almost all scrupulously avoid harming others in any way."[54] Even among those who advocate the use of confrontational tactics, there exists a recognition that some lines ought not be crossed, such as in the communiqué issued by the Acme Collective after the World Trade Organization protests in Seattle: "We contend that property destruction is not a violent activity unless it destroys lives or causes pain in the process."[55] As Gordon observes, "even the heaviest street fighting [today] does not involve anarchists taking up arms, as they would and did a hundred years ago," and thus "armed struggle seems to be for now a self-defeating prospect" (Gordon does leave open the possibility that it could become necessary in the event of widespread social collapse or due to "a final, violent attempt by the state" to maintain its authority).[56] Chaz Bufe argues that even in the most repressive situations, "armed resistance should be undertaken reluctantly and as a last resort, because violence is inherently undesirable due to the suffering it causes . . . and because, as history has shown, the chances of success are very low."[57] The authors of the pamphlet "You Can't Blow Up a Social Relationship" refer to proponents of indiscriminately taking up arms as "vanguardist and authoritarian," pointing out that "armed struggle means people would be killed and there is no getting away from the fact that violence threatens humanism."[58] And in a particularly poignant narrative, Judi Bari—herself a victim of terrorist violence for her anti-logging and forest preservation efforts—rejected the use of such incidences of physical force:

> The person who bombed me was a monster. . . . But what I realized is that if you gave me the same bomb, and you gave me the person's car who did this to me, I don't have it in me to do that back to him. What I have discovered is that there's a level of violence, there's a level of terrorism that's really unacceptable to me, and I think that's one of the things that we really need to change in the world. The existence of this kind of violence in the world and this kind of terrorism, this is part of the problem.[59]

In this light, the arguments advanced by armed struggle advocates appear sophomoric at best and reckless at worst. Churchill contends that non-violence has *never* brought about a "substantial social reorganization" and that, in every instance where it is alleged to have done so, it is actually the case that "violence has been an integral *requirement* of the process of transforming the state."[60] He concludes that while it is a desirable end, unfortunately "in order to achieve nonviolence, we must first break with it."[61] For his part, Gelderloos begins from a premise that "violence is inherent in social revolution," concluding that "our options have been violently constrained" to either do nothing and thus support a violent system, or "pursue new and original ways to fight and destroy that system."[62] In the end, Gelderloos, like Churchill before him, laments the fact that "peace is not an option until after the centrally organized violence that is the state is destroyed."[63]

Unfortunately, these formulations are hardly new and original in their call to arms, and they tap directly into a sense of pervasive violence that already defines the culture we are supposed to be struggling against. "The violence and warfare which are characteristic conditions of the imperialist world," as de Ligt observed, "do not go with the liberation of the individual and of society."[64] Anarchists have long rejected the statists' and militarists' arguments that "if we would ensure peace we must prepare for war; that peace can only be guaranteed by force of arms."[65] Anarchism offers a moral and practical critique of war, rejecting the state's violence in all forms including "the cruel and indiscriminate nature of war."[66] Throughout history, anarchists "have opposed wars between states and adhered to anti-militarist agendas," since "the war-making tendencies of the state are closely related to their socially disintegrative characteristics" and "war is seen as one of the ways in which the institutions of the state corrode and inhibit spontaneous social order."[67] With the most notable exception being the Spanish Civil War, in which anarchists took up arms against a fascist regime (tragically so, in the end), the broader stance of anarchism has long decried war as part and parcel of the state's repressive apparatus.

Still, proponents of armed struggle argue that they are simply being realistic in following Berkman's dictum that "there is no record in history of any government or authority, of any group or class in power having given up its mastery voluntarily. In every instance it required the use of force, or at least the threat of it."[68] The problem is that even a cursory review of history reveals that the sum total of "violent revolutions" has merely served to deliver us into the hands of even more totalitarian and militaristic structures of authority. This is a major flaw in the "realist" school of thought, namely that it takes an "absolutist position" about the primacy of "authoritarian modes of organization or violent methods of protest and struggle" as being the only authentic ones for a radical political praxis.[69] "Dogmatic pacifism bothers me," notes one Black Bloc activist, "but there's also dogmatic violence, based on the view that violence is the only means of carrying on the struggle."[70] As Graeber cogently observes, "the 'reality' one recognizes when one is being a 'realist' is purely that of violence."[71] Thus, as Read counsels, "our practical activity may be a gradual approximation towards the ideal, or it may be a sudden revolutionary realization of that ideal, but it must never be a compromise" of the inherent connectedness of means and ends if we are to bring about an anarchist social order.[72]

Was Gandhi an Anarchist?

Contrary to the militant view, pacifism is neither passive nor cowardly, and in fact it has a deep historical association with anarchism; as Brian Morris has asserted, "most anarchists have been against violence and terrorism, and there has always been a strong link between anarchism and pacifism."[73] In Starhawk's lexicon, "nonviolence has been the tool of choice of precisely those people who face overwhelming violence in their daily lives," and pacifism represents a dynamic posture based on "the refusal to obey unjust laws, the willingness to act and to risk, to disrupt business as usual, not through violence but through noncompliance."[74] For Graeber it is thus clear that "in the larger perspective, [anarchist] ideas and practices emerged much more from [the pacifist] tradition than from any other" and moreover that "in terms of overall approach, Gandhi's 'become the change you wish to see' seems a thousand times more in keeping with the anarchist spirit than Malcolm X's 'by all means necessary.' "[75] Graeber points out that "Gandhi himself recognized a strong philosophical affinity of his own ideas and anarchism" and that the " 'by all means necessary' [idea] seems an awful lot like the very ends-justifies-the-means logic which anarchism has consistently rejected."[76]

Throughout history, many anarchists have overtly embraced a pacifist ethos, including Henry David Thoreau, Dorothy Day, Ammon Hennacy, Alex Comfort, Paul Goodman, and, perhaps most notably, Leo Tolstoy. Despite revisionist attempts to exclude him from the milieu, Tolstoy was unquestionably anarchistic in both his words and deeds: "Tolstoy is an anarchist—and a vigorous one at that—because he specifically called for a society without government and the State."[77] "The State is a conspiracy designed not only to exploit, but above all to corrupt its citizens," he wrote in 1857, and "henceforth I shall never serve any government anywhere."[78] He staunchly rejected violence as a precept of his nonhierarchical reading of Christianity, famously asserting that "government is violence" and concluding that "a protest which permits itself the use of violence has not a leg to stand on and is, as a consequence, doomed to failure."[79] Tolstoy's sophisticated view included the notions that "to take up armed struggle is to fight the State on its own ground where it is strongest," and that the state will not hesitate "to make use of agents provocateurs and to orchestrate fake terrorist attacks" as a means of discrediting radicals, hypnotizing the public with fear, and further strengthening its position in the end.[80]

Tolstoy sought to embody a "moral revolution" based on the refusal to cooperate with authoritarian structures, and he saw the personal dimensions of our lives as a critical (yet largely ignored) locus of revolutionary potential. In his own actions, Tolstoy renounced the copyrights on much of his published work, gave up his estates, and founded 13 "free schools" for peasant children based on "purely libertarian principles," including that "the pupil has always the right not to come to school, or, having come, not to listen to the teacher."[81] "The best policy and administrative system for a school is to allow the scholars perfect freedom of learning and of governing themselves as they like," he wrote in 1862.[82] Tolstoy's life and work as an anarchist and pacifist had a profound impact on a young Mohandas K. Gandhi, and the two corresponded briefly at the end of Tolstoy's life. "It was forty years ago, when I was passing through a severe crisis of skepticism and doubt," Gandhi wrote in his autobiography, "that I came across Tolstoy's book *The Kingdom of God is Within You*, and was deeply impressed by it. I was at that time a believer in violence. Its reading cured me of my skepticism and made me a firm believer in *ahimsa* (non-violence)."[83]

Known of course as an iconic figure of non-violence, Gandhi likewise borrowed from and advanced many aspects of anarchism in his social and political philosophies. As described by Josh Fattal in the journal *Peace Power*, Gandhi's anarchism was made plain in myriad ways:

> Mohandas Gandhi opposed the State. The State is the military, police, prisons, courts, tax collectors, and bureaucrats.... "The State represents violence in a concentrated and organized form. The individual has a soul, but as the State is a soulless machine, it can never be weaned from violence to which it owes its very existence." ... Reiterating the idea of Anarchy, Gandhi said, "In such a state (of affairs), everyone is his own ruler. He rules himself in such a manner that he is never a hindrance to his neighbor." ... Gandhi's concept of swaraj elucidates the connection between the individual and society. Swaraj translates into "self-rule" or "autonomy." ... The principle of swaraj ultimately leads to a grassroots, bottom-up, "oceanic circle" of self-ruling communities.[84]

Anarchists will recognize many familiar themes here, including a strong preference for autonomy, self-governance, decentralization, self-sufficiency, and a federated network of horizontal communities—as Gandhi's ultimate vision of a new society embodies:

> Independence begins at the bottom.... It follows, therefore, that every village has to be self-sustained and capable of managing its own affairs.... In this structure composed of innumerable villages, there will be ever-widening, never ascending circles. Life will not be a pyramid with the apex sustained by the bottom. But it will be an oceanic circle whose center will be the individual. Therefore,

the outermost circumference will not wield power to crush the inner circle but will give strength to all within and derive its own strength from it.[85]

In addition to Tolstoy's influence, Gandhi also took much from Peter Kropotkin's anarchistic teachings, embracing "his vision of a decentralized society of autonomous village communities."[86] As Peter Marshall has further observed, "on several occasions [Gandhi] called himself a kind of anarchist and always opposed the centralized State and the violence it engendered."[87] Indeed, in a 1916 speech, Gandhi straightforwardly proclaimed that "I myself am an anarchist," even as he disavowed the violent (i.e., killing in the name of liberation) wing of the movement.[88] Still, Gandhi was not in fact an absolute pacifist—although his personal peccadilloes do suggest a kind of spiritual puritanism and moral orthodoxy that some find troubling. Yet on more than one occasion he expressed the view that it is better to fight than be a coward: "Where there is only a choice between cowardice and violence, I would advise violence."[89] In the end, Gandhi's legacy asks us to deeply consider the nexus of means and ends and points toward his conviction that "the ideally nonviolent state will be an ordered anarchy."[90]

Toward a Complementarity of Tactics

From pacifism and building alternatives to revolution and insurrection, anarchism represents a rich tradition of diverse tactics and strategies aimed toward achieving the widely shared goal of building societies upon a foundation of autonomy, equality, and voluntary association. The pointed debates about the means to be employed in sociopolitical struggle can at times be rancorous, but they are also a strength of anarchist movements, likewise reflecting the sense of pluralism and heterogeneity that underscores anarchism in general. In seeking to reconcile the nascent movement rifts over methods of engagement, anarchists have largely settled upon a collective framework that embraces a "diversity of tactics." As Starhawk observes, there is an operative ethic involved in this resolution, namely that "people should be free to make their own choices; that a nonauthoritarian movement doesn't tell people what to do; and that we should stand in solidarity even with people whose choices we disagree with."[91] In this sense, "the respect for tactical diversity thus relates to an ideal of autonomy centered on a radical definition of the principles of freedom and equality."[92]

Critics may contend that diversity of tactics is merely a "euphemism for violence,"[93] and not all anarchists embrace the concept, but it has served for over a decade to forestall the splintering of movements into abject factionalism. Perhaps more importantly, it has also spawned greater dialogue and new levels of understanding among activists across a range of perspectives and identities. Yet at the same time, viewpoints about "violence versus non-violence" have begun to harden, and the pressure on movements to police themselves has increased as a function of official repression and public perception alike. While observers such as Jensen assert that "the question of whether to use violence" should be secondary to the motivations for a better world that underscore the struggle, there remains a sense (as Gelderloos expresses) that "people have, for the most part, not even figured out whether our goals are compatible, and whether our strategies are complementary or counterproductive."[94] Indeed, a central open issue for anarchists is contained within the observation that even "the total collapse of this society would provide no guarantee about what replaced it."[95] In this sense, *diversity of tactics* has functioned as an "agree to disagree" approach without prompting a deeper discussion about what comes next.

Taking up Gelderloos's challenge, a compelling argument can be made that it is time for anarchism to move beyond a mere tactical-diversity approach. A starting point might be to reaffirm the shared values and visions that have drawn people to anarchism in the first place. At this juncture, anarchists might look for ways to support and bolster those places where there in fact may be broad agreement: mutual aid, anti-statism, anti-capitalism, egalitarianism, autonomy, and so on. Rather than repeating useful but tired mantras about diversity of tactics, which can bring with it a sense of resignation and the preclusion of continued discussion, anarchists could instead seek to generate a "complementarity of tactics," in which the choices made are mutually-reinforcing and reflective of the myriad shared values that pervade the anarchist tradition. By shifting the conversation from "I don't necessarily agree with what you're doing but I respect your freedom to do it" to "I want to learn more about what you hope to accomplish with this action and how it fits with your vision for the future," anarchists could develop stronger bonds of solidarity—and thus more effective movements—in the process. Indeed, for many, "the essence of revolution is not armed conflict with the state but the nature of the movement which backs it up, and this will depend on the kinds of relationships and ideas amongst people in the groups, community councils, workers councils, etc. that emerge in the social conflict."[96]

It is apparent that this is a matter of some urgency for anarchist movements. The sense of "violent anarchists" becoming the justification for an escalating police state, and all of its retributive techniques against activists in general, has become palpable—even as we may recognize it as obviously fallacious and disingenuous. What are the available alternatives? We might remain on the same course, but that is increasingly looking like one bent on public alienation, increased repression, and perhaps ultimately oblivion. Anarchists throughout history have been known for their innovation, flexibility, and boldness; I would submit that this is a moment to bring all of those qualities to the fore and focus more pointedly on how to contest the present while building the future—always bearing in mind the means-ends nexus that is part and parcel of anarchism's dynamic ethos. Far from constraining action, this perspective offers the potential for greater harmonization between actions and visions, between anarchists and other activists, and among anarchists themselves.

As a starting point, anarchists would do well to remind people that the state (including its corporate partners) is inherently violent, both overtly and structurally—and since anarchists above all reject the state (and capital), they can undertake actions that highlight this fundamental contrast. "The state is violent, and we are not" might be a good start to the discussion. Another central point for advancing the dialogue would be to refocus activist energies beyond their sometimes-narrow sectarian interests, most directly by cultivating an ecological perspective that speaks to the pressing global issues of the day. This will be the focus of the next chapter.

CHAPTER 4

Anarchist Ecologies

One of the galvanizing forces among anarchists of all stripes throughout history has been a strong focus on property rights, most often taking the form of advocating for the abolition of privatization and the promotion of communal interests as to the management of basic human resources. This emphasis on property gives anarchism a decidedly environmental bent, insofar as it draws our attention to the essentials of food, energy, shelter, and land as critical areas of intervention and engagement. While anarchists have debated the precise formulations for access to and distribution of resources, the rejection of private property interests in the land and the overall means of production has represented a sine qua non of anarchism for generations.

Some of anarchism's central figures, such as Peter Kropotkin and adopted brethren like Henry David Thoreau, are historical forebears of the modern environmental movement.[1] Indeed, following Kropotkin and Thoreau, among others, anarchism has long included an impetus toward *naturalism*, in the sense of locating human ethics and sociopolitical structures firmly within the larger processes of natural systems. Many of the most-cited anarchist experiments in history have explicitly embraced a strong "back to the earth" ethos, including the advocacy of small-scale agriculture, village life, and vegetarianism or veganism. Even those experiments more often associated with revolutionary politics (such as the Spanish Civil War) have still counted "many adepts of naturism and vegetarianism among its members," in the recognition that "these ways of living were considered suitable for the transformation of the human being in preparation for a libertarian [anarchist] society."[2]

Anarchists today have extended these environmental themes to include critiques of technology, visions of bioregionalism, efforts toward food justice, and strategies for coping with climate change, among other contemporary issues. Sometimes these undertakings reflect an affinity with a perceived natural harmony that is viewed as dynamic, spontaneous, and self-organizing—much like anarchism strives to be in itself. At other points, anarchists' ecological engagement is more pragmatic, working to ameliorate the harsh effects of capitalism's unequal distribution and, simultaneously, to develop evolutionary (if not revolutionary) alternatives to a dominant order that fosters dependency and exploitation rather than self-rule and cooperation. At still other moments, the environmental emphasis is even more visceral, essentially entailing a direct assault by "ecological anarchists" on the "megamachine" of destruction that is bound up with modern civilization and its dual tendency to dominate nature and subjugate humankind all at once. Indeed, for many anarchists, the assertion of human supremacy over nature and the domination of humans by other humans are thoroughly intertwined processes, and both sets of forces are seen as contributing to widespread environmental degradation that inexorably pushes the world toward the brink of apocalypse. For some in the milieu, it is rapidly appearing that the choice before us is "anarchism or annihilation"—meaning that the effort to achieve an anarchist social order is no longer a mere idyllic vision but is an urgent necessity for human survival.[3]

Anarchists have long been on the cutting-edge of ecological thinking, having at many points anticipated the profound sense of pervasive and escalating crises that we presently face. As an inherently revolutionary system of thought, anarchism seeks to dismantle structures of oppression and disharmony at all levels, from the personal to the global. In so doing, it strives to reformulate the conditions of human existence at its most basic echelons, including the essentials of life such as sustenance, shelter, energy, and space. Through its efforts to resist privatization and promote democratization of resources, both materially and ideologically speaking, anarchism sees human liberation as part and parcel of ecological revitalization. Beyond simply speaking the language of sustainability, anarchists focus on nature's resiliency and dynamism, oftentimes highlighting its capacity to regenerate and create abundance. In order to realize these natural tendencies, humankind must build a social order upon similar foundations, which have consistently been embraced by anarchists in their penchant for decentralized, spontaneous, and cooperative endeavors. Indeed, this convergence of anarchy and ecology is not accidental, and in fact it comprises a longstanding (if not predominant) aspiration of anarchistic thinkers dating all the way to prototypical exemplars such as Lao-Tzu and Zeno of Citium.

This putative convergence, however, does not end the inquiry. Anarchism and environmentalism have a complex, and at times conflictual, relationship. On the one hand, as noted above, anarchism is inherently ecological in its aims and desires. Yet the modern environmental movement is often construed as being bound up with reformist pursuits, electoral politics, lobbying efforts, "corporate responsibility," and other forms of what more radical environmentalists sometimes refer to as "greenwashing" (i.e., the tendency to repackage innately unsound policies, practices, and products as new, improved, and environmentally-friendly). As David Watson has opined, "lacking a perspective that challenges the capitalist order, environmentalists have seen their rhetoric captured and employed by the contaminating corporations and the state."[4] Anarchists do not merely seek to sustain the current paradigm of state control and capitalist production and consumption, nor to attain a more durable system of resource exploitation and distribution. Anarchism envisions a world where production is for use, not profit, and where people situated in their locales can decide how best to manage their material lives. The workings of the global corporate economy are thus incompatible with anarchism, and any attempt to prolong this system's stranglehold on people and nature alike is seen as untenable. That said, anarchists maintain an affinity for nature that partly embraces (yet also goes beyond) the conservationist and sustainability efforts that define much of environmentalism today.

A Hidden Harmony?

Works documenting the grave and escalating character of the environmental crises confronting humankind are by now legion. In recent years, there has been greater public consciousness of issues including climate change, loss of species, soil depletion, drought, pollution, food shortages, toxicity, and other symptoms of widespread degradation across the globe. In addition, a growing number of people have begun to connect these burgeoning crises with the machinations of corporate capitalism and the nation-states that sponsor and enable it to progress unfettered; indeed, the coincidence of the rapid destabilization of the environment and the rise of the global, technocratic economy has not been lost on many observers.[5] As Joel Kovel poignantly observes, the choice before us increasingly appears to be whether we will opt for "the end of capitalism or the end of the world."[6] As a sociopolitical theory that is staunchly anti-capitalist, anarchism has long embraced these sentiments, back to its earliest roots as a political theory and well before the full effects of today's crises were widely anticipated. As the anarchist geographer Elisée Reclus wrote in his famous 1891 essay, "Evolution and Revolution":

> It will be salvation, and there is none other. For if capital retains force on its side, we shall all be the slaves of its machinery. . . . If capital carries the day, it will be time to weep for our golden age; in that hour we may look behind us and see like a dying light, love and joy and hope—all the earth has held of sweet and good. Humanity will have ceased to live.[7]

Such nascent ecological notions are deeply embedded in the theory and practice of anarchism. In the contemporary milieu, for example, Graham Purchase observes that "the overriding cause of hunger, starvation, and environmental degradation . . . is the corporate capitalist system under which we are forced to live."[8] As Purchase concludes, it is "no accident that Emma Goldman chose to call her long-running anarchist journal *Mother Earth*" (following the early work of Reclus, simply titled *The Earth*), which represents a "poetic and well-crafted description of the ancient and time-honored metaphor of the Earth as mother and pro-vider."[9] According to Peter Marshall, Reclus "spent a long life of scholarly research and militant agitation to bring about the equilibrium of the natural order of anarchy."[10] Goldman herself referred explicitly to anarchism as "the teacher of the unity of life, not merely in nature but in man," and she advocated for a version of natural law (to replace man-made law) that would assert itself "freely and spontaneously with-out any external force in harmony with the requirements of nature."[11] And Kropotkin, of course, famously based his divination of "mutual aid as a factor of evolution" on exhaustive biological research, concluding that the processes of mutuality, cooperation, and sociability are simply "what Nature teaches us."[12]

All of this has led Purchase to conclude that anarchism devolves upon the critical insight that "a hidden harmony exists between the earth and the people it supports."[13] The Green Anarchist International Association premises its "Ecoanarchist Manifesto" explicitly on the ways in which humankind is embedded within "the ecological interrelatedness of the world around us," concluding that "there will be no real anarchism without ecology [and] no real ecology without anarchism."[14] In this vein, Brian Morris likewise opines that "anarchism implies and incorporates an ecological attitude towards nature."[15] For Cindy Milstein, "an ecological perspective within anarchism ... sees the world holistically [and] translates into the very openness that characterizes anarchism."[16] Ira Chernus thus poses the summative question: "What do anarchists see when they look at nature?"—and concludes as follows:

> Nature is organic. All its parts are interconnected and constantly interacting, so each part influences all others. Nature is spontaneous. ... Because it is organic and spontaneous, nature is diverse [and] any attempt to stifle that diversity stifles the flow of life itself. Nature is cooperative. ... This cooperation, like everything else in nature, is spontaneous, not commanded by a central authority. Yet the result is not chaos. When individuals are totally free, they spontaneously create the forms of order that are best for them.[17]

In the end, as Purchase notes, anarchists are defined most directly by "their relentless quest for justice, equality, and harmony among all living things"—including humans and nature alike.[18]

But that does not entirely settle the matter, since anarchists—as is their wont—disagree over the implications of these naturalistic underpinnings. While it is the case that anarchists by and large embrace environmental issues as part and parcel of critiquing the workings of capital and the state, likewise in formulating liberatory and egalitarian alternatives, there also exists a strong secularist-rationalist current in anarchism that resists any attempts to turn naturalism into an incipient spiritualism. In other words, the oftentimes quasi-mystical manner of expressing ecological virtues is thoroughly rejected by some anarchists—including the Green Anarchist International Association (despite their acronym of "GAIA"), who specifically dismiss any "new age and/or Skippy & Disney" formulations, including "guru-hierarchies [or] spiritual ecology."[19] As David Orton more soberly contends, "contrary to anarchist thinking, there cannot be very definite lessons drawn from Nature, in how humans should organize themselves ... because most humans lack both the knowledge and wisdom to understand fully the organization of the natural world, and to draw the appropriate lessons for ourselves."[20] Philosophers sometimes refer to arguments of the "appeal to nature" variety as a form of "naturalistic fallacy" in which conclusions about how humans *should* act are derived from observations of how nature *does* act. While such argumentation threatens to degenerate into anarchist esoterica, the implications have partly defined major rifts in the field.

Ecology, Social and Deep

Despite many points of agreement about the development of ecological crises and their genesis in state-bound and capitalistic modes of organization, two of the primary camps with the "ecoanarchist" milieu have diverged over what is to be done, resulting in a longstanding "acrimonious dispute between social ecologists and deep ecologists."[21] In actuality, this rift might be more about intellectual territorialism and personal antipathies, and accordingly a number of observers have found more points of convergence than rupture between the competing schools known as *social ecology* and *deep ecology*. Still, this ostensible (and at times publicly displayed) conflict has served to highlight the existence of multiple approaches to contemporary anarchist engagement with the environmental aspects of human existence. The result has been a fruitful reigniting within anarchism of critical debates about praxis, teleology, ethics, and worldviews, plus tangible inquiries into areas such as technology and economic alternatives. As a theory of integrative tension, anarchism is capable of synergizing the insights put forth by various schools of thought, and the emerging cosmology of *ecoanarchism* reflects this tendency.

The leading exponent of social ecology as a system of thought was Murray Bookchin, whose complex vision of "libertarian municipalism" weaves together strands of classical anarchism, humanism, Hegelian dialectics, and modern environmentalism. Bookchin argued that patterns of domination and hierarchy in society are part and parcel of the domination of nature and thus drive the current ecological crises. In seminal works such as *Post-Scarcity Anarchism* (1971) and *The Ecology of Freedom* (1982), Bookchin propounded a critique of repressive and exploitative structures in contemporary society, positing that only a social order that had abolished them in favor of egalitarian and communal processes could achieve a balanced, sustainable relationship with the larger environment. In this view, as Bookchin contends, "the *idea* of dominating nature has its primary source in the domination of human by human," thus prioritizing the realm of society as the locus for addressing ecological issues.[22] Still, Bookchin understood that nature is also a participant (perhaps even a teacher to an extent) as to how human communities evolve and that, in the right context, humankind could attain a "material abundance" that would overcome the false scarcity and repressive drudgery of capitalism in a manner that might reformulate society's relationship with the balance of the environment. The operative concept in this non-prescriptive vision is an organic "unity in diversity" among federated, regionalized communities that both reflects and constitutes the basic human-nature dialectic. In the end, as John Clark observes, social ecology envisions "a comprehensive *holistic* conception of the self, society, and nature" based on interdependence and "mutualistic naturalism."[23]

While it continues to factor significantly in anarchist views on environmental issues, social ecology has been criticized for its prioritization of human affairs vis-à-vis nature, as well as the instrumentalism and even anthropocentrism potentially suggested in its formulation. Moreover, Bookchin's well-known caustic responses to competing theories and/or potential detractors contributed to a sense of rigidity that did not always cast his theories in a positive light. Perhaps Bookchin's most pointed attacks were reserved for deep ecology, which he dismissed as misguided mysticism and a dangerous inversion of the human-nature balance. Derived from the biospheric environmentalism of Arne Næss, and later popularized by figures such as Bill Devall and George Sessions, deep ecology essentially inverts Bookchin's formulation and instead begins from a premise of radical egalitarianism that extends to humans and nature alike.[24] Explicitly rejecting anthropocentric views, including those implicit in social ecology, deep ecology devolves upon an anti-instrumentalism that regards humankind as one aspect of an interconnected natural system that is balanced equally by all of its components. As such, for deep ecologists, humankind is always already part of nature, and therefore it cannot diminish natural diversity without destroying the very system in which it is enmeshed.

The ensuing debate between social and deep ecology need not be recounted here in detail, except to note that it has largely served the double-edged purpose of promoting anarchist engagement with ecological issues while simultaneously contributing to greater factionalism. In a sense, the "social versus deep" ecology schism is reflective of similar rifts in anarchism that break along the lines of materialist/spiritualist, syndicalist/lifestylist, and revolutionist/evolutionist tendencies in the milieu. On the one hand, there is the view that concrete political conditions and mass organizing around the means of production and consumption define the priorities of human society and the prospects for ecological balance. On the other is a perspective advocating for a baseline reformulation of human perceptions regarding nature, as well as an injunction to manifest this egalitarian vision in every sphere of life. In reality, the theories are complementary in the sense that humankind certainly can strive to be mindfully situated and materially satisfied at the same time—and perhaps even more to the point, we can *only* attain the one in conjunction with the other.

In this light, figures such as Gary Snyder—the erstwhile Beatnik, Buddhist poet, and sharp critic of the state's imperialism and capitalism's growth-obsession—have sought to harmonize social and deep ecology by recasting the discussion less in terms of whose prioritization of domination is correct and more so on what the effects (and stakes) are. Snyder advocates a bioregionalist approach based on the pursuit of an "organically rooted local and regional culture" that replaces the totalitarian and ecocidal state with human communities striving for social harmony and ecological balance.[25] One significant contribution to the ways in which anarchists have subsequently come to evolve their ecological sensibilities has been Snyder's distinction between nature, wilderness, and the wild as loci of human activity as well as overlapping terrains for considering the dimensions of our collective existence.[26] Indeed, for some contemporary anarchists, the desire to "rewild" and/or "go wild" has become an overarching compulsion, and it likewise comprises an expression of living outside the repressive bounds of the state and the destructive impetus of corporate capitalism.

Born to Be Wild

For Snyder, following the social ecologists, "both humans and the non-human are an expression of nature," meaning that human social constructs are not in fact unnatural.[27] The *wilderness* then represents that "part of the physical world that is largely free of human agency" (such as a pristine forest or the ocean depths), and *the wild* is a "complex process of becoming" in which one's "wild nature" is reclaimed as against the realm of human greed and ecological despoliation.[28] In this sense, as Snyder argues, "nature is ultimately in no way endangered; wilderness is," and thus the opportunity to reclaim wildness as a human value is increasingly diminishing.[29] From this insight there has sprung a contemporary version of "ecological anarchism" that tends to "place emphasis on *wildness* rather than wilderness *per se*," and which has come to believe that "the salvation of the world lies in wildness."[30] With roots in deep ecology's invocation of a biospheric egalitarianism that decenters human societies as the linchpin of existence, proponents of what is often referred to as *primitivism* generally celebrate "the wildness of an unconstrained and untrammeled nature, of an unexploited world not yet entirely subject to commodification and domestication."[31] As Mick Smith concludes, in this view, "wildness is regarded as synonymous with creative freedom from social constraint."[32]

Extending the point, wildness becomes the essence of anarchism, and vice versa. "Anarchism, understood as freedom from constraint, *is* wildness and that wildness is the living, creative, principle of nature, both wild nature and human nature, now dominated and repressed by the civilizing process."[33] The issue for primitivists, then, is less about whether human-human domination or human-nature domination is prior, since both humans and nature are equally dominated by the domesticating, routinizing, and exploitative practices that have come to be associated with *civilization* itself. Proponents of neoprimitivism as an expression of ecological anarchism include Fredy Perlman, whose landmark work *Against His-story, Against Leviathan!* (1983) sets forth an eclectic and wide-ranging critique of the "Western Spirit" that subsumes the practices of the state, capitalism, and more broadly the sum total of human civilization as an enterprise that stands against Mother Earth.[34] Similarly, in *Endgame: The Problem of Civilization* (2006), Derrick Jensen predicts (and advocates for) the collapse of advanced, developed society (i.e., civilization), reflecting upon the imminent threat to existence posed by human interventions and the urgent need to eliminate this threat through direct action.[35]

Perhaps the best-known articulation of such notions comes from John Zerzan, who, in works such as *Against Civilization* (2005), rejects the wars, mechanization, dehumanization, environmental destruction, and the "mass psychology of misery" inherent in modern society.[36] For Zerzan, settled human existence began to become the dominant norm around the same time as the advent of agriculture as a widespread means of procuring sustenance, and along with this propertarian, dominating turn came the impetus for sociopolitical stratification as well as the increasing degradation of the environment. Moreover, this perspective contains a concomitant valorization of pre-civilizational hunter-gatherer societies, as Zerzan has argued: "Now we can see that life before domestication/agriculture was in fact largely one of leisure, intimacy with nature, sensual wisdom, sexual equality, and health. This was our human nature, for a couple of million years, prior to enslavement by priests, kings, and bosses."[37] For many anarcho-primitivists, civilization "in all its various guises [is taken] to be inherently destructive to biological and cultural diversity and to individual freedoms," and the very notion of "progress" is little more than "an ideological smoke-screen used to justify the increasing domestication and enslavement of human populations and ecological landscapes."[38] This view thus rejects the "ecological humanism" of social ecology and its inherent progressivism as well.

Bookchin, in response, leveled many of the same critiques against primitivism as he did against its ideological cousin, deep ecology. With its tendency to place human needs on a par with those of non-human systems, Bookchin saw primitivism as denying the unique capacity of humankind to transform its environment, as well as denying the responsibility this quality carries with it to do so in positive ways. In calling for a return to pre-agrarian lifeways and (by Malthusian implication) far lower levels of human population, primitivism at times has been equated with a kind of *ecofascism* that callously ignores the special needs and powers contained within human existence. And in romanticizing pre-civilizational cultures, primitivism has (for Bookchin) taken on a cult-like, mystical, pre-rational aura that is titillating in its eccentricity but short on concrete programs for confronting the major crises in our midst. "Whereas anarchists wish to eliminate the state and give the means of production to the hands of the people, primitivists want to get rid of production itself," and since "it is unrealistic to expect modern people to become tribal … primitivism can play a part in the marginalization of anarchistic thinking."[39]

Despite these criticisms, primitivism has enjoyed a resurgence of support in recent years, as the contemporary anti-globalization and anti-war movements have come to challenge the imperialistic, hierarchical, technocratic, and exploitative aspects of modern life—and thus of civilization itself. Anarchist publications such as *Fifth Estate*, *Green Anarchy*, and *Green Anarchism* have cultivated a strong primitivist undercurrent in the milieu, laying a foundation for today's radical environmental movement and interposing a "critical examination of the society in which we live right now and the ways [in] which it systematically alienates our life-activities and denies our desires for a more unitary and satisfying way of life."[40] To those arguing that primitivism is anti-human and regressive in its diminished-population implications, proponents note that "civilization hasn't done a very good job of helping to keep alive the tens of thousands in the (under)developed world currently without access to clean water and adequate food," moreover asserting that civilization has not forestalled the harsh realities of warfare, impoverishment, and genocide—not to mention the urgency that comes with the realization that we are now living through "an ecological crisis that is unprecedented in the history of humanity."[41] In this view, "civilization itself is inherently violent and unsustainable and can only be remedied by an end to industrialism and return to a more harmonious way of life."[42]

Primitivism often includes a call for *rewilding* our lives by recovering "lost knowledge" of how to live in harmony with the earth, serving to vividly remind us of "what it is possible to reclaim about human culture and history" and yielding lessons that merit consideration if we are to successfully navigate today's compound and escalating social-ecological crises.[43] As one commentator has observed, "if one doesn't at least deeply sympathize with the primitive, you must really be on the side of the mega-tech, controlled as well as controlling mega-population, mega-authority as against real as well as ideal alternatives. One should be properly skeptical about any libertarianism that lacks considerable primitivism."[44] Still, as Bookchin has contended, "to oppose activities of the corporate world does not mean that one has to become naively romantic and 'bio-centric.' "[45] As Jason McQuinn likewise intones, "the critique of civilization doesn't have to mean the ideological rejection of every historical social development over the course of the last 10 or 20,000 years."[46] Setting up the terms of what is yet another substantial point of debate within contemporary anarchism, Bookchin valorized the potential of new technologies that might "begin to provide food, shelter, garments, and a broad spectrum of luxuries" without denigrating human dignity or destroying the environment.[47] Once again, a potentially polarizing issue offers great insight into the contours of today's anarchism.

We Have the Technology

Is technology a potential savior or merely another tool of our enslavement? Social ecologists such as Bookchin see a liberatory role for modern technology in promoting alternative energy sources, increasing food production, remediating degradation, and processing wastes, among other positive potentials. It is also contended that the reasoned application of appropriate technology could yield greater decentralization and local control, thus harmonizing with many of anarchism's core aspirations. Proponents of such a progressive perspective assert that technology is value-neutral—that it is how we use it and for what purposes that determine its character. Indeed, some of the most high-tech forms of computer hacking possess strong anarchist tendencies, and likewise some of the cutting-edge proposals for "green energy" and "direct democracy" extrapolate a future that is reliant upon modern technologies. Against this, many primitivists, deep ecologists, and green anarchists "claim that it is not the use or kind of technology which is the problem today, but the technology itself."[48] Sometimes this position results in a form of neo-Luddite engagement that actively seeks to "smash television and surveillance screens" as a revolutionary statement against the totalization of modern life.[49]

In their book *Welcome to the Machine: Science, Surveillance, and the Culture of Control* (2004), Derrick Jensen and George Draffan explore the ways in which today's pervasive technologies are used to control individuals and the environment alike.[50] Comprised of equal parts political economy and personal lamentation, *Welcome to the Machine* "defies our willingness to submit to the institutions and technologies built to rob us of all that makes us human: our connection to the land, our kinship with one another, our place in the living world."[51] While Jensen's anarcho-primitivist critique of technological civilization has generated much discussion, there remains for some a sense that "he offers us no clear way forward" beyond simply destroying the oppressive, exploitative infrastructure in the name of reclaiming an authentically feral human wildness that embodies the virtues of nature itself.[52] As a rhetorical device, such provocative musings call our attention to the baseline ways in which our lives are increasingly dependent upon alienating and destructive technologies, yet this also leaves many unanswered questions about how humankind is to survive in the world as we now find it—not to mention the apparent hypocrisies reflected in the fact that authors like Jensen and Zerzan mass-publish their works, as well as the irony that "anarcho-primitivists are well-organized on the web."[53]

For Zerzan, in a world in which our experiences "are processed, standardized, labeled, and subjected to hierarchical control, technology emerges as the power behind our misery and the main form of ideological domination."[54] A particularly cogent take on all of this has been propounded by David Watson (aka George Bradford) of the *Fifth Estate* cadre, who has written extensively and eloquently on the inherent dangers of the *megamachine* and how it posits itself as the only viable solution to the very problems it has manufactured in the first place:

> The authority of the modern state cannot find a solution, of course, because it has come to encompass every aspect of the problem itself. In fact, disaster tends to fuel the system that generates it, which means that we must also abandon the pathetic hope that perhaps this latest horror will be the signal that turns the tide (as Chernobyl was supposed to be, and Bhopal). . . . Because they are isolated, localized events, or because they are generalized, global ones, the calamities of industrialism erode the common conditions of life without necessarily posing any alternatives . . . In fact, urban-industrialism no longer needs to justify itself with claims to be good or eternal; it appears eternal because it's the only game in town—according to this ideology, either we continue technological development (we can argue about who administers it or reaps the profit) or we'll face collapse and all the horsemen of the apocalypse.[55]

Directly confronting some of the potential inconsistencies inherent in the virtual impossibility of practicing a fully primitivist lifestyle in the modern world, Watson revealingly observes that while "we may have nothing to lose but our urban-industrial chains," it is equally the case that "they are our own pathological behavior patterns, and conform to an enormous social and material terrain, a terrain we tend to reproduce even as we question it."[56]

The complexities of coming to grips with pervasive technologies of communication and control—in which contemporary anarchists are equally likely to embrace "various forms of hacktivism, electronic civil disobedience and culture jamming" and the tenets of primitivism all at once—reflects a deep-seated historical schism dating to the earliest days of industrialism, in which anarchists oscillated between an anti-technology Luddism and the potentialities of social experiments that sought to draw upon the liberatory benefits of new technologies.[57] In elucidating an inevitable technological ambivalence for contemporary anarchism, Michael Truscello opines that "the technicity of everyday life, the naturalization of complex technological systems, the *total phenomenon* of the technological society, cannot be critiqued and dismantled from a single position of insurrection, but must instead be confronted from multiple, disparate nodes in a network of communicative and strategic orientation."[58] In the face of pervasive technologies that simultaneously constrain and enable communications and communities alike, Truscello concludes that "only a multiplicity of mechanical discontinuities in everyday life can foster conditions consonant with anarchist politics."[59] Rather than offhandedly rejecting all appearances of technology (which is an impossibility in any event), this "post-anarchist" view suggests that we should reframe the inquiry toward establishing "the congruence of anarchism, anti-corporate globalization and environmentalism" as a means of deciding how to proceed.[60]

One of the most diverting and instructive recent interventions into these issues has come from Uri Gordon, in a chapter subtitled "Anarchism and the Politics of Technology" in *Anarchy Alive!* First, as to the nature of the problem, Gordon observes that "one does not need to be an anarchist to see that the constraints created by the existing socio-technological complex and its infrastructures have a specifically exploitative and authoritarian nature."[61] Among contemporary theorists, it is by now uncontroversial to note that "technology expresses hierarchical social relations and fixes them into material reality [thus] sustaining and enhancing inequalities of wealth and power."[62] Declaring his sympathies with the anarcho-primitivist perspective, Gordon nevertheless acknowledges that "some technologies have inherent features that encourage decentralization and localism," citing solar and wind energy as examples that can be deployed on a relatively small scale with a minimal degree of specialization required to operate them.[63] The problem is that certain other aspects of modern life have become bound up with high technologies that cannot easily be decentralized, and thus at the end of the day anarchists are simply "going to have to bite the bullet" in terms of embracing a "process of decentralization that amounts to a quite significant roll-back of technology."[64] This potential transition, as Gordon concludes, will undoubtedly necessitate "something of a revolution" for its ultimate realization.[65]

Eco-Revolution and the "Green Scare"

Enter the more militant wing of ecological anarchism. Responding to an increasing sense of concern and even desperation, a decentralized network of autonomous groups and individuals has taken it upon itself to directly confront not only the symbols of civilizational oppression but its actual workings as well. Underground entities including the Animal Liberation Front (ALF) and the Earth Liberation Front (ELF) have emerged in recent years, attacking targets such as animal testing facilities, genetic engineering laboratories, SUV dealerships, and high-end developments in sensitive habitats. The logic of these actions—which trace part of their origins to earlier *monkeywrenching* initiatives undertaken by networks such as Earth First!—is the twofold recognition that (a) nature is in grave jeopardy but lacks the capacity to defend itself, and (b) the technocratic, capitalist system can be undermined by inflicting economic damage on strategic targets within it that likewise emblematize its repressiveness. The basic premise is that economic sabotage can educate the public by highlighting unjust enterprises, while at the same time conveying a spirit of empowered resistance through direct action. The decentralized organizing strategy of these efforts "codifies an anarchist ethic: the name provides only a framework for conducting actions, rather than constituting a formal clandestine organization. Any act consistent with the guidelines can be claimed in the name of the ALF or the ELF."[66]

Many of the tactics associated with these efforts aimed at *eco-revolution* can be traced to the influence of Edward Abbey's 1975 fictional work *The Monkey Wrench Gang* and its application to real-world situations. As popularized in the 1980s by groups such as Earth First! and memorialized by advocates including Dave Foreman, monkeywrenching is a set of practices that can be undertaken by individuals or groups "to put a monkeywrench into the gears of the machine that is destroying natural diversity."[67] The aim is to develop tactics that can be "effective in stopping timber cutting, road building, overgrazing, oil and gas exploration, mining, dam building, powerline construction, off-road-vehicle use, trapping, ski area development, and other forms of destruction of the wilderness, as well as cancerous urban sprawl."[68] The basic tenets of the practice include a number of value-laden and strategic intentions that possess decidedly anarchistic qualities, including that monkeywrenching is specifically constructed as: individual, not organized, dispersed, diverse, deliberate and ethical.[69] Interestingly, these tactics are not taken to be revolutionary in nature, but they rather are seen as a defense of the wild that does not seek to overthrow the social order. Moreover, monkeywrenching is expressly coded as non-violent, in that it is "never directed against human beings or other forms of life. . . . Care is always taken to minimize any possible threat to people."[70]

These precursors have served to inform subsequent, and ostensibly more militant, entities such as the ALF and ELF, whose recent history is worth recounting here. In early December 2005, six individuals were arrested across the United States in a nationwide sting on alleged "ecoterrorists," in what was termed "Operation Backfire." They were accused of various federal crimes involving arson or explosive devices dating back to 1997, including the destruction of a wildlife research facility, wild horse corrals, a farm reputedly growing genetically modified trees, an SUV dealership, and most notably a ski lift expansion in Vail, Colorado. Invoking provisions of the USA Patriot Act to conduct the investigations, searches, and seizures, the U.S. government billed this as a major salvo in the War on Terror. Indeed, in 2002 while testifying before the U.S. Congress, James F. Jarboe, then-chief of the FBI's Counterterrorism Division, referred to the ALF and ELF as "a serious terrorist threat" that would be considered on a par in terms of investigative priorities with "the recent focus on international terrorism."[71] In the summer of 2005, FBI Deputy Assistant Director John Lewis proclaimed ALF/ELF the "number one domestic terrorism threat," despite the fact that "no one has died from any of these attacks"—a point echoed by Chief Jarboe in noting that these groups adhered to an "operational philosophy [that] discourages acts that harm 'any animal, human and nonhuman.' "[72] In 2007, FBI Director Robert Mueller III testified before Congress that: "Animal rights extremism and eco-terrorism continue to pose a threat. Extremists within these movements generally operate in small, autonomous cells and employ strict operational security tactics making detection and infiltration difficult. These extremists utilize a variety of tactics, including arson, vandalism, animal theft, and the use of explosive devices."[73]

It soon became apparent that the initial wave of arrests was merely the beginning of a larger operation, comprising "the government's most dramatic and heavy-handed use of repression to date against the counter-cultural, anarchist milieu that came of age over the past 10 years."[74] Activists have termed this the "Green Scare" to indicate its demonizing, witch hunt-like qualities, akin to the Red Scare against suspected Communists in the Cold War era. Since 2005, numerous arrests have been effected, subpoenas served, organizations infiltrated, and pressures to plead guilty brought to bear on environmental activists (many of whom openly identified as anarchists) across the United States.[75] One of those initially arrested in December 2005 was William (Bill) Rodgers, co-proprietor of the Catalyst Infoshop in Prescott, Arizona, and a personal friend. In court hearings after his arrest, the government anointed him the "mastermind" of ecoterrorist operations in the United States.[76] During the preliminary phase of his case, it became apparent that the legal deck was stacked against him. For instance, the single charge upon which he was indicted (a 1998 arson at the National Wildlife Research Center offices in Olympia, Washington) carried a presumption of incarceration pending trial. In denying him bail, the court credited unsupported hearsay testimony from an FBI agent who implicated Bill in a number of other arsons, including the ski lift expansion at Vail that was the most costly act of ecoterrorism in the United States at the time, with damages totaling $12 million. On December 21, 2005, Bill was found dead in his jail cell, an apparent suicide by asphyxiation; he was accompanied by a note directed to his "friends and supporters to help them make sense of all these events that have happened so quickly." It read in part: "Certain human cultures have been waging war against the Earth for millennia. I chose to fight on the side of bears, mountain lions, skunks, bats, saguaros, cliff rose and all things wild. I am just the most recent casualty in that war. But tonight I have made a jail break—I am returning home, to the Earth, to the place of my origins."

Even before the onset of the Green Scare, it was apparent that ecological anarchists figured prominently in the post-9/11 mix. In testimony given before Congress in 2002, Chief Jarboe defined ecoterrorism as "the use or threatened use of violence of a criminal nature against innocent victims or property by an environmentally-oriented, sub-national group for environmental-political reasons, or aimed at an audience beyond the target, often of a symbolic nature."[77] Jarboe cited a number of examples of ecoterrorism, including some that were unsolved at the time but were later attributed to the initial wave of ecoarrestees, including Bill Rodgers. Of particular note in this formulation of the definition of terrorism is the inclusion of acts done solely against "property" for political, social, or environmental purposes. In assessing the efficacy of monkeywrenching tactics, one scholar has affirmed that for many radical environmental activists, "the destruction of property is not considered to be a 'violent act,' " and furthermore many contend that "actions against property ought to be judged in terms of broad political purposes and not on the moral distinction between violent and non-violent behavior."[78] Addressing these concerns, Elaine Close, a spokesperson for the ELF, opined: "Property destruction targets the motive behind environmental destruction: profit. ... I don't consider damaging property to be violence. The end goal of the ELF is to save life on this planet, to stop violence. If we are concerned about violence, then we have to be serious about stopping environmental destruction."[79]

Pre-dating the events of 9/11, there was already significant hysteria about ecoterrorism. In 2000, Rep. Randy "Duke" Cunningham (R-CA), who later pleaded guilty to accepting bribes, proposed H.R. 5429 (the Researchers and Farmers Freedom from Terrorism Act of 2000), which was designed to increase penalties and establish a national clearinghouse for ecoterrorism incidents. In support of the bill, Cunningham argued: "All across America, animal rights terrorists have declared war on our nation's farmers and researchers. These terrorists claim that they are fighting for a noble cause. However, their violent reign of terror is not a noble or just cause; it is a threat to all Americans' security and liberty. ... These groups advocate the harassment of people that have a prime goal for the betterment of mankind."[80] In June 2001, Rep. George Nethercutt (R-WA) introduced the AgroTerrorism Prevention Act of 2001 H.R. 2795 which was designed to impose and increase mandatory minimum sentences, even including the death penalty in certain cases. "Is it harsh?" Nethercutt rhetorically asked. "Certainly it's harsh. But I think if there isn't a harsh response there will be harsh activity on behalf of the terrorists."[81]

Subsequent to 9/11, in 2004, Sen. James Inhofe (R-OK) submitted a 30-page report to Congress calling for investigations into groups such as the ALF, ELF, and any of their potential sources of funding: "Just like al Qaeda or any other terrorist organization, ELF and ALF cannot accomplish their goals without money, membership and the media," Inhofe declared.[82] In October 2005, Inhofe introduced S. 3880 (the Animal Enterprise Terrorism Act of 2005), which created penalties up to and including death for acts undertaken "for the purpose of damaging or disrupting an animal enterprise," including actions that intentionally damage, disrupt, "or cause the loss of any property (including animals or records)," or that contemplate "a course of conduct involving threats, acts of vandalism, property damage, trespass, harassment, or intimidation." In this context, an "animal enterprise" means "a commercial or academic enterprise that uses or sells animals or animal products for profit, food or fiber production, agriculture, research, or testing" and includes zoos, furriers, and rodeos in addition to entities such as research facilities and factory farms. The Animal Enterprise Terrorism Act was passed and signed into law in 2006, and it has been used to prosecute a number of animal rights and environmental activists, including most notably members of the decentralized grassroots entity known as "SHAC" (aka Stop Huntingdon Animal Cruelty).

In response, many ecological anarchists have argued that true ecoterrorism is precisely what it sounds like: *terrorizing the environment*. In this view, the targets confronted by the ALF and ELF would actually be the terrorists, since they generally involve animal research, genetic modification of plants, and the promotion of ecologically unsound practices such as driving SUVs. As Earth First! activist Rod Coronado (who spent over three years in prison for fur industry arsons) contended: "I personally consider myself an anti-terrorist, because everything I oppose I see as acts of terrorism. When I think of eco-terrorists, I think of corporate executive officers in high-rise buildings."[83] Jeff "Free" Luers, who was given a 22-year sentence for burning three SUVs, succinctly intoned during his sentencing hearing: "I did this because I'm frustrated that we are doing irreversible damage to our planet, our home. . . . I fight to protect life, all life, not to take it."[84] Luers's co-defendant, Craig "Critter" Marshall, likewise was motivated by the belief that "if the current technological state progresses or even carries on at the rate it is currently destroying the eco-systems all life depends on, [then] life on this planet is doomed."[85] These questions of moral justification and tactical efficacy comprise points of significant debate among radical environmentalists and anarchists in particular; while they merit robust analysis, the effect of branding someone a "terrorist" generally forestalls any such meaningful discussion, disabling cultural reflection and instead fostering reactionary views.[86]

Against this official backlash, many ecological anarchists remain steadfast in their belief that drastic action is required in order to avert grave calamities, even including potential extinction. As Leslie James Pickering, former spokesperson for the North American press office of the ELF, wrote: "I unwaveringly support revolutionary action to bring about the liberation of the Earth and its animal nations, including the liberation of the human race. . . . I consider the ELF a loose network of clandestine guerrilla groups struggling for revolution on a global scale."[87] In assessing the state of ecological anarchism in the wake of the Green Scare, CrimethInc. inquired: "What qualifies as a situation that calls for action to be taken outside the established channels of the legal system, if not the current ecological crisis?"[88] Others in the contemporary anarchist milieu, while generally embracing this sense of urgency and the need for drastic action, extend the scope of potentially revolutionary action to include tactics such as "civil disobedience, outspoken criticism, protest, pacifism, voluntary poverty, and even gentle violence."[89] Still others focus their revolutionary intentions on less overtly militant actions that devolve upon the basic necessities of everyday life, seeking to manifest an anti-hierarchical and community-building prefigurative strategy to bridge social and ecological issues.

Free for All

"The sources of life, and all the natural wealth of the earth, and the tools necessary to co-operative production, must become freely accessible to all," wrote Voltairine de Cleyre in 1912.[90] Goldman likewise defined anarchism as "an order that will guarantee to every human being free access to the earth and full enjoyment of the necessities of life"; Kropotkin worked out an integrative anarchist vision for the production of "the necessaries of life" that would stand in opposition to the Malthusian resource-controlling perspective of "the wealth-possessing classes"; and Rudolf Rocker viewed anarchism as having "for its sole purpose the satisfying of the necessary requirements of every member of society."[91] Decades later, Bookchin opined on the radical nature of such sentiments, observing that "daily life itself must be viewed as a calling in which we have an ethical responsibility to function in a state of unrelieved opposition" to the prevailing norms of a "depersonalized, mindless system that threatens to absorb us into its circuitry."[92] Continuing in this vein, Bookchin expounded upon the now-familiar anarchist insight that the realm of everyday life is rife with ecorevolutionary potential: "The things we need, how we acquire them, whom we know, and what we say have become the elements of a battleground on a scale we could not have foreseen a generation ago."[93] Extending this point, Watson rejects the false logic posed by capitalism "as the only solution to the ecological crises it has created," and he argues that in the end "it won't be enough to get rid of the rulers who have turned the earth into a company town;

a way of life must end and an entirely new, post-industrial culture must also emerge."[94] And in a manner that connotes the prefigurative tendencies of anarchism, in which future visions are modeled in the present, Purchase asserts that revolution "involves direct physical actions such as the planting of trees, gardens, and fields, the devising of new, nonpolluting and ecologically integrated ways of meeting humanity's many needs."[95]

Their theoretical and pragmatic differences notwithstanding, these anarchist voices from the past century reflect a point of convergence that resonates deeply for many contemporary anarchists: humankind must live differently if we are to (a) be free and (b) survive. In this sense, both our fulfillment and salvation are conditioned on the capacity to resist the forces of totalization and instead create a dynamic order that infuses social and ecological processes with an equivalent spirit of radical egalitarianism. For anarchists, the reason that the essentials of life must be "free for all" is more than a matter of morals or ideals—it is bound up with the historically informed insight that unless this aim is assiduously pursued, society will find itself on a sure path to institutionalized inequities and rampant degradation of its habitat. Equality and freedom are not antagonists, as mainstream political theorists often suggest, but rather are necessarily conjoined aims. In essence, the anarchist view is that people must be *equally free*, or none will truly be either equal or free. In order to achieve this condition of equal freedom at higher states of engagement (including politics and economics), it must be manifested in particular at the level of basic human necessities such as food, energy, shelter, and other essential resources. Once power skews within the realm of necessities, as it does within the state-capital mode of production, a system of virtual blackmail and *enforced dependency* sets in that is misguided, self-defeating, and potentially cataclysmic, as Tina Lynn Evans describes:

Enforced dependency is a form of reliance upon external resources or externally created conditions. For such dependency to function as enforced dependency, it must, once established, progressively undermine the self-sufficiency and resilience of the dependent person, community, institution, or government, making the dependent party increasingly vulnerable to exploitation. . . . Typically, dependent parties are also progressively co-opted into supporting the system of enforced dependency upon which they have come to rely, even as the system progressively robs them of freedom, independence, and resiliency. . . . Dominant parties may increasingly constrain the decisions and actions of dependent parties in order to enhance their opportunities to gain material and financial wealth and increase their social power. Though dominant parties may gain substantial wealth and power through enforced dependency, over the long term, their own resiliency may be negatively impacted as the socio-ecological capacity of dependent parties to serve as sources of wealth and power for dominant parties declines.[96]

Anarchist communities are distinguished by their maintenance of an economic safety net in which members are at least guaranteed access to essentials such as sustenance and shelter. Zerzan, for instance, has observed that "food sharing has for some time been considered an integral part of earliest human society," allowing members to realize "the benefits of being part of a society where everything is shared." Gandhi's anarchistic vision included strong currents of "material simplicity, localism (*svadeshi*), the sanctity of 'bread labor' . . . and nonviolence towards others and the earth itself."[97] Bookchin advocated the adoption of "a decentralized, ecological system of food production" as a means of promoting "cooperation with nature" and the development of healthy human "ecocommunities." Starhawk has likewise fostered a vision of "an economy of true abundance" in which the "basic means of life, growth, and development" are assured for all members of the "human community."[98] And anarchists today are involved in a broad range of similarly situated initiatives, including free food distribution (e.g., Food Not Bombs), alternative economies (e.g., the Really, Really Free Market), community gardens (e.g., the Victory Gardens Project), and permaculture (e.g., Earth Activist Training).[99] In seeking to restore the society-environment relationship, anarchists grasp that this requires the maintenance of egalitarian and mutually supportive relations among community members as well.

The operative principle here is that humankind "must make enormous changes in society" in order to halt the downward spiral of exploitation and degradation that defines the modern era.[100] As Purchase discerns, "these changes will not be realized without a local and global social-ecological revolution—the success or failure of which will involve every member of our species."[101] Affirming the radical nature of the required change, Purchase concludes that "the ecorevolution will affect and necessitate a change in virtually every aspect of our everyday life."[102] Throughout history and into the contemporary era, one of the primary tenets anarchists have maintained for promoting this vision of social harmony and ecological balance is the federated network of self-governing units—sometimes construed at the level of community, city, or bioregion. Clark envisions "small communities of liberation" that could serve to bring about "a new just, ecological society."[103] Purchase focuses his vision on the "ecologically-integrated and autonomous city" that fosters the capacity of people to "deeply identify with the natural ecology of their local place and to protect that place while developing industrial and agricultural practices that are adapted to its ecological characteristics."[104] Watson eschews the temptation to "deliver a program" but cites as positive examples "myriad activities ranging from land restoration to urban gardens to fair trade cooperatives to solidarity networks."[105]

In each case, the salient point is that people ought to be free to form associations at every level of the loci of their lives, from the local to the global, through processes of autonomy and equality both within their societies and vis-à-vis the balance of life on the planet. To fail to do so is not merely an unfortunate situation or a condition to lament—it is a matter of survival. This sense of informed urgency, which is becoming undeniable and increasingly widespread, animates much of contemporary anarchism's action and vision alike, posing the definitive question of whether the future will be one characterized by community or cataclysm, by ecology or eschatology, and, ultimately, by anarchy or annihilation.

Back to the Garden, or Gone with the Wind?

At present, the stakes for humankind are extraordinarily high. While modern society tends to mask the scale of the current environmental crises beneath a facade of plenty and the functional distractions of mass culture, the sense of urgency for many around the world has been steadily rising in recent years. The frequency and magnitude of "natural disasters," the loss of habitats and species, the displacement of people from their lands, the adulteration of the food supply, and shortages of essential resources including water have inculcated an ecological consciousness in many of the planet's inhabitants, including an increasing number from the privileged settings of the global north. In particular, the ravages of climate change are beginning to appear in the present through hurricanes, floods, tsunamis, and more—and not merely as issues to be dealt with in the future. Against this, many have been actively searching for "secure moorings," including a greater voice in the decisions that affect their lives, community bonds and cooperative endeavors, local control rather than corporate globalization, self-sufficiency as to basic resources, and appropriate technologies that do not contribute further to the problems.

In short, whether they use the word or not, people and communities across the globe have been seeking the practical lessons of *anarchy* as methods for ordering their lives and bringing balance to their relationships with nature. The exigencies of the modern era have further rendered these anarchist aims not simply as good ideas but rather, as Bookchin once wrote, as "preconditions for human survival."[106] Accentuating this sensibility, Clark has described anarchism as "both a strategy for human liberation and a plan for avoiding global ecological disaster."[107] Clark's prescient words were published in 1984, and today we are living through their unfortunate realization as the combined footprint of humanity is pushing the planet's carrying capacity to its limits. But the benefits and burdens in this calculus are not equally distributed, with poor people contributing less to the problem yet being more directly impacted. The anarchist project of directly linking "the domination of humans by humans with the attempt to dominate nature" is critical to ameliorating this.[108] In this sense, the choice collectively before us increasingly appears to be one between the "alternatives of anarchism or annihilation."[109]

Perhaps nowhere are these concerns more keenly felt than around climate issues. "The problems of deforestation, water and air pollution and chemicals in the food supply may only be overshadowed by the effects of catastrophic climate change."[110] Chief among the drivers of the crisis are global capitalism and its profiteering, perpetual-growth ethos. Climate summits have been convened by state actors, but their interlocking interests with corporations have prevented any tangible results; in fact, the rate of change is worsening and such elite summits serve as little more than a palliative. As Peter Gelderloos has observed, "it would be unconscionable to allow the world leaders who just five and ten years ago were denying the reality of climate change to be entrusted with solving the problem today."[111] To meaningfully address the roots of the problem, "we will need to do nothing short of changing who holds power in society, and how decisions are made; to change the way our culture views the planet, from seeing it as a dead thing that can be exploited and toyed with, to understanding it as an interconnected, living system upon which we are dependent for our survival."[112] Gelderloos contends that this "will require a decentralization of economy and decision-making" akin to that prefigured by anarchist networks emerging around the globe, ultimately devolving upon the creation of "an ecological, anti-authoritarian society" premised on bioregional consciousness and localized power.[113]

Social ecologist Brian Tokar likewise chronicles the rise of a growing "climate justice" movement that is "challenging the expanding scope of commodification and privatization, whether of land, waterways, or the atmosphere itself."[114] In communities, towns, and cities, people are mobilizing to regain political and environmental power, working in locales everywhere "to regenerate local food systems, develop locally controlled, renewable energy sources and, sometimes, to build solidarity with kindred movements around the world."[115] Unfortunately, too many people still seek "least painful" reforms rather than confronting the "destructive development of global capitalism," even as it has become clear that "our survival depends on our ability to challenge this system at its core."[116] Following Bookchin, Tokar counsels that working solutions can be found in practicing participatory decision making, cultivating land-based societies, reclaiming (and updating) pre-industrial social relations, and developing alternative institutions for the provision of essential resources.[117] In the end, this anarchist perspective asks that we remain engaged and even hopeful, in the belief that the current crises can serve to "help us envision a transition toward a more harmonious, more humane and ecological way of life."[118] The locus of much of this transformative potential will necessarily occur at the level of *community*, whose critical lessons for realizing the virtues of anarchism—and thus forestalling an impending ecological annihilation—are the subject of the next chapter.

CHAPTER 5

"Do It Yourself"—Together

In terms of theory and practice alike, anarchism throughout history has struggled to reconcile personal liberty with social organization. Indeed, the scope of anarchism ranges from the highly individualistic to the unabashedly communitarian. Whereas other political theories are often defined by where they stand on the individual-community spectrum, anarchism is uniquely instructive in its sophisticated integration of both perspectives. Anarchists today prioritize values including *solidarity* and *affinity*, and contemporary modes of anarchist organizing often take the form of a *collective* or *network*. Despite the caricature of anarchy as lacking any order or coordination altogether, it is actually the case that anarchists have developed alternative methods of cooperation and even governance apart from the hierarchical, centralizing, and exploitative set of sociopolitical arrangements embodied by the state. Anarchism does not reject all order—merely that which inhibits voluntary participation, promotes repressive power relations, and undermines the development of individual conscience. In short, anarchists work to foster horizontal, egalitarian, spontaneous, and organic communities and forms of coordination that serve to challenge present conditions while steadily building toward a viable alternative.

As we have seen, this dualistic sense of contestation and constructivism largely defines the anarchist project. At times within the milieu there are fierce debates about lifestyle-level action versus open insurrection as the best expression of anarchism's inherently revolutionary tendencies. Similarly, tensions are evident around issues of scale, sometimes taking the form of nascent schisms about whether local, community-based initiatives or more coordinated workers' syndicates are better situated as the locus of prefigurative organizing. Tactically, some anarchists maintain that spontaneous and autonomous actions undertaken by self-directed individuals (sometimes in concert with others) are the most effective methods of confronting the hegemony of capital and the state, whereas others prioritize large-scale mobilizations that exert political and moral suasion on issues including war and the economy. Some anarchists seek to drop out, while others dig in; some refuse to participate, while others actively infiltrate; and some ignore the state, while others seek to smash it. In all of these cases, from the highly individualistic to the strongly coordinated, anarchists walk a fine line between autonomy and solidarity, seeking a productive balance of tensions that reflects anarchism's highest aspirations as a social theory.

Anarchists are collectivists, in the sense that they believe in the innate sociability of humankind and the rational desire to live, work, and play among others. Yet anarchism never asks that we forsake the self in the process, arguing instead that it is precisely the practice of radical individuality that enables non-oppressive forms of association. If one believes in a social order premised on "equality in all things" (as Peter Kropotkin envisioned), rather than a system where some are more "equal" than others, it must be grounded in the actualization of ourselves as unique beings entitled to dignity, respect, opportunity, and compassion.[1] What distinguishes anarchism from other political theories is the vigorous embrace of individualism *and* communitarianism as mutually reinforcing processes that, when balanced in a supportive system, render one another possible at all; indeed, when this balance is lacking and one pole dominates the other, the results can be disastrous. Neither capitalism nor communism, in their mutually destructive antagonism, has satisfactorily accomplished this dynamic equilibrium between the self and the collective, and thus it remains true that "the case of those who argue that individual autonomy and community life are incompatible remains unproven."[2] For its part, the nation-state often appears as the top-heavy enemy of both, treating us as individuals when it wants to undermine solidarity, while appealing to our sense of communal pride when seeking jingoistic compliance with exploitative and repressive policies.

Against these dominant forces, anarchism posits a world in which freedom and responsibility naturally co-exist and where the impetus to "do it yourself" is equivalent to the practical necessity to "do it together." A century ago, Kropotkin critically asserted that "unbridled individualism is a modern growth," whereas "the feeling of solidarity is the leading characteristic of all animals living in society."[3] Anarchists today find themselves in a world that seeks to constrain individual expressions of identity, morality, sexuality, and the like, when they conflict with the mores of capitalist reproduction. At the same time, practices of solidarity are dissuaded by way of a combination of economic impracticability (such as through the disadvantaging of cooperative structures) and legalisms that turn anti-authoritarian associations into criminal conspiracies when it is convenient to do so (such as with the case of the "RNC 8" who were arrested before the 2008 Republican National Convention).[4] Despite this, contemporary anarchism includes myriad collaborative enterprises, from infoshops and publishing collectives to coordinated prisoner-support projects and academic associations. As such, the working definition proffered by the Active Resistance network in 1998 remains apropos in the quest to reconcile and harmonize the interests of the self and society at once, and thus it serves as a meaningful point of departure for analyzing anarchist relationships in practice:

> **Anarchy:** A self-governed society in which people organize themselves from the bottom up on an egalitarian basis; decisions made by those affected by them; direct democratic control of our workplaces, schools, neighborhoods, towns and bioregions with coordination between differing groups as needed. A world where women and men are free and equal and all of us have power over our own lives, bodies and sexuality; where we cherish and live in balance with the earth and value diversity of cultures, races and sexual orientations; where we work and live together cooperatively.[5]

The Moral Self

The anarchist tradition has always reflected an uneasy tension between the priority of the individual and the necessity of community, even at times referring to the same as the "genuine dilemma of anarchism," in which it often appears that "community negates itself, or at least is either unstable or compelled to resort to unanarchistic methods of social control."[6] Murray Bookchin opined on "anarchism's failure to resolve this tension, to articulate the relationship of the individual to the collective," and in response he asserted the primacy of *social anarchism* as superior to the appearance of an individualistic *lifestyle anarchism* that is based on "preoccupations with the ego and its uniqueness and its polymorphous concepts of resistance."[7] Bookchin specifically derided notions of "personal autonomy [that] stand at odds with concepts of social freedom," arguing that "if individual 'autonomy' overrides any commitment to a 'collectivity,' there is no basis whatever for social institutionalization, decision-making, or even administrative coordination. Each individual, self-contained in his or her 'autonomy,' is free to do whatever he or she wants."[8] Conversely, L. Susan Brown affirmatively cites "anarchism's uncompromising and relentless celebration of individual self-determination and autonomy," concluding that "it is not the group that gives shape to the individual, but rather individuals who give form and content to the group."[9]

Such tensions might be abated somewhat by envisioning a common moral apparatus, something universally attendant to existence and consciousness, that is sufficient to hold together a community of individuals—but without a rigid ethical code in place, no privileging of one set of principles over another, a morality "that will issue no commands."[10] From place to place and at different times, community standards and expectations will change; likewise from person to person the urges of conscience will vary. In this sense, we might conceive a personal, subjective imperative of morality, yielding "a social order in which each is able to live and act according to his or her own judgment."[11] At the same time, anarchists surmise that in a great many circumstances, autonomous individuals will reach similar moral conclusions—in the recognition that people are more alike than different, and that sociability and reciprocity are fundamental impulses manifested in "the consciousness of an overriding human solidarity."[12] Thus, Kropotkin grounded his moral theory in this basic notion: "In that constant, ever-present identification of the unit with the whole, lies the origin of all ethics, the germ out of which all the subsequent conceptions of justice, and still the higher conceptions of morality, evolved."[13]

Indeed, as Kropotkin sought to demonstrate through his extensive research, the moral impulse in nature precedes the existence of human life. Early humans, according to Kropotkin, developed the moral urge by observing the processes around them, "and as soon as they began to bring some order into their observations of nature, and to transmit them to posterity, the animals and their life supplied them with the chief materials for their unwritten encyclopedia of knowledge, as well as for their wisdom, which they expressed in proverbs and sayings."[14] For Kropotkin, the moral lessons that humans have derived from nature include sociability; a prohibition against killing one's own kind; the clan, kinship, or tribal structure; the advantages of common endeavor; play; and a notion of reciprocity in addressing wrongful acts.[15] In this view, the overarching tendency in nature toward *mutual aid* has principally enabled the survival of species in the animal kingdom, including of course species of the genus *Homo*. The basic formulation suggested by Kropotkin, still influential among contemporary anarchists, is that an inherent mutualism serves as an effective counterbalance to the potential limits of individualism. Todd May likewise begins with what he terms the "*a priori* of traditional anarchism: trust in the individual" in validating the sentiment that "left to their own devices, individuals have a natural ability—indeed a propensity—to devise social arrangements that are both just and efficient."[16] As John Zerzan has observed, the anarchist aim is to foster a community of individuals based on "egalitarianism and personal autonomy in the context of group cooperation."[17]

Still, we can almost hear critics forming the tried-and-true query: "But won't the lack of specific laws, codes of conduct, and punitive enforcement lead to chaos, violence, and anarchy?" Anarchists from time immemorial have been quick to point out that the state already does a pretty fair job at promoting chaos and violence through its practices of warfare, criminal justice, and institutionalized inequality. As for the notion that there will be *anarchy* in the absence of formal laws and the coercion brought to bear on individuals to comply with them, anarchists obviously would welcome such an eventuality as preferable to the stifling, destructive conditions fostered by the current set of sociopolitical arrangements. As Kropotkin famously argued:

> We are not afraid to forego judges and their sentences. We forego sanctions of all kinds, even obligations to morality. We are not afraid to say: "Do what you will; act as you will"; because we are persuaded that the great majority of [hu]mankind, in proportion to their degree of enlightenment and the completeness with which they free themselves from existing fetters will behave and act always in a direction useful to society.[18]

In this sense, one begins to see the state as a self-fulfilling prophecy: by creating coercive institutions to stave off the potential ravages of inherently untrustworthy individuals, we find ourselves living in a world that is (a) defined by the speculative behaviors of the worst among us, and (b) continually producing the very sorts of people it was ostensibly designed to remediate. "By flinging overboard law, religion and authority, [hu]mankind can regain possession of the moral principle which has been taken from them," as Kropotkin presciently wrote in 1892.[19]

For anarchists, it is the very presence of a coercive state apparatus that disables individual moral reasoning as an effective principle for organizational engagement; in such a paternalistic state, the net effect over time is to produce subjects whose abilities to coordinate spontaneously and equally will either atrophy or never develop. Michael Taylor has discerned that "the more the state intervenes…the more 'necessary' it becomes, because positive altruism and voluntary cooperative behavior atrophy in the presence of the state and grow in its absence."[20] Moreover, people "who live for long under government and its bureaucracy, courts and police, come to rely upon them. They find it easier (and in some cases are legally bound) to use the state for the settlement of their disputes and for the provision of public goods, instead of arranging these things for themselves."[21] Similarly, Zygmunt Bauman notes that "the bid to make individuals universally moral through shifting their responsibilities to the legislators failed, as did the promise to make everyone free in the process."[22] Again, Kropotkin offers his famous insight:

> We are so perverted by an education which from infancy seeks to kill in us the spirit of revolt, and to develop that of submission to authority; we are so perverted by this existence under the ferrule of a law, which regulates every event in life—our birth, our education, our development, our love, our friendship—that, if this state of things continues, we shall lose all initiative, all habit of thinking for ourselves.[23]

These inquiries present some of the most challenging sociopolitical questions; anarchism at least possesses the virtue of confronting them directly and being willing to accept the ambiguities and even potential consequences of living without official coercion as the basis for social order. "Anarchists understand that freedom is grounded in the refusal of the individual to exercise power over others, coupled with the opposition of the individual to restrictions by any external authority"— or, in Kropotkin's plain words: "We do not wish to be ruled. And by this very fact, do we not declare that we ourselves wish to rule nobody?"[24] Anarchism is thus a condition of maximal human freedom, whose "sensitivity to all forms of domination is tied to a fundamental concern for the individual as a whole person, a creative, active agent, not simply a producer or a citizen."[25] Still, anarchists do not accept that this inevitably leads to a notion of "rugged individualism [that] fosters competition and a disregard for the needs of others," focusing instead on developing a sense of "true individuality, which implies freedom without infringement on others' freedom," in the inescapable recognition of "the close dependency of everyone's happiness upon the happiness of all."[26] Thus, as Teoman Gee articulates, "within an anarchist commitment to *individuality for all*, freedom and equality have to go hand in hand."[27]

Balancing these interests has been an overarching aim of the anarchist project, and it continues into the contemporary milieu. Whereas the state grants individual rights (oftentimes even to the exclusion of the exercise of group rights), and capitalism seeks to tap into its subjects' strong sense of individuality as a means of marketing styles and constructing demands, anarchism prioritizes a version of the self that is at once autonomous and interconnected—one that sees its own capacity to be free as bound up with the freedom of others, that recognizes the basic premise that *none* can free unless *all* are free. "To understand oneself as oneself, yet at the same time as an integral part of a collective that shelters one's own existence, demands an *individual responsibility* for this collective," as Gee counsels.[28] Herein lies the twofold anarchist recognition that the collective enables the experience of individuality, and that it is the individual's responsibility to remain free within the context of a dynamic social order. This basic order is inevitable, necessary, and desirable—it is, in short, the highest expression of *anarchy*.

Action in Concert

In exploring anarchism as a collective endeavor, we thus recall at the outset that "anarchy is a form of social life which organizes itself without the resort to coercive authority."[29] Moreover, "the rules and behavioral norms that ensure social harmony would be arrived at collectively," and "social cohesion would be ensured as people replaced the competition and antagonism that typify market-driven societies with cooperation, solidarity and mutual aid."[30] In seeking to achieve this vision, a principal aim of anarchist praxis has always been the abolition of codified, formal laws. Instead, anarchist communities are regulated by informal *norms* including "customs, habits and usages," as well as the individual urges of conscience experienced by each member.[31] The anarchist view is that reference to rigid, abstract laws represents an abdication of the individual's capacity for moral self-direction and responsibility—an essential element of a social order without institutional coercion. Moreover, codified laws require official administration and enforcement, whereas internalized social norms can serve to cultivate deeper instincts of sociability by promoting broader access to the community's moral pulse. Further, in anarchist communities "laws" as such would scarcely be required, since the greater part of formal law has "but one object—to protect private property"; much of the rest serves to "keep up the machinery of government."[32] As to the balance of the space occupied by law, namely "the protection of the person and the detection and prevention of 'crime,' " informal norms of conduct and the urges of the moral self can fill the space and provide a framework for social order—without replicating the intrinsic cruelty of state-bound methods.[33]

Restoring Order

In exploring alternatives, anarchists unflinchingly begin from the radical premise that the present "law and order" paradigm ought to be abandoned entirely. Indeed, it is axiomatic in the anarchist lexicon that the coercive, authoritarian, and ineffective workings of "criminal justice" must be wholly rejected. While this is a view that I have echoed and endorsed in previous works, it is nonetheless crucial to understand the full implications of such a position.[34] After all, while there is a certain seductive quality to the belief that, once freed from the shackles of law, human communities will spontaneously develop egalitarian and inclusive social practices, it is still often the case that "the aspect of anarchist ideas of social organization which people find hardest to swallow is the anarchist rejection of the law, the legal system, and the agencies of law enforcement."[35] To merely accept the abolition of law as an anti-authoritarian inevitability, then, is to oversimplify the issue and to risk speaking a language that is counterintuitive to many whom anarchists would hope to reach with their words and deeds.

One point of departure that anarchism has increasingly begun to embrace is *restorative justice*, which operates from a place of empathy, compassion, and mutual respect in seeking to resolve the inevitable conflicts that arise in any human community. "Restorative justice fits with anarchist views that seek to replace the State through the creation of a multitude of voluntary associations."[36] Two of the earliest advocates for explicitly linking anarchism and restorative justice are Larry Tifft and Dennis Sullivan, who contend that "we can never find meaning or freedom in living if we consider life processes from the floundering orbits of law, the state or corporate economy, but only through lifting ourselves to the warmth of experience and human community."[37] Amplifying their point and tapping into longstanding anti-authoritarian and anarchist tenets, Tifft and Sullivan are unabashed in their rejection of *criminal justice*:

> All law, authority and institutions of state are based on force, violence and the fear of punishment.... The function of law historically has been to deny some people the right to their personal journey, to detain us, by demanding that we resolve our contradictions within the confines of law and the state.... Law prohibits us from freeing

ourselves, experiencing ourselves in the struggle to be human. . . . To accept law, therefore is to accept a reality in which there is imposition of person upon person. It is to accept the reality of enslavement, the plantation of the welfare state. It is to accept the division of the world into parts that translate into subject and objects, and the mechanisms to manage this hierarchical division, denying autonomy to everyone.[38]

These sentiments serve to locate the authors specifically within the anarchist tradition, reflecting the tendency in the milieu to favor a negotiated, lived experience of justice in our communities.

In this sense, highlighting the hierarchical and oppressive nature of law is an important initial endeavor, but it also leaves the harder question of how human communities will sustain and regulate themselves in the absence of formal law. Drawing upon anarchist examples from history, Tifft and Sullivan call for communities grounded in "mutual aid, co-operation, spontaneity and peace," as well as "self-reciprocity, equity, and love."[39] Taken together, these strands serve to trace the boundaries of the authors' vision of "a moral order in accordance with which people, from their inner convictions, act towards others as they desire that others should act toward them."[40] Yet the pragmatic question remains: "Can a society exist in which nothing limits the individual, where all regulation is an affair of the individual and not of the collective will?"[41] Answering his own query, Alexei Borovoi states the basic premise:

There has not been a single society, even prior to the birth of the State, that has not made certain demands upon its members. While specific regulations may vary from society to society, some form of regulation is always necessary. Aside from legal codes, there exist in all societies what can be called codes of convention. The force of these codes is perhaps greater than the force of laws. The fundamental difference is that these codes are based on a collective accord.[42]

As Giovanni Baldelli has likewise noted, "no society is ethical in which each member does not naturally absorb its governing principles of right and wrong. Written law represents a generally unsuccessful substitute for a universal understanding of ethical principles."[43]

Here we see the ambivalence anarchists have toward concepts such as *regulation* and *social control*—and thus toward communal enterprises in general. Are we to grant such primacy to the individual that no form of collective intervention is acceptable? If we do allow collective intervention, how do we keep it from becoming authoritarian and destructive of individual liberty? In short, how do we avoid the pitfalls of law and the state while preserving the integrity of our communities? Struggling with such queries, Tifft and Sullivan recognize that even "social custom, religious dogma and moral codes are yet more subtle forms of domination which, like education and official propaganda, are harnessed by the state to perform as ancillary functions of law."[44] And yet, it is equally acknowledged that anarchist communities will be regulated not by laws but by "mutual agreements" and by "a sum of social customs and habits."[45] Expanding on this instructive ambivalence within anarchism, Colin Ward similarly endorses "values and norms" as substitutes for law, whereas the anarchist anthropologist Harold Barclay cautions against "the confusion of the term *law* with *norm* or *custom* in such a way as to claim that anarchist societies have law."[46] Barclay further notes that "there are on the one hand rules which are imposed by the state through its government—in other words, laws—and there are other kinds of rules not imposed by the state. . . . An anarchist society is clearly different from a state society in that in it there would be no penal sanctions—no law."[47] As Borovoi finds, "anarchism admits social norms. The norms of a free society resemble neither in spirit nor in form the laws of contemporary society. These norms will not seek the detachment of the individual from the collectivity. Anarchist norms will not be a torrent of decrees from a higher authority."[48]

Tifft and Sullivan thus envision a dynamic sense of order that devolves upon the humanistic application of "face-to-face justice," "the airing of conflicts," and "the reality of returning to work and living with the other person."[49] Jeff Ferrell has likewise reflected upon the development of an anarchist criminology that "argued for replacing state/legal 'justice' with a fluid, face-to-face form of justice grounded in emerging human needs."[50] For Tifft and Sullivan, the essence of restorative justice as an anarchist project is that "we must move to create personal relationships, social arrangements, and communities that promote patterns of interaction that are non-hierarchical, non-power-based."[51] The central notion is that "justice-done restoratively requires that participants continually remain open to each other's concerns, ideas, needs, feelings, desires, pain and suffering, so that each can see the other not as a resource to be used or exploited or as an object to be derided or scorned, but as he or she is, similar to oneself, a person engaged in an unending struggle to become human, with dignity."[52] This relational view of autonomy, community, and respect is at the cutting edge of contemporary anarchist inquiry, even as we recognize its deep historical roots: "Anthropologists of every ilk have shown us multitudinous examples of societies that have neither laws nor a state but which are every bit concerned about justice, reparation, and human well-being."[53]

Anarchists have long comprehended the outlaw nature (literally) of what it means to take these teachings to heart, to stand against the majesty of the state in favor of the messiness of community, to be an outsider vis-à-vis mainstream society, to be viewed as a lawbreaker and even a heretic. Adherents in the modern era are at least in excellent company, including the legendary musings of Henry David Thoreau in "Civil Disobedience": "Law never made men a whit more just; and, by means of their respect for it, even the well-disposed are daily made the agents of injustice. . . . But if it is of such a nature that it requires you to be the agent of injustice to another, then I say, break the law."[54] As Robert Paul Wolff inquired in *In Defense of Anarchism*,

> on what grounds can it be claimed that I have an obligation to obey the laws which are made in my name by a man [sic] who has no obligation to vote as I would, who indeed has no effective way of discovering what my preferences are on the measure before him? . . . The citizens have created a legitimate state at the price of their own autonomy! They have bound themselves to obey laws which they do not will, and indeed even laws which they vigorously reject. Insofar as democracy originates in such a promise, it is no more than voluntary slavery.[55]

Tifft and Sullivan further observe that "laws are so numerous that no one could possibly not break them. There are laws that individuals choose to break and laws which individuals are forced to break. . . . If all laws were strictly enforced, everybody would be criminalized."[56] Indeed, as things stand today, we may not be far from such a condition of universal criminalization, with modern society increasingly coming to represent a "panopticon gulag."[57]

The societal obsession with "law and order" renders the anarchist project all the more urgent, and the impetus to simultaneously reclaim individual conscience and community solidarity becomes nothing less than essential. Far from merely rejecting the need for order in an offhand manner, anarchists have instead proposed a working set of social relations based on "healthy education," "mutual aid," "fraternal treatment," and "moral support," in the belief that "liberty, equality, and practical human sympathy are the only effectual barriers we can oppose to the anti-social instincts of certain among us."[58] Recalling the false solutions offered by the state, Kropotkin reminds us that "such means will be far more powerful to protect society from anti-social acts than the existing system of punishment which is an ever-fertile source of new crimes," concluding that "the remedy [state mechanisms] offer is worse than the evils they pretend to cure."[59] As Graham Purchase concurs, "if the State is supposed to resolve violence and conflict then it really has proved to be an extremely poor mechanism for doing so."[60] The anarchist perspective on social order thus rejects the criminal justice apparatus, indicating a commitment to extra-legal mechanisms for managing the trespasses that take place in any human community.

Sanctioning, Diffusely

As such, the next step in understanding anarchist collectives is to consider what forms of "crime and punishment" exist in the absence of the state and its associated socioeconomic logic. Following the work of Barclay, Tifft and Sullivan, and of course Kropotkin, it becomes evident that punishment in anarchist settings is more likely to be directly and instrumentally responsive to a particular transgression, not to serve the larger purposes of fostering fear as an instrument of deterrence and statecraft. When intervention is required and punishment meted out, any anarchist *sanction* "typically protects the life of relationships [and] is more remedial than accusatory."[61] In this sense, "the aim seems to be not so much to determine guilt as to re-establish group harmony."[62] Although anarchist communities may at times levy sanctions, it is essential to note that they always aspire to be "crime free" by creating a space where community norms are subjective and voluntary, where each member is equally entitled to define the parameters of the group's moral boundaries, where "there are personally equivalent inputs and mutual confidence," and where "people hold all goods in common and take what they need."[63]

As Ward explains, "there must be room for deviance in society, and there must be support for the right to deviate."[64] There are of course risks in pushing too far beyond the moral boundaries of the group, and even in anarchist settings sanctions can ensue in such cases. Barclay, for example—analyzing anthropological studies of a number of indigenous cultures, as well as modern examples such as intentional communities—observes that "anarchists use a variety of diffuse sanctions [including] gossip, name calling, arguing, fist fighting, killing and ostracism."[65] Donald Black likewise notes the presence of social control devices ranging from "banishment and beating to ridicule and teasing," as well as "revenge, compensation, and voluntary exile."[66] Purchase discusses a range of devices, from "simple sanctions" including shaming, ridicule, and gossip, to "more extreme sanctions" including excommunication, ostracism, duels, and combat, concluding that the dominant social sanction in stateless societies is "the withholding of essential forms of economic cooperation."[67] And Taylor, in his study of anarchy and community, similarly considers sanctions including gossip, shaming, ostracism, denial of benefits, and expulsion (which is rarely utilized).[68]

While it is clear, then, that anarchist communities can employ mechanisms of punishment and social control, it is crucial to grasp the *diffuse* nature of these processes. "This is the meaning of diffuse: responsibility for and the right to impose the sanction is spread out over the community. Society as a whole has the power. There is no special elite which even claims a monopoly on the use of violence as a sanctioning device."[69] As Purchase further observes, "diffuse sanctions can be applied by any member, [yet] the control of anti-social acts in stateless societies [is] maintained by the community itself, through the continued action of all its members."[70] Put another way, in an anarchist community every member possesses the executive authority of the "law" and is charged with the task of cultivating positive conduct and discouraging anti-social acts—tempered, of course, by the ubiquitous possibility of "reciprocal justice," which can have a distinct chilling effect on one's readiness to sanction another frivolously or spitefully.[71] While these sorts of fluid, situated, and ambiguous processes may seem troubling at first glance, they pale in comparison to the blatant brutalism of state-bound policies. Thus, while it is apparent that anarchist communities sometimes sanction repressively, they more often do so restitutively or restoratively—with the critical point being that in anarchist settings there is no state or other institutional apparatus to carry out such punishments, only actual people with ostensible ties to their fellow community members. When sanctioning does ensue, the face-to-face nature of relations in anarchist communities at least gives social control a more humane quality than the mediated, institutional, and repressive methods of the state.

Conflicts and Resolutions

Beyond occasionally imposing diffuse sanctions, it is also the case that "all societies, even the most cooperative of them, have to find methods of resolving conflict, [since] conflict is just one part of social life. It is a natural and integral dimension of human interaction and activity."[72] Closely related to sanctioning practices, then, we must consider those social processes often denoted as *conflict resolution*—which is not a distinct sphere in anarchist settings but merely another mode of negotiating the constant (and largely positive) tension between individual autonomy and communal existence. Are instances of theft or assault, for example, "crimes" against the community, or are they better conceived as personal disputes between individual parties? In anarchist settings, without a central state apparatus for administration and enforcement, acts of trespass or aggression are more likely to be treated as disputes of a civil nature, with the added dimension that the community itself is directly involved in the resolution process. What is left that we might term *crime* is conduct that violates social norms and for which there is no specific victim except the community itself, such as the theft of shared food supplies or betraying the community's confidence to authorities for personal gain.

But for the bulk of human interactions, the daily incursions we face when living in community and acting in concert are of the interpersonal variety: ideological disputes, personality conflicts, power plays, territorialism, romantic triangles, cultural antagonisms, and the like. Of critical importance, then, are the processes by which disputes are resolved in anarchist communities—since the methods adopted serve both as a means of resolving conflict and as a fluid, participatory form of social control. In this regard, Tifft notes that

> experiences of personal conflict are essential to creative assessment and change. It means that we must restore life and the settlement of disputes to a direct face-to-face and collective process. This means no institutionalization of conflict resolution. It means airing the complexities of the dispute situation and of all our collective futures to reach toward new understandings. . . . Face-to-face justice is an outgrowth of life, needing no special or permanent personages or languages, no office of authority or imposition. [Therefore,] a response to interpersonal conflict cannot be reasonably articulated before the conflict has arisen, only afterwards and after it has not been resolved to the mutual satisfaction of the persons involved.[73]

Thus, the first level of anarchist conflict resolution is the affected parties themselves working out a mutually agreeable and socially productive arrangement; only in cases of genuine impasse is a more formal process (i.e., community involvement) required.[74] Barclay cites numerous anthropological examples, including those in which the entire community is involved in resolving intractable disputes—those in which "disputes are to be settled by mediation, and no violence is tolerated," and those in which "go betweens" serve to facilitate mediation.[75] Black similarly analyzes processes including the appointment of a mediator and the presence of "local influentials, chosen for wisdom and diplomacy," who work with interested parties to resolve disputes—concluding that, "whether an individual or a group ... the third party typically is more an agent of compromise than of judgment."[76] Purchase likewise notes that the hallmark of mediators is that they possess "no power or authority to enforce [their] decisions."[77] So who then, if anyone, possesses power in anarchist collectives?

Authority, Power, and Consensus

As with the maintenance of social order as a whole, anarchist communities do not entail the elimination of attributes such as power and authority; rather, they contemplate new applications of these endemic tendencies. In such settings, authority might be characterized as "recognized competence within a certain field, and the right to take and carry out decisions with the assent of every person whom the decisions affect. Authority thus defined is not the opposite or the enemy of freedom but its necessary complement."[78] In *Social Anarchism*, Giovanni Baldelli provides initial guidance as to how this might look:

> "coercive power must be reduced to a minimum and put in as many hands as possible"
> "claims to authority must be rejected if they are established by force"
> "each authority must be answerable to several others that are equally responsible to several more"
> "no person in his relationship with another should be exempt from judgment by a third"
> "overwhelming power should always be with the third party"; and
> "access to a third party, available to everyone, should be to many third parties, not to one only."[79]

Compare Bookchin's discussion of *authority* in "organic" societies, which devolves essentially upon "guidance, lacking the usual accouterments of command. Its 'power' is functional rather than political," and those possessing it are generally viewed more so as "advisors, teachers, and consultants, esteemed for their experience and wisdom."[80]

Putting all of this together, a vision begins to emerge of an anarchist community in which individuals are free to exercise authority in areas of particular skill or interest while following, assisting, and learning in other spheres, creating a space "where reputations and other statuses fluctuate from one day to the next."[81] As Michael Bakunin described it, in an anarchist community, "each directs and is directed in his turn. Therefore there is no fixed and constant authority, but a continual exchange of mutual, temporary, and, above all, voluntary authority and subordination."[82] Thoroughly diffuse and decentralized, power is free to course through the conduits of the community, finding its way into action through those best attuned to its resonance for the task at hand; power thus conceived fosters an air of spontaneous creative energy, in which chores become "happenings" and works are events—and still somehow structures are erected, people fed, fires fought, decisions made, and children reared.[83] In this way, an anarchist community gets the most out of the energies of its members, maximizing its human potential, while preserving both individual autonomy and group consensus as well.

On this point, it has often been observed that absent central authority, practices of social order are generally established by *consensus*, in which community norms and decisions are unanimously agreed upon through processes of active participation and open debate. Kropotkin was an early advocate of such methods, analyzing the historical preference for unanimity in community decision making, whereby "the discussions continue until all present agree to accept, or submit to, some decision," since there exists "no authority in a village community to impose a decision."[84] Perhaps somewhat ironically, consensus is not universally accepted among anarchists, yet it has been an important part of anarchist praxis that represents a potentially horizontal form of group decision making by seeking "input and guidance from all participants in a project," likewise by striving to minimize group pressure at the expense of individualism by ensuring that "no one is coerced into taking part in a course of action that they have not agreed to or of which they do not approve."[85] While some find it to contain subtle forms of oppression, consensus nonetheless enjoys significant popularity in anarchist settings, and it actively works to "include specific practices to recognize and address the silencing of marginalized and oppressed groups."[86] In so doing, consensus recognizes that "all persons have some part of the truth," and thus they ought to be included in exercising any use of collective power that might impact them.[87]

As with the concomitant processes of sanctioning, dispute resolution, and authority, the appearance of power in anarchist settings is diffuse in the sense that every member of the group is equally entitled to be a direct and active participant in the creation of community norms and in the entire decision-making process itself. In this way, individuals acquire a deeper sense of the meaning and purpose of the "rules" extant in the community, rendering superfluous the need for institutionalization and even codification. The benefits of conceiving *social order* as an organic, ongoing agreement derived through direct participation and consensual processes are manifold, not the least of which is to encourage an environment in which cooperation and not competition becomes the predominant aim of both the group and its individual constituents. As Tifft concludes, under such conditions people will by and large "institute the principle of justice—to each according to need, taking into account the resources available to the community."[88] It is not an exact science by any means, but it stands in marked contrast to the incidence of poverty, neglect, inequality, and even genocide that we see in a world dominated by nation-states and market ideologies. Beyond merely constituting a set of potential alternatives in theory, contemporary anarchism presents a number of collaborative examples that merit closer attention.

Cases in Point

While a comprehensive listing of anarchist collaborations and collective experiments would be impossible to produce, the primary categories in which these exemplars fall are *intentional communities*, *autonomous zones*, *egalitarian collectives*, and *decentralized networks*. Some anarchist alternatives exist between or among these spheres (such as the "free skool" concept that is discussed in the following section), whereas others are squarely identified—sometimes by their very name—with a particular form of organizing. It will be useful here to consider a few of these examples of anarchist action-in-concert in order to move from theory to practice, and likewise to deepen the analysis of how anarchism's do-it-yourself ethic is often balanced by a strong desire to do things together as well. As one commentator notes, "there is some burden to show how an anarchist vision might function in reality."[89] Fortunately, the contemporary milieu provides us with many intriguing examples.

Intentional Communities

One of the longest-running communities based expressly on anarchist principles is Freetown Christiania in Copenhagen, Denmark. Founded in 1971 on the site of a former military barracks, the space quickly drew an eclectic mix of squatters, hippies, collectivists, and anarchists to its straightforward, egalitarian mission based on a "magical mixture of anarchy and love": "The objective of Christiania is to create a self-governing society whereby each and every individual holds themselves responsible over the wellbeing of the entire community. Our society is to be economically self-sustaining and, as such, our aspiration is to be steadfast in our conviction that psychological and physical destitution can be averted."[90] The community has endured numerous controversies and conflicts (both within its confines and with the larger society) over issues including drugs, violence, and other governmental pressures brought to bear on its existence. Nonetheless, Christiania still survives into its fourth decade, and today it even includes a community radio and television station, a vegetarian restaurant, an organic market, and even its own internal currency.

An ethnography of the community, conducted in 1976 and sponsored by the National Museum of Denmark, described Christiania as "a relaxed and tolerant form of village life, which is opposed to the norms of the surrounding society," manifesting a "positive tolerance . . . towards what is traditionally called deviant behavior," where even crimes such as theft are "seen as an act that is necessary for the offender, an act caused by certain social and economic circumstances, a problem which can only be solved collectively," and in which "there is a close connection between the decisions that are taken and the people they apply to."[91] A 2003 assessment of this unique community further found that "government is fully democratic, and all major decisions are reached at open meetings to which everyone residing in Christiania is invited. When a general meeting is in progress, the shops and cafes close down and discussion of items on the agenda continues until a consensus is reached."[92] While cautioning that "Christiania is not to be imagined in terms of an anarchist idyll," it remains the case that this "bold and enduring social experiment" has been in operation for decades, and in that time its members have "built houses, schools, playgrounds, opened shops and restaurants, galvanized social awareness, hosted some memorable musical events, run a variety of cooperatives, established recycling programs and wind and solar power projects, and developed a participatory form of direct democracy and administration of financial funds and communal resources."[93]

Perhaps the best-known communal system is the Israeli kibbutz, but less widely perceived are its anarchist underpinnings. James Horrox has reclaimed part of that narrative, describing the kibbutz as a "voluntary, self-governing community, administered democratically by its members with neither legal sanction nor any framework of coercive authority to ensure conformity to its collectively-agreed upon behavioral norms."[94] In 1910, the first settlement was founded, comprising "a cooperative community without exploiters or exploited," in which members enjoyed "political and material equality, freedom and democracy, [and] the elimination of all forms of hierarchy."[95] The day-to-day workings of the kibbutz are based on "communal ownership of all property, including the means of production and consumption, mutual responsibility and mutual aid, communal production and consumption, and directly democratic self-management [with] no need for formalized rules and sanctions enforced by a specialized body of coercive legal institutions"—resulting in a remarkable condition in which crime is virtually non-existent.[96] Despite external pressures of militarism and nationalism, including the steady co-optation of the kibbutz into an authoritarian mythos, a new generation of kibbutzim are "consciously reinvoking the movement's anarchist progenitors as inspiration for its future directions," including the appearance of "an anti-authoritarian, consensus-driven structure rising up within the Israeli state—*alongside* it—in a federated alliance of communal groups."[97]

Autonomous Zones

Hakim Bey popularized the notion of the "temporary autonomous zone" as something akin to "an uprising which does not engage directly with the State, a guerilla operation which liberates an area . . . and then dissolves itself to re-form elsewhere/elsewhen, *before* the State can crush it."[98] While this may work well as poetry to fuel anarchist imaginations, "one must be careful not to underestimate the rather large amounts of real labor required to keep such autonomous zones running," as Jeff Shantz observes.[99] "Despite their heterotopian character, such spaces are constructed of the mundane, the everyday. . . . In the end, it is how well the demands of the everyday are met that can determine the success or failure of autonomous zones."[100] The notion of liberating a space in which anarchy can "break out" for any length of time beyond the purely ephemeral is a complex task fraught with myriad challenges, both internal and external. One of the more successful attempts to liberate and hold space in this manner is the Old Market Autonomous Zone (A-Zone) in Winnipeg, Manitoba, Canada. Founded in 1995, the A-Zone is located in Winnipeg's Exchange District, "an area of the city with a deep tradition of class struggle and anti-fascist organizing, going back to the 1919 General Strike, the 1930s street fights between workers and fascists, not to mention the visits of well-known anarchists such as Peter Kropotkin, Emma Goldman, and Rudolf Rocker."[101] The basic idea is to link "like-minded individuals and organizations, activists, as well as alternative worker-run businesses" and "to enhance the activist movement by helping to nurture a community of solidarity and resistance, and by recognizing the interrelatedness of all our struggles."[102]

The centerpiece of the A-Zone is the Mondragon Bookstore and Coffeehouse, "a political bookstore, vegan restaurant and home to Sacco & Vanzetti's organic grocery store [that is] organized as a workers collective. We have no manager, and all worker members, regardless of starting skill or seniority, earn the same rate of pay."[103] Mondragon's *Policy Handbook* memorializes its commitment to open information, participatory decision making, consensual organizing, egalitarian distribution, and an anti-oppression agenda: "We work to uproot instances of racism, sexism, homophobia, transphobia, classism, ableism, and other forms of oppression in our workplace and to provide a space safe from oppressive practices."[104] Mondragon (and the A-Zone in which it is located) has become "a focal point for activism in Winnipeg, and has contributed to a larger community and culture of resistance in the city. Its existence and example has also inspired activists in other cities, across Canada and the United States, who have written wanting advice and information about starting up their own projects."[105] In this sense, Mondragon and the A-Zone have moved beyond the "temporary" liberation of space and have thus served to perpetuate a working model of co-operative anarchism in practice.

Egalitarian Collectives

ABC No Rio is a "collectively-run center for art and activism" in New York, "known internationally as a venue for oppositional culture."[106] It was founded in 1980 "to facilitate cross-pollination between artists and activists" and to create a "place where people share resources and ideas to impact society, culture, and community."[107] The community is "committed to social justice, equality, anti-authoritarianism, autonomous action, collective processes, and to nurturing alternative structures and institutions operating on such principles"; it includes "punks, nomads, squatters, fringe dwellers, and those among society's disenfranchised."[108] In addition to its networking venue, art gallery, and event space, ABC No Rio sponsors a number of ongoing "affiliated projects," including Books Through Bars ("an all-volunteer project which sends free books and reading material to prisoners nationwide"), Food Not Bombs (which "prepares and serves healthy vegan food to the homeless in Tompkins Square Park, and often serves at protests and demonstrations in the New York City area"), and the Lower East Side Biography Project (which "trains individuals in all aspects of digital video through the production of video biographies of long-term Lower East Side residents").[109] ABC

No Rio is one of the longest-running collectives in North America and has deep roots in its local community.

Founded in December 2003, the Iron Rail library and bookstore "is committed to anarchist, anti-authoritarian, feminist, anti-racist, queer-positive and class-conscious politics, and to providing alternative literature and information to the people of New Orleans."[110] The Iron Rail is "a collectively owned and operated, all-volunteer, non-profit reading room, lending library, bookshop, and community space with over 7,000 titles for free borrowing"; the vast collection includes works on "anarchist action, anarchist theory, and the histories of overlooked groups, struggles, and individuals," plus numerous texts on "feminism, gender, race, class, sexuality, sex work, how-to books about crafts and DIY—bike fixing, cooking, monkey-wrenching, gardening."[111] The Iron Rail is "one of the largest collectively-run radical libraries in the country [and] was the first library in metro New Orleans to re-open after the disastrous failure of the government levees in 2005, and for several months [was] the only functioning library in the city."[112] The organization of the collective reflects its values:

> We believe in a world without domination and oppression and in working to undermine authoritarian structures of power. As an anarchist collective, the Iron Rail has no bosses or managers. Group decisions are made collectively in weekly meetings, and members are encouraged to be creative in initiating individual projects. The bookstore is operated by volunteers who believe in the importance of establishing alternatives to capitalism, while creating new public spaces and supporting community projects.[113]

The collective offers the following "Policies and Points of Unity" that further serve to define the scope and mission:[114]

1. We are working towards the creation of a new society based on participatory economic and social structures as a replacement for capitalism and the state.
2. We believe that helping to provide wider access to education and information will help us build this society.
3. We recognize capitalism and the state as inherently oppressive, exploiting us all to various degrees and in different ways depending on our age, gender, skin color, sexual orientation, abilities, culture and class. We therefore oppose all forms of oppression and are committed, in part through education and the development of personal

    support systems, to their abolition in society and in our own collective.

4. We believe that making our decisions collectively in a non-hierarchical, anti-authoritarian manner empowers our members through worker self-management and is the only way to organize a project based on collective liberation. Putting our principles into practice, we strive to serve as an example of the kind of society we are working to create as anarchists.

Decentralized Networks

In Chapter Two, a sample of networks were described in which local autonomous units link with similar efforts elsewhere (even worldwide) to create a decentralized "whole" that functions as a bottom-up, horizontal quasi-organization; specific examples cited included Food Not Bombs, CrimethInc., and Indymedia. To those we can add the Anarchist Black Cross (ABC), which traces its earliest roots back to the coordinated provision of materials and support to anarchist prisoners at the turn of the twentieth century. Like other decentralized networks, the ABC is a concept and not a top-heavy organization, meaning that anyone doing work within its basic principles can adopt the moniker. In the case of the ABC, this led to rifts and splintering to some extent, but it also yielded an expansion of the mission and a wider variety of prison support mechanisms. In 1995, a small group of ABC collectives merged to form the Anarchist Black Cross Federation (ABCF), with the specific intention to support people who are in "prison as a result of conscious political action, for building resistance, building and leading movements and revolution . . . for making change."[115] The ABCF has a fairly elaborate structure for maintaining and operating the federation, with the overarching aim being the establishment of "tactical unity" among the various collectives.[116] In 2001, a parallel and less formal entity was formed, called the Anarchist Black Cross Network (ABCN); whereas the ABCF focuses on political prisoners and regulates its membership, the ABCN was designed to confront prison issues in a more general sense (e.g., as connected to poverty, racism, and human rights violations) and opened the network to any entity working on prison abolition in general. At a 2003 conference, the ABCF and ABCN attempted to resolve their differences and reclaim the original spirit of the ABC.

    There are many additional examples of anarchist networks, federations, collectives, and the like—far too many to cite here (the notion of "global networks" in particular will be discussed in Chapter Six). In terms of broad categories of engagement, there are clusters of infoshops, bookstores, and publishing houses; archives, databases, and listservs; community centers, social spaces, and performance sites; neotribal gatherings and anonymous high-tech cadres; alternative currency exchanges, free economy groups, and work equity co-ops; activist workshops, book fairs, and academic associations. In each instance, and to varying degrees, the navigation of individual expression and collective cohesion is always in play, as is the dual tendency to critically engage the dominant order while modeling a viable alternative as to both methods and substance. In fact, for many contemporary anarchists working collaboratively, there is no clear distinction between the processes employed and the group's substantive aims; rather, the two spheres are mutually reinforcing and contribute equally to telling a story about anarchism's efficacy and desirability as a mode of living in—and learning about—our world.

Teach Your Children Well (and Vice Versa)

In this sense, all of the entities noted above embody an educative function in terms of communicating the practical workings of anarchism as a dynamic form of social order. Indeed, one of the central features of anarchist praxis throughout history has been an emphasis on liberating *education* from its restrictive, compulsory, and dehumanizing fetters.[117] Anarchists have long recognized that education in its broadest sense can be a double-edged sword, containing not only an emancipatory impulse but an authoritarian one as well; as Joel Spring has observed, "schools came into being as a means of shaping the moral and social beliefs of the population for the benefit of a dominant elite."[118] In this context, it appears that "schools are an extension of the state; they reproduce the class, sex, race and other divisions on which the state is built."[119] Like many others schooled in formal settings that are licensed and/or administered by the state, anarchists apprehend the normative strictures of the educational system, the obligatory nature of public schooling, and the problematic appearance of the teacher as a "secular priest."[120] As Ivan Illich explains in his classic work *Deschooling Society*, the repressive potentials of formal education oftentimes increase as one advances up the scholastic ladder:

> The university graduate has been schooled for selective service among the rich of the world. ... Schools select for each successive level those who have, at earlier stages in the game, proved themselves good risks for the established order. Having a monopoly on

both the resources for learning and the investiture of social roles, the university coopts the discoverer and the potential dissenter.[121]

Despite such moments of co-optation, there are possibilities for dissidence presented in the university setting; although, as Illich cautions, there are serious limitations as well:

> There is no question that at present the university offers a unique combination of circumstances which allows some of its members to criticize the whole of society. It provides time, mobility, access to peers and information, and a certain impunity—privileges not equally available to other segments of the population. But the university provides this freedom only to those who have already been deeply initiated into the consumer society and into the need for some kind of obligatory public schooling.[122]

Picking up on these themes and challenges, contemporary critics often seek to construct practical visions of liberatory education that avoid the pitfalls identified by Illich. Working from the premises that "the nature of most schooling is anti-dialogical, breeds dependency, subserviency or identification with those who already hold power, [and] sustains the existing power arrangements," Larry Fisk calls for a "problem-posing education" that begins with a self-critical "awareness of one's own oppressed or flawed consciousness and conditioning."[123] Fisk posits a framework that fosters "moral intelligence and peacemaking skills" and that can "provide a holistic climate within which the sense of powerlessness or fatalism can be challenged."[124] Focusing upon familiar themes such as "process, critical thinking, and self-discipline," this type of education "erodes dependency and fatalism by allowing us to see and experience the world as problematic, unfinished, and exposed to the change which we can help bring about."[125] Specifically, Fisk calls for an educational paradigm in which "people learn values and attitudes which move them to act effectively in particular ways: against war, for environmental protection," and which "actively promotes justice, conflict resolution, service-training, and non-violent action."[126] Such sentiments mirror Illich's earlier insight that "the inverse of school is possible" and moreover that

> a desirable future depends on our deliberately choosing a life of action over a life of consumption, on our engendering a lifestyle which will enable us to be spontaneous, independent, yet related to

each other, rather than maintaining a lifestyle which only allows us to make and unmake, produce and consume—a style of life which is merely a way station on the road to the depletion and pollution of the environment.[127]

Illich, whose anti-authoritarian critique of formal education has strongly influenced the development of contemporary anarchist perspectives, desires a society in which "we can depend on self-motivated learning instead of employing teachers to bribe or compel the student to find the time and the will to learn" and, further, one where "we can provide the learner with new links to the world instead of continuing to funnel all educational programs through the teacher."[128] In many important respects, this is a decidedly anarchistic approach to learning, since anarchism has always sought to let "a thousand flowers bloom" rather than impose a specific blueprint for social change.[129] Sensitive to such themes, the anarchist critique of formal education reflects larger concerns about the nature of hierarchy and official coercion, as Ward bluntly concludes:

> Ultimately the social function of education is to perpetuate society: it is *the* socialising function. Society guarantees its future by rearing its children in its own image. . . . The educational system is the largest instrument in the modern state for telling people what to do. . . . Compulsory education is bound up historically, not only with the printing press, the rise of Protestantism and capitalism, but with the growth of the idea of the nation itself. . . . It is in the *nature* of public authorities to run coercive and hierarchical institutions whose ultimate function is to perpetuate social inequality and to brainwash the young into the acceptance of their particular slot in the organized system.[130]

As Bakunin plaintively inquired in the late nineteenth century, "must we, then, eliminate from society all instruction and abolish all schools? Far from it!"[131] Instead, Bakunin envisioned the positive and proactive creation of "schools of human emancipation":

> From these schools will be absolutely eliminated the smallest applications or manifestations of the principle of authority. They will be schools no longer; they will be popular academies, in which neither pupils nor masters will be known, where the people will come freely to get, if they need it, free instruction, and in which, rich in their own experience, they will teach in their turn many things to the

professors who shall bring them knowledge which they lack. This, then, will be a mutual instruction, an act of intellectual fraternity between the educated youth and the people.[132]

Following Bakunin, perhaps the quintessential early model of anarchist education was the Modern School founded in Spain by Francisco Ferrer in 1901, who launched this effort with due regard to the fact that "rulers have always taken care to control the education of the people; they know better than any that their power is based entirely on the school, and they therefore insist on retaining their monopoly of it."[133] To counter this oppressive, indoctrinating force, Ferrer proposed and implemented a school built on humanistic, naturalistic, and holistic principles:

> We are convinced that the education of the future will be of an entirely spontaneous nature; certainly we cannot as yet realize it, but the evolution of methods in the direction of a wider comprehension of the phenomena of life, and the fact that all advances toward perfection mean the overcoming of restraint—all this indicates that we are in the right when we hope for the deliverance of the child. . . . We can destroy all which in the present school answers to the organization of constraint, the artificial surroundings by which children are separated from nature and life, the intellectual and moral discipline made use of to impose ready-made ideas upon them, beliefs which deprave and annihilate natural bent. Without fear of deceiving ourselves, we can restore the child to the environment which entices it, the environment of nature.[134]

In this sense, as Ward infers, "the anarchist approach to education is grounded, not in a contempt for learning, but in a respect for the learner."[135] Indeed, the anarchist vision contemplates that "the pupil must be trusted to determine his [or her] own curriculum," thus embracing Paulo Freire's pedagogical insight that "education must begin with the solution of the teacher-student contradiction, by reconciling the poles of the contradiction so that both are simultaneously teachers *and* students."[136] In attempting to depict how such a "community of scholars" might function, Paul Goodman conceived a working anarchist model in which

> a core faculty of about five professors secede from a school, taking some of their students with them . . . and set up a small unchartered university that would be nothing but an association. Ten teachers

would constitute a sufficient faculty for such a community of scholars. With individual classes of about fifteen . . . the students and teachers create a small university where they can associate in the traditional way, *but entirely dispensing with the external control, administration, and bureaucratic machinery and other excrescences that have swamped our communities of scholars.*[137]

In his corollary call for an "education of the aesthetic sensibility," Herbert Read assessed the qualities that "the good teacher" in such a setting ought to embody:

> He [sic] will try to establish a relationship of reciprocity and trust between himself and his pupil, and one of co-operation and mutual aid between all the individuals within his care [so that] the group develops spontaneously a social life and cohesion which is independent of the teacher. We can aim at making our teachers the friends rather than the masters of their pupils; as teachers they will not lay down ready-made rules, but will encourage their children to carry out their own cooperative activities, and thus spontaneously to elaborate their own rules. The teacher must be primarily a person and not a pedagogue, a friend rather than a master or mistress, an infinitely patient collaborator.[138]

Similarly, Leo Tolstoy—who took part of his personal fortune to found over a dozen schools for peasants based on "purely libertarian principles"—focused on the voluntaristic aspects of anarchist pedagogy, bringing on teachers who were "young radical students" themselves:

> The school has evolved freely from the principles introduced into it by teachers and pupils. . . . The pupil has always had the right not to come to school, or, having come, not to listen to the teacher. . . . Obeying only natural laws, flowing from their nature, [the pupils] revolt and grumble when they have to obey your untimely interference. They do not believe in the legality of your bells, rosters and rules. . . . The best policy and administrative system for a school is to allow the scholars perfect freedom of learning and of governing themselves as they like.[139]

In this light, we can discern—in addition to the quest to secure individual autonomy—that it is equally the case that "higher education" in the anarchist lexicon "is ideally based upon a long and laudable tradition of autonomous, 'anarchically self-regulating' communities."[140] In other words, just as individual pupils will learn to be self-regulating, so too will the learning communities they create, as Ward observed in describing the student revolts of the 1960s:

> What a delicious, but predictable irony, that *real* education, self-education, should only come from locking out or ignoring the expensive academic hierarchy. The students' revolt was a microcosm of anarchy, spontaneous, self-directed activity replacing the power structure by a network of autonomous groups and individuals. What the students experienced was that sense of liberation that comes from taking your own decisions and assuming your own responsibilities. It is an experience that we need to carry far beyond the privileged world of higher education, into the factory, the neighborhood, the daily lives of people everywhere.[141]

As the image comes into sharper focus, we see that over time "learning and teaching will become an integrated element of life itself. ... Everybody will be a student and a teacher at the same time. The transmission of wisdom, know-how, theories, styles will always accompany all productive or reflective processes."[142] In this manner, "a kind of school system can be organized," one that "will be completely voluntary" and for which "there will be no standardization of school systems, no official programs."[143] And thus we enter the *free skool*.

In recent years, a new movement has arisen, based on the lessons of history and the tenets of anarchism. Often intentionally misspelled as "skool" to indicate its anti-school and anti-formalistic tendencies, this burgeoning phenomenon counts dozens of exemplars, primarily in the United States, Canada, and the United Kingdom. Its purpose is inherently revolutionary:

> A free skool is a decentralized network in which skills, information, and knowledge are shared without hierarchy or the institutional environment of formal schooling. Free skools are explicitly rooted in an anarchist tradition of collectivism, autonomy, and self-reliance, and feature informal, non-authoritarian learning outside of the monetary economy. From the Free Skool Santa Cruz website: "More than just an opportunity to learn, we see Free Skool as a direct challenge to dominant institutions and hierarchical relationships. Part of creating a new world is resistance to the old one, to

the relentless commodification of everything, including learning and the way we relate to each other."[144]

Free skools often embrace the basic philosophy of "we are all teachers, and we are all students," striving to exist outside the structures of state regulation and capitalism's profit motive. Education in the free skool is offered and received without expectation of payment, and the settings for the informal "classes" themselves are often decentralized throughout the community.

In all of these active visions from history and into the contemporary anarchist milieu, there is a penchant for processes that are voluntary, non-hierarchical, self-directed, informal, open-ended, non-commercial, and spontaneous. At the end is a form of schooling that transcends any particular meeting time or classroom setting, instead conceiving *education* as part of the everyday experience of life itself, as a mutually supportive and socially reflective set of conditions that constitutes an ongoing "experiment in human living."[145] In a strong sense, young people (and children in particular) can be seen as natural anarchists, and it is through cultivating these attributes rather than squelching them with compulsion and discipline that the emancipatory potential of education is most readily realized. Moreover, the individuals that emerge from such settings are likely to be engaged and not disaffected, action-oriented and not apathetic, dissident and not conformist, community-minded and not egocentric. This anti-authoritarian approach to education views "all people as capable and worthy of curiosity, learning, teaching, and creation."[146] In this manner, the lessons learned in anarchist educational settings can serve to infuse and inform our relationships at every level of social interaction.

Identities and Relationships

In the end, tensions about individualism and collectivism are really just another way of talking about relationships. Similarly, the contours of education, labor, socialization, politics, and more are strongly influenced by the nature of the relations upon which they are premised—for example, whether they are predominantly horizontal or vertical. Anarchism strives for the former as the surest way to preserve autonomy and promote cooperation, in the view that freedom and equality are thoroughly conjoined aims. As such, some contemporary anarchists have begun to shift the inquiry toward a "relational ethics" that focuses on "the process of mutual discovery and knowing one another . . . through relations of friendship, solidarity, and empathy."[147] In this light, "the question of whether or not people are immediately capable of self-organization without rigid structure or control is, then, perhaps not the most relevant one. Anarchists, instead, might ask: what do people need to learn, what do I need to learn, to practice, to become more capable? How can we support each other in those practices, in that learning?"[148] Extending the analysis, we come to understand anarchism as "an ethics of relationships"—and perhaps more to the point, "as affirming alternative relationships to those of states (and equally, to intertwined hierarchical relationships including capitalism, patriarchy, heteronormativity and colonialism)" through the development of "sustainable, empowering and egalitarian relationships."[149]

Recalling Gustav Landauer's famous (and oft-quoted) words, the inherently revolutionary potential of his insight begins to fully emerge: "The state is a social relationship; a certain way of people relating to one another. It can be destroyed by creating new social relationships; i.e., by people relating to one another differently."[150] Viewing anarchism as a theory and practice of *relationships* enables us to see beyond the mere political economy of materialist conceptions of *revolution*, instead moving toward a truly subversive reclaiming of our essential humanity in the face of dehumanization and our innate conviviality as against the state's "multitude of opportunities for intimacy lost."[151] As Horrox observes, "humanity's natural bonds of empathy and fraternity, corrupted by the influence of the capitalist state and the trappings of modernity, need to be restored in order to create a new kind of society."[152] Accordingly, contemporary anarchism has increasingly engaged relational issues of family structure, sexuality, parenting, household management, cohabitation, polyamory, "free love," conflict transformation, non-violent communication, listening, and becoming—as well as matters of social location and identity construction bound up with race, class, gender, sexual orientation, ability, age, and more.

Conceiving anarchism in relational terms as a paradigm of *radical horizontalism* that privileges no set of attributes (e.g., white, male, heterosexual) over another provides a ready basis for rethinking individuality as both difference *and* equivalence, likewise for reconstructing community as a form of rediscovered intimacy. Being rendered *equal* does not serve to denigrate the unique self; rather, it elevates each of us to a place of inherent integrity and mutual respect. Extending this horizontalism further, we come to see that including *nature* in the calculus similarly places humankind in the advantageous position of being part of an intricate and supportive web, rather than appearing as its enemy in a fit of self-defeating egocentrism. And finally, by bringing this maximal, relational, and revolutionary egalitarianism to bear on all of humankind, we glimpse a vision of a world without militarized borders, where poverty and profligacy have been eliminated, and where networks of mutual aid can operate globally absent the historical baggage of nation or station. This is where the next chapter strives to take us.

CHAPTER 6

From the Local to the Global

Anarchism is sometimes viewed (even by sympathetic evaluators) as a nice idea that could only apply in small-scale settings, if at all. At the same time, anarchist principles of theorizing and organizing are present worldwide in both activist and academic circles. An exploration of some of the key local initiatives emerging out of contemporary anarchism suggests that a nascent global movement may be in the offing; indeed, anarchism possesses an inherent internationalism that reflects a complex balance of local action within a globally connected network. Additionally, the basic anti-state and anti-capitalist premises of anarchism present an opportunity for considering different geopolitical configurations than those promulgated by powerful interests—which have largely brought to the world increasing warfare, impoverishment, and environmental degradation. Anarchism does not seek to reform the state (and its associated processes) or win power within its confines, but to abolish it altogether—raising critical questions including what would take its place, how to address "people power" struggles for national liberation, and whether emerging networking technologies can be deployed in the name of emancipation. Contemporary anarchism directly engages all of these queries.

At the outset, anarchism's history reflects a remarkably internationalist spirit, dating to its anthropological roots in the myriad "stateless societies" found worldwide that possessed "no formal leaders"—from the Inuit of the polar north to the San of the arid south.[1] Rich histories have been produced on anarchist organizing in Mexico, Cuba, Uruguay, Brazil, Argentina, and other nations in Central and South America.[2] Anarchism traces part of its origins (at least metaphysically) to Lao-Tzu and the naissance of Taoism and has found expression in China, Japan,

Korea, India, and Indonesia, among other Asian settings.[3] James C. Scott has written a particularly fascinating "anarchist history" of Zomia, a vast stateless region in Asia populated by "self-governing peoples" who represent what was once "the great majority of humankind."[4] Likewise, in concluding that "anarchism as a way of life is in large measure indigenous in Africa," Sam Mbah and I. E. Igariwey locate contemporary "outright anarchist movements" (to varying degrees) in countries including South Africa, Nigeria, Zimbabwe, Ghana, and Egypt.[5] Anarchist praxis has been indicated in the "Arab Spring" uprisings in the Middle East, and anarchists have maintained a strong presence in the central global hotspot that is Israel and Palestine.[6] In addition to anarchism's influential presence in Russia and Eastern Europe, which produced many landmark thinkers, there are of course well-known examples from across Europe, including strong manifestations in Greece, Italy, England, and perhaps most notably Spain, where anarchists fought against fascism in the 1930s and set up a model society in the process. Confirming this global scope, a 2010 book (in German) on "worldwide anarchism" includes interviews with anarchists from 50 countries, covering all continents in the process.[7]

All of this portrays a thoroughly global anarchism, even as it remains the case that a Eurocentric, U.S.-centric, and/or "Western" perspective tends to dominate the field. This eventuality has clear roots in the legacy of colonialism, as well as the unequal distribution of education and opportunity that skews to the benefit of "First World" nations in the global north versus those often pejoratively coded as the "Third World" countries of the global south. Despite the fact that anarchist writers (myself included) at times perpetuate this imbalance by virtue of their sociocultural and geographical locations, it is also true that anarchism as a set of theories and practices works specifically to ameliorate such effects through concrete efforts bent on decolonization and egalitarianism. One of the key methods for pursuing these aims is the establishment of horizontal networks of exchange and solidarity across national borders, which often include in their development a thoroughgoing deconstruction of privileges and hierarchies attendant to race, gender, class, and other attributes. Moreover, anarchists labor diligently to oppose the workings of nation-states and corporate globalization alike, thus seeking to eradicate two of the most pernicious impediments to a world of equal justice for all its inhabitants.

A critical point of reflection for anarchists today is to envisage what forms of human association would take the place of nation-states in any potential anarchist global system. Whereas a liberal-internationalist perspective might advocate for a world governmental structure as a means of surmounting militarized borders and perpetual national conflicts, and a neoconservative model might devolve upon a single hegemonic superpower subsuming the world in its orbit as a path to stability and prosperity, anarchists generally reject both formulations in favor of "bottom-up" processes that are organized from below by individuals and communities. As we have seen, the primacy of personal autonomy is central to anarchism, as is the productive necessity of living in community with others; beyond this, anarchists grow increasingly suspicious of forms of association that expand the scope of governance in such a manner as to render direct participation unwieldy. This does not necessarily preclude city-level units of analysis or even bioregional perspectives, and indeed anarchists at times have argued for both as reasonable alternatives to the rigidity and brutality of the state as the arbiter of world order. The crucial ingredient for anarchists in establishing a global model is how these anti-authoritarian units will "federate" and coordinate their efforts; in many ways, this process will be analogous to the ways in which individual liberty and collective processes are balanced, reflecting the longstanding anarchist premise that freedom and equality are mutually inclusive endeavors.

Global Anarchism: A Primer

Perhaps the leading figure in recent decades bringing a global perspective to anarchism (and vice versa) has been Noam Chomsky. His trenchant analysis of world politics and current events, coupled with his critical reading of recent history through a lens of U.S. imperialism in particular, has served to inform and inspire generations of anarchists. In his impressive body of work, Chomsky has elucidated the stark parameters of geopolitics, empire building, realpolitik, and ongoing attempts by nation-states to capitalize on ostensible "threats" as a means of expanding their internal control and external hegemony at once. As Chomsky observes, the concept of the "enemy" is often used to brand "people who are committed to these dangerous heresies, such as using their resources for their own purposes or believing that the government is committed to the welfare of its own people."[8] Taking the analysis further, he concludes that "the United States quite consistently tries to create enemies . . . because that justifies us in carrying out the violent attacks which we *must* carry out, given the geopolitical conception under which we organize and control much of the world."[9] In the end, Chomsky discerns that the greatest actual threat to U.S. dominance may well be "successful social and economic development in one area," which can have the effect of encouraging others to extricate themselves "from the system of misery and oppression that we've helped to impose."[10]

Chomsky's analysis provides a useful point of departure for interpreting global politics in the age of empire building, likewise for understanding (at least in part) the attempt to crush examples of intransigence and insurgency—including those fomented by anarchists around the world. But it also leaves many unanswered questions and points in need of further refinement, including what exactly is to be done (or perhaps more to the point, *undone*) in the face of a rapidly escalating global hegemony that is being facilitated by new technologies and the combined effect of military-economic conquest. To some extent, despite his radical approach and major influence, Chomsky remains entrenched within the Westphalian order that (a) constructs geopolitical insights (even critical ones) around nation-states as the essential pieces of the puzzle, (b) views ideological rifts as key battlegrounds, and (c) takes institutional political power as the prime mover of world events. This is not to say that Chomsky prefers it this way but merely that it is the paradigm in which he is working—and there remains much to be said for this line of thought. Still, as John Clark counsels, the landscape is rapidly changing: "The prevailing world systems . . . no longer offer us a hopeful prospect of resolving the vast social and ecological crises which now confront humanity. . . . What is necessary is an alternative vision of society, the future, and indeed reality itself: a vision which departs from the traditional ideologies."[11]

For Clark, that new vision is in fact *anarchism*. Interestingly, it is more often the case that international relations are said to be typified by *anarchy*, in the disparaging sense of representing chaos and potential violence, since there is no formal executive authority at the global level to enforce laws and impose coercive sanctions as a means of securing compliance. The United Nations is not such an entity, nor is the force of an incipient international law and its relatively toothless tribunals. The operative premise in international theory is actually a projection of the logic of the nation-state, that is, that left to their own devices, individual units (states themselves, in the international order) are fundamentally untrustworthy and bent on asserting their power for personal (or national) gain. Perhaps ironically, in the case of nation-states vis-à-vis the international community, this Hobbesian logic often appears true. Assertions of superior power by global hegemons like the United States are thus tolerated (if not celebrated) as necessary—if at times unfortunate—attempts to fill the vacuum and impose a police-like sense of order upon an anarchic state of world affairs. However, as Richard Falk contends, the purported "solution" has by now become a primary driver of the problem: "The modernist reliance on the sovereign territorial state … is increasingly anachronistic and dysfunctional when it comes to global policy and problem-solving. The primacy of the state as the foundation of human community and the state system that continues to constitute the operative framework for world order needs to be superseded, or modified, ideologically and behaviorally as rapidly as possible."[12]

This realization has led Andrej Grubacic, implicitly following Clark's insight, to conclude that "the answer to 'global anarchy' … is 'global anarchism.' "[13] Simply put, an anarchical world order composed of nation-states is not a condition of *anarchism* but one of opportunistic authoritarianism, in which state and corporate elites jockey for position among themselves, while neither power nor wealth genuinely circulates among the masses. As Falk notes, it increasingly appears that we have reached a tipping point defined by "the ideological exhaustion of state-centrism as a transformative nexus"—with the bare teeth of empire and nascent fascism steadily being reasserted in response, through means including "hyper-nationalism, intensified militarism, xenophobic immigration policy, and an endless search for enemies within and without state boundaries."[14] Against this, Falk concludes that the "genuine challenge for a revived tradition of anarchism [is] to develop a global vision that allows its overriding concern with freedom of the individual, autonomy of the group, and harmony among groups to be responsive to the planetary imperatives of a sustainable social life in the early 21st century."[15] Anticipating the coming challenge, Clark has sketched an anarchist vision based on

> the replacement of nation-states by federations of communal and workplace associations; replacement of corporate capitalist and state ownership by self-management of production by the producers; replacement of the patriarchal authoritarian family by libertarian family and living arrangements; replacement of the megalopolis and centralized population distribution by decentralized, ecologically balanced population patterns; and replacement of centralized, high technology by more humanly scaled alternative technologies, which are compatible with decentralized, democratic decision making, and which are not destructive of the social and natural environments.[16]

In this sense, by exposing regimes of domination at every level and "offering paths to their dismantling that places the autonomy of the individual and the collective at its heart," anarchism "provides a useful intellectual toolkit for scholars of the global, and brings a new perspective" of rigorous critique and imaginative reconstruction.[17] Recognizing that anarchists in general have engaged in too little "sustained analysis of 'the international' " in favor of more micro-level considerations of individuals and communities, Alex Prichard has worked to develop a "deeper anarchism; one that does not ignore the international nor retreat to the utopian visions of the transformative powers of revolutionary class struggle anarchism."[18] Prichard is responding to anarchism's historical impetus toward international workers' solidarity as a means of promoting global revolution. This trend in anarchism has been greatly informed by Michael Bakunin's collectivist, insurrectionist approach, which has been both complemented and counterbalanced by Pierre-Joseph Proudhon's mutualist federalism that included the possibility of "constitutionalized anarchy" as a basis for political order.[19] In practice, while neither Bakunin's nor Proudhon's formulation was ultimately successful in surmounting state/corporate power, the lessons of their examples serve as important reminders of anarchism's simultaneous anti-statism and internationalism.

While these (and other) approaches from the classical era certainly served their purposes and have influenced generations of anarchists in the process, today the emphasis for engaging the international frame is more on the "translation or circulation of struggles [and] the elaboration of cooperation among people in the struggle."[20] The path to globalism, in this view, is to become more deeply rooted in local struggles and to find ways to link them together. As Clark explains, "unless the inhumane, bureaucratic, objectifying relationships created by the state, capitalism, and high technology are replaced by personalistic, cooperative relationships arising in the primary communal group, it cannot be hoped that people will have a deep concern for humanity as a whole."[21] Clark wisely discerns that anarchists—far from being insufficiently attentive to international concerns—have in actuality infused them within the context of everyday existence, communal relationships, and local struggles for dignity, justice, and ecologically balanced lives. This reflects anarchism's penchant for grassroots, bottom-up organizing as a means of promoting an "organic interdependence beginning with the most basic social units and building, through federation, to humanity as a whole."[22] The question thus becomes what level of affiliation we will take as the unit of analysis; despite the geopolitical dominance of nation-states (even in the age of corporate power), anarchists reject their utility as a basis for association.

Beyond the State

Anarchists by and large consider the state to be a poor choice for managing human and environmental affairs. Nation-states exist within the confines of artificial boundaries, often acquired and maintained through processes of warfare or colonialism. States are militaristic, capitalistic, and governed through hierarchical processes that at best claim the problematic mantle of "representation" and at worst devolve upon naked fascism. Anarchists were early critics at the dawn of industrialism to point out how state and corporate interests were intertwined and mutually reinforcing despite at times conveying a public face of opposition that serves to generate a false sense of "checks and balances" and spirited political debate as a means of placating the populace. *Anarchy* by definition rejects the state, as we know, and likewise all forms of rule based on coercive authority and pyramidal power structures. But as we have also seen, anarchists do not reject *governance* per se, and in fact they are ardent proponents of self-management, community-based decision-making processes, and the active participation of all who will be impacted by any particular course of action contemplated by the group. In this sense, anarchism is not governance-averse but rather *government*-averse, and thus it abhors the state.

Interestingly, this critique of the state comes from two directions, as Clark observes: "There are two sides to the anarchist rejection of the nation-state: one is communalism, and the other is internationalism."[23] On the one hand, the state does violence to individual autonomy and communal relationships by imposing "law and order" from above, under penalty of punishment (or worse); unlike an anarchist community in which people live and work as relative equals and no authority is ever reified in coercive power, the state is an abstraction that mandates universal obedience (at least as to the governed) without equal voice in the process of governance. On the other hand, the state refuses to yield its sovereignty in globally cognizable matters such as the environment and human rights, asserting its plenary powers over its resources and peoples alike. In this sense, the anarchist denunciation of the state is both bottom-up and top-down, that is, the state is insufficiently local *and* global at the same time—representing an "unhappy medium" that has served more often than not as an agent of oppression, and even genocide, rather than as a locus for human dignity and oft-invoked rights of "life, liberty, and the pursuit of happiness."

There is a popular notion in international relations and peace-building circles about how nation-states, particularly ones that are ostensibly "democratic" in nature, do not generally wage war upon one another.

There is also the view that most global conflicts are actually internecine and that cross-border wars are the exception. Despite the force of these concepts, they are limited by interpretation and the intrusion of reality, as even a cursory glance at U.S. foreign policy over the past century alone (in which the nation has been at war continuously) might reveal. The creation of nation-states has not served to forestall conflict, and in fact it has mainly exacerbated it; simply put, the state did not save the world from the scourge of violence, but merely normalized its use. A well-known aphorism from Randolph Bourne counsels that "war is the health of the state," and the bloody history of the twentieth century aptly confirms this. Ultimately, the rise of the nation-state as the locus for promoting conflict resolution in the Westphalian world order simply has not brought much of it. As Thorstein Veblen once famously noted, "Born in iniquity and conceived in sin, the spirit of nationalism has never ceased to bend human institutions to the service of dissension and distress." Grasping this, anarchists reject the state and its nationalistic software "as an ideology that is ultimately rooted in authoritarianism and bigotry, recognizing that it is an ideology that came into its own with the flourishing of the capitalist state."[24]

A 2011 article by Falk raises the central question "Is the State a Monster?" and observes that "for many the state becomes an idol to be unconditionally obeyed as if an infallible god, a forfeiture of freedom, a renunciation of citizenship in a humane political community, and a voluntary acceptance of subjugation of the spirit. Such a 'patriotic' process has drastically diminished the quality of democratic life almost everywhere, and has given the state a green light to wage wars of choice, regardless of their bloody consequences."[25] Falk cites chilling historical examples, including "the Nazi death camps, the atomic bombs dropped on Japanese cities, the genocidal dispossession of indigenous peoples throughout the world, the cruelties of colonial rule, the long siege imposed on the people of Gaza," asserting that a global superpower such as the United States "remains ready to incinerate tens of millions of innocent civilians for the sake of regime survival for itself and allied governments. What could be colder? What could be more anti-human?"[26] As Crispin Sartwell concurs, "the state is a self-referential history, a self-reinforcing infinite spiral of oppression. . . . The modern nation-state is an absolutely necessary condition for the wars and exterminations of the twentieth and the present century that have expended human beings as if they were inanimate. . . . It may well be, when all is said and done, that the nation-state is responsible for the extermination of our species or the extinction of our planet."[27]

Despite this legacy, nation-states have largely retained their legitimacy by eradicating viable alternatives, from the local to the global, and by fomenting antipathies between people based on groundless nationalistic passions. Against this, anarchism "advocates internationalism to break down ideologically imposed national divisions in order to reveal the real divisions which our rulers are constantly trying to mask: the division between rich and poor, between capital-owners and workers, between the international financial elites and the rest of us."[28] The anarchist tradition, in the view of the authors of *Black Flame*, has thus devolved upon "an internationalist movement; it strove to unite the popular classes across all state borders, stressed the common interests of the working class and peasantry of all countries, and aimed at an international social revolution."[29] Reflecting this universality of human interests and allegiances, the Mexican revolutionary Ricardo Flores Magón stated in a Los Angeles federal courtroom in 1916: "We are aliens to no country, nor are we aliens to any people on earth. The world is our country and all men are our countrymen."[30] Anarchists embrace such notions of obliterated borders and common humanities and thus oppose the state as the enemy of such pursuits.

Whatever historical utility the nation-state model may have represented appears to have run its course. Perhaps it was a necessary step away from absolutism and toward liberty and democracy, but the rubric by now appears to be working at cross-purposes to these aims. States are repressive, militaristic, authoritarian, expansionist, opportunistic, and intolerant. Even in the best case scenario, the state breeds dependency, obedience, and centralization of power; in the end, the rise of nation-states has yielded precisely what it was alleged to forestall. Conversely, as anarchists have long maintained, abolishing nation-states would encourage people to live and work together regardless of territorial boundaries, allowing for a freer exchange of communities and cultures.[31] Localities would become the locus of peoples' lives and in that sense would promote more sustainable lifestyles. The tendency to simplify conflict into "us versus them" would be severely undermined, and the ability of hardliners to hijack the "will of the people" for destructive purposes greatly diminished. Permanent war economies would be rendered impracticable if not impossible, and the pervasive leveraging of corporate power over democratic governance would become a virtual nullity. While some believe that the waning influence of nation-states would yield greater corporate power, it appears instead that the two are in fact jointly operational and that the obsolescence of one could bring about an end to the other. Beyond both governments and corporations lie individuals and communities—seemingly forgotten entities that may well reemerge if given sufficient room and encouragement to do so.

Even so, anarchists do not suggest that the abolition of nation-states would be a panacea, or that this would not bring about its own set of difficulties. There is also some ambivalence in the milieu, such as with Falk himself, who has argued that

> even most of those among us who try to be citizens in the proper sense would still not opt for the chaos of an ungoverned social order if given a free choice. Our task is to build a just and ethically accountable state, not to abandon the enterprise as futile. ... We also need to resist the temptation to fall into a deeper sleep by adopting a posture of unrealizable and unacceptable negation of this strange political creature called the state. In the end, the state is not a monster, but a work in progress.[32]

Others have likewise recognized the implicit, pragmatic dilemma that "in a situation where state power more or less extends to every corner of the globe, anarchy becomes practically impossible."[33]

Another critical question concerns the appearance of "struggles for national liberation [that are] frequently infused with nationalism," something that anarchists that have grappled with as embodying both revolutionary and nationalistic potentials.[34] Indeed, anarchists throughout history have fought in national liberation struggles, from Nestor Makhno in the Ukraine to Buenaventura Durruti (among many others) in the Spanish Civil War. Yet given today's climate, in which an increasingly integrated global system has shown a remarkable capacity to co-opt and/or crush resistance that remains too firmly rooted within its statist confines, "it could equally be argued that national liberation efforts can only end up creating new state-sponsored nationalisms."[35] Should anarchists thus reject popular uprisings against dictators, such as those evidenced by the Arab Spring in countries like Egypt, on the basis that they seek not to abolish the state but to reform it? Shall anarchists navigate the Israel-Palestine conflict by seeking a multiplicative "two-state solution" or through some other mechanism?

We will consider these particular examples in more detail below. The salient point for now is that anarchist engagement with the nation-state is complex, defined by the realities of living in a state-bound paradigm yet also recognizing that this must be resisted if we are to achieve a sustainable world based on freedom and equality. Whereas some anti-capitalist activists have "tended to underplay the relevance of national state practices as part of globalization" in the belief that corporations and emerging technologies are eroding the centrality of the state in driving world affairs, anarchists have been quick to point out that "nation-states have provided the military force for the expansion and institution of capitalist ventures."[36] In this sense, for many anarchists, paradoxically, "the state needs to be returned to the center of critical analysis and oppositional politics," and thus any temptation to see it as a bulwark against the ravages of corporate capital must be forcefully resisted.[37] Anarchists likewise reject the tendency (sometimes reinforced by national liberation struggles that seek to win support of the military) to view "self-defense" through a statist lens of militarism, instead seeking communal forms such as the popular militias of the Spanish Civil War that were organized on egalitarian principles.[38] As we have seen throughout this volume, anarchists instead embrace bottom-up, do-it-yourself, and loosely affiliated modes of association that seek to preserve autonomy and promote community.

From Federations to Networks

As noted in the Introduction to this volume, anarchism has enjoyed a dramatic resurgence in recent years, seeing its core values and methods of organizing infused throughout global movements against corporate globalization, Western militarization, and elite inaction on climate change, among other pressing issues. It would be an overstatement to say that these movements of the new millennium are in themselves anarchist by nature, since they are comprised of diverse individuals, organizations, and coalitions that do not necessarily agree on methods and goals, let alone on their visions for what an alternative global society would look like in practice. Still, from tactical diversity and affinity groups to solidarity actions and large-group consensus models, there is no doubt that anarchism has been at the heart of movement culture in the era of globalization. As Richard J. F. Day surmises, this is due in part to the realization that "the struggle between community . . . and state and corporate forms is indeed *the* struggle of the (post)modern condition," and anarchism's longstanding and uncompromising rejection of both the state and capital have placed it in good stead to be at the fore of this contest.[39] David Graeber further finds that "anarchist principles—autonomy, voluntary association, self-organization, direct democracy, mutual aid—have become the basis for organizing new social movements from Karnataka to Buenos Aires," even if the word "anarchist" is not always explicitly utilized.[40]

One of the remarkable features of this emerging global anarchism is that, as Day notes, "those on the margins are showing the way [in] exploring the possibilities of non-statist, non-capitalist, egalitarian modes of social organization."[41] The reasons for this may be self-evident, including that for many of the planet's inhabitants who live and work in slums, shantytowns, and maquiladoras—with little hope for the future and having seen their already-tenuous material footholds eroded in rapid fashion—it is clear that the apparatuses of the state and capital have utterly failed them. The purported "rising tide" of corporate globalization has not served to "lift all boats," as the saying goes, but rather for many in the margins it has threatened to drown them altogether. Unsurprisingly, then, many of these people have been "working to reverse the colonization of everyday life by taking control over—and responsibility for—the conduct of their own affairs," most directly by "building, linking, and defending autonomous communities."[42] This combination of autonomy and community, of self-management and responsibility, is part and parcel of anarchism, and thus it has served as a natural place from which to resist oppression.

In previous chapters we have considered many examples of global anarchist networks, including Food Not Bombs, the Anarchist Black Cross, and Indymedia. A particularly intriguing exemplar of emerging autonomist resistance is Peoples' Global Action (PGA), a global network of grassroots groups that "build local alternatives to globalization; reject 'all forms and systems of domination and discrimination'; have a confrontational attitude towards dominant (governmental and economic) structures of power; organize based on principles of decentralization and autonomy; and employ methods of direct action and civil disobedience."[43] The PGA "is an instrument for co-ordination, not an organization," and thus "no organization or person represents the PGA, nor does the PGA represent any organization or person."[44] The PGA was formed in 1998 out of *encuentros* (encounters) that drew thousands of people in opposition to neoliberalism; key entities comprising the foundations of the PGA include the Zapatista Army of National Liberation (which launched an uprising in Chiapas, Mexico, on January 1, 1994, the day the North American Free Trade Agreement took effect), the Brazilian Landless Workers' Movement (which occupies unused lands and uses them to create farms), and the Karnataka State Farmers Union from India (which utilizes direct action campaigns on behalf of traditional agricultural methods). As an umbrella entity, the PGA spells out its aims in "hallmarks," the first of which sums up its basic shared value: "A very clear rejection of capitalism, imperialism and feudalism; all trade agreements, institutions and governments that promote destructive globalization."[45]

The Zapatistas themselves have been instrumental in pointing the way toward resistance to globalization and modeling constructive, anarchistic alternatives. Since taking up arms for a brief period in 1994 and thus announcing their presence to the world, this autonomist movement has looked like no other "army" in recent history. The Zapatistas have focused less on confrontation with the state than on "the creation of autonomous, democratic, self-governing communities," always conscious of the necessity to work "in alliance with a global network of like-minded democratic revolutionaries."[46] As Graeber notes, the Zapatistas are "about the least violent 'army' imaginable," mirroring a pattern in evidence with other groups that are part of the PGA: "In moving away from military tactics they often also ended up—often rather despite themselves —moving towards much more anarchistic forms of organization."[47] What these entities (in particular, the sustained example of the Zapatista Army of National Liberation and its capacity to preserve village life and indigenous lifeways in the face of hegemonic forces) have demonstrated is "that municipalities can strive to become autonomous from statecraft and capital, to put human and ecological concerns first, while retaining regional and global links of solidarity and mutual aid."[48] What the Zapatistas recognized in the mid-1990s turned out to be the key insight that helped launch the global movement against neoliberalism, namely, that any struggle for self-determination (at any scale of engagement) will wind up confronting the workings of the entire system and not just the local authorities or apparatuses of the nation-state.

Anarchists at the dawn of industrialization focused more specifically on creating *federations* of self-managing communities, both within nations and internationally, rejecting the state as the basis for federalism but remaining wedded to a framework in which individual units might remain relatively separate in their affairs and would always possess "the right of secession."[49] As Bakunin asserted in 1868, "we will never recognize any rights or duties other than those founded upon freedom. The right to free assembly and equal freedom to secede is the prime and most important of all political rights: without which confederation would be nothing more than centralization in disguise."[50] Bakunin's vision is still germane, including his insight that a unity could be achieved through the "federation of autonomous parts into the whole, in such a way that the latter, no longer the graveyard where all local prosperities are forcibly interred, becomes instead the confirmation and well-spring of all these autonomies and all these prosperities."[51] The presumption in Bakunin's time was that individual units could *choose* whether to become imbricated within the larger workings of a global system, or they could simply opt out; in this manner, autonomy and decentralization would be grounded in the power of the local community versus the imposition of the global federation. This is a worthwhile perspective, to be sure, but the realities of the modern era have rendered at least parts of it effectively moot.

Today's world is inherently global, and communities are thus necessarily (rather than optionally) incorporated into its matrix. This is due in large measure to the force of globalization and its impetus to interlink economies and technologies, creating the web of telecommunications and international finance that now encircles the world even out to its farthest reaches. Additionally, many of the byproducts of the industrial age have contributed to conditions of inescapably global import, including climate change, loss of arable lands, food shortages, drought, and the escalating toxification of the biosphere. Local communities simply no longer have the option of wholly "opting out" since the character of the crises being confronted is increasingly global in nature. In the face of this eventuality, and coupled with the Zapatistas' insight that local struggles are necessarily global ones as well, anti-state and anti-capitalist activists in the contemporary milieu often begin from a premise of interconnectedness that has moved the discussion from a vision of voluntary federation to one of requisite networking.

In this light, decentralized entities such as the PGA may be less innovative than they are mere survival strategies; they represent an effort to create a counter-network to the one being plied by neoliberalism, the one that seeks to erase differences and eradicate non-commercial vestiges. In other words, if we are forced to become integrated, then the optimal strategy is to do so in a manner that preserves and promotes autonomy, community, self-governance, diversity, and solidarity—in short, *anarchism*. As such, an emerging network like the PGA "can be seen as a significant step in the possible construction of an anarchist counter-hegemony, as it tries to deepen the political linkages between various radical groups in order to strengthen both feelings of collective solidarity and anarchists' capacity to resist repression by acting as a tool of communication and co-ordination."[52] Today's movements "call simultaneously for self-determination and global connectivity [in order to] develop creative strategies to organize against the local agents of local capital, including nation-states, while seeking to create political spaces and communities beyond appeals for state protectionism."[53] Sometimes this is reflected in anarchists' rejection of national borders, a tack which has the dual (and seemingly contradictory) effect of strengthening local communities by allowing them to become more integrated within global networks—akin to what Falk has described as "achieving self-determination above and below the level of the state."[54] In this manner, the local and the global converge, creating a space for the potential development of "shared ethico-political commitments that allow us to achieve enough solidarity to effectively create sustainable alternatives to the neoliberal order.... The goal is not to 'strive to be one community' ... but to build many linked communities."[55]

We might call this attempt to preserve local/community autonomy in the face of a relentlessly globalizing world something like "scaling down and linking up." As Jeffrey S. Juris has observed, such efforts represent a confluence "between anarchist principles and a wider networking logic associated with late capitalism."[56] In fact, for Juris, anarchism *is* the "cultural logic of networking," which is ironically reflective of "the logic of informational capitalism."[57] Still, "there is nothing *inherently* anarchist or even progressive about network forms," but rather their efficacy (and anarchy) are determined largely by the spirit in which they are deployed.[58] This is not so much a question of technology (hardware) but more so one of values (software); for anarchically inclined entities such as the PGA, the latter includes horizontalism, diversity, autonomy, decentralization, consensus, self-direction, and the "free and open circulation of information."[59] In an interview discussing his book *Networking Futures*, Juris distinguishes

> between two ideal organizational logics: a vertical command logic and a horizontal networking logic, both of which are present to varying degrees, and exist in dynamic tension with respect to one another, within any particular network.... PGA reflects a particular commitment to new forms of open, collaborative, and directly democratic organization, thus coming closer to the horizontal networking logics.... PGA does reflect something of an anarchist ethic, although this has more to do with the confluence between networking logics and anarchist organizing principles than any kind of abstract commitment to anarchist politics per se.... The network structure of PGA thus provides a transnational space for communication and coordination among activists and collectives.... PGA provides the kind of communicational infrastructure necessary for the rise of contemporary networked social movements.[60]

As Juris concludes, "the global justice/alternative globalization/anti-capitalist frame is a good one in that it encompasses an array of movements and struggles, while maintaining a focus on systemic inter-connections. I think it would be an error to revert back to single issue politics and struggles at this point, as such connections would be obscured and the social, political, and cultural capital of the global justice movement would be squandered."[61]

Here again we find the implicit recognition that in an inevitably inter-linked world (at least as things presently stand), the choice is not so much *whether* to be networked, but *how* we will do so. By choosing proactively to embrace the decentralized and autonomist potentials of the global age—always cognizant of the ever-present potential for co-optation and linearization—anarchists (and their associated movements) have boldly stood up in the midst of a maelstrom, counter-posing "voluntary associa-tion" to "free trade," "conscious community" to "conspicuous consump-tion," and, ultimately, "global anarchism" to "global anarchy." Taking such transformative lessons seriously, there may be no other region of the world where these quasi-heroic pursuits are more pointed, challeng-ing, and revolutionary than in the Middle East.

In the Middle of the Action

As prophetically predicted by Graeber, among others, "anarchist ideas and imperatives have become more and more important everywhere in the world," and accordingly, "revolution will, in the twenty-first century, take on increasingly unfamiliar forms."[62] More than a century ago, anar-chists recognized the coming interconnectedness of *revolution*, even as today's modes of global networking were not yet imagined, let alone implemented: "An isolated national revolution cannot succeed. The social revolution inevitably becomes a world revolution."[63] Some anarchists in the historical milieu could see the seeds of contemporary dilemmas being sowed in the early stages of industrialism, as did James Guillaume, writ-ing in 1876:

> The Revolution cannot be confined to a single country; on pain of death, it is obliged to subsume into its movement, if not the whole world, then at least a considerable portion of the civilized countries. Indeed, today no country can be sufficient unto itself: international relations are a necessity of production and consumption, and they could not be severed. Should the neighboring States around a coun-try in revolution manage to impose an impregnable blockade, the Revolution, being isolated, would be doomed to perish.[64]

What Guillaume was reflecting upon—the necessity of an international perspective and active global solidarity in matters of revolutionary praxis—has been aptly demonstrated in the set of popular uprisings comprising what has become widely known as the *Arab Spring*.

Across the Middle East and Northern Africa during much of 2011, peoples' revolutions confronted dictators (oftentimes those emplaced or supported by the United States) and sought to implement substantial democratic reforms. While not necessarily anarchist in their demands and visions, these uprisings appeared "to require no guardian intellectual authority, no political leadership, no organized parties [and] there is no party of the revolution anywhere, no leader emerges to embody its historical spirit."[65] Viewing these loosely interlinked uprisings (which have taken place in nations including Egypt, Tunisia, Yemen, Syria, Algeria, Jordan, and Libya) through a lens of "anarchist technique," Mohammed Bamyeh summarizes the dramatic import:

> The Arab revolutionary experiments seem to be based on the newly shared presumption that ordinary individuals are capable of enlightenment without leadership or guardianship, without even organizations in the common sense of the word. . . . The agent of this revolutionary enlightenment is the little person, not the historical figure, the hero or the savior. It is in this sense that the current Arab revolutionary wave is closest to anarchist ideals, which highlight spontaneous order and posit the principle of unimposed order as the highest form of a rational society. . . . The revolutionary style is anarchist, in the sense that it requires little organization, leadership, or even coordination; tends to be suspicious of parties and hierarchies even after revolutionary success; and relies on spontaneity, minimal planning, local initiative, and individual will much more than on any other factors.[66]

Bamyeh's cogent analysis highlights the critical factors for revolutionary success, including spontaneity, solidarity, conviviality, anti-authoritarianism, non-violence, organic expression, and a historical sensibility.[67] In noting that the aim of these movements is less than an anarchist "total revolution" in favor of more liberal reforms constrained by the unit of the nation-state and international norms, this assessment also signals in part the processes of retrenchment that have been observed following the initial waves of rebellion.[68]

These real-time lessons have encouraged movements around the world to consider matters of means and ends, practicability, and solidarity in an instructive light. Perhaps nowhere have these processes been more starkly projected (for anarchists in particular) than in Egypt. Writing in *Waging Nonviolence*, Nathan Schneider reflects on a statement by the Egyptian then-President Hosni Mubarak that "if I resign today there will be chaos"—to which Schneider responds: "This is a claim dictators love to make, that they are the only ones maintaining order, and that without them, everything would fall apart. [But] you're the one creating the chaos. The thousands upon thousands of your people in the street against you today are behaving quite well in contrast."[69] In a subsequent article specifically considering anarchist potentialities in the Egyptian uprising, Jake Olzen posited alternatives to the potential "democratic tyranny" that could ensue if the people "re-brand themselves as passive citizens of the Egyptian state rather than direct participants in society." [70] Olzen notes that in the context of an organic mass mobilization such as that in Egypt, which seemingly caught the world by surprise, "it is remarkable the anarchy that emerged—that is, rule and organization without a consolidated authority, NOT chaos and disorder," and he further cites the positive, anarchistic potential in the movement as represented by "the creation of make-shift clinics, protester-organized security, and the youth leadership networks [that] indicate the real possibility of alternative institutions paving the way forward."[71]

As explained by Egyptian anarchist Nidal Tahrir, people spontaneously organized *committees* for security and solidarity during the uprising: "Anarchists in Egypt joined both protests and popular committees to defend the streets from thugs. Anarchists in Egypt put some hope in [these] councils. . . . For us, as anarchists, we are anti-capital and anti-state too—we will try to strengthen the committees that have been formed to protect and secure the streets, and try to turn them into real councils."[72] A subsequent analysis explored the key role of images adapted from the film *V for Vendetta* (which chronicles an anarchistic anti-hero's efforts to bring down an Orwellian government and foment an anti-authoritarian peoples' movement) in helping to spark the revolution: "The potent imagery and eminently quotable lines from the film permeate individual Facebook pages and the 'We are all Khaled Said' [a youth killed by Mubarak's forces in 2010] Facebook Fan Page. . . . What is certain is that the idea for change has been firmly planted and cannot be eradicated. Ideas after all, as V proclaims, are bulletproof. The struggle continues."[73] Finally, in a piece looking back on the "groundswell of decentralized but well coordinated opposition [that had] overpowered the Egyptian regime's main coercive institutions," the difficulties of maintaining a post-revolutionary praxis were reaffirmed: "Outside of the polar opposites of post-Apartheid South Africa (a good outcome none can replicate) and Iraq (a catastrophe no one wants to recreate), there is scant guidance about the conditions that best enable citizens to retrench coercive institutions, punish or reconcile with torturers and killers, and convert ministries of interior into civilian departments."[74]

At the Nexus of Global Conflict

This brief look at the Egyptian case underscores several themes that are familiar to anarchists, most notably the dualistic, prefigurative spirit of simultaneously contesting authoritarianism and modeling the alternative society in the process. For anarchists in Israel and Palestine, this task has been (quite fittingly) both enormously challenging and inspiring at once. A 2006 blog described some of the anarchist activities in Israel and provides a useful overview:

> The small anarchist movement in Israel is very active in the wider movement of radical anti-occupation activists. There are a number of collectives that organize in many forms, including protests and street theatre, education and direct action. Many have served jail time for refusing their compulsory service in the Israeli army. Additionally, many Israeli anarchists are also involved in the small Israeli animal rights and environmental movements. The largest group is Anarchists Against The Wall. AATW works with Palestinian communities and organizations to oppose the barrier Israel is building around (and within) the West Bank. . . . Many members of AATW are also involved in a group called Black Laundry, a radical queer anti-occupation group that has been involved in both direct actions in the occupied territories and street theatre within Israel. . . . Another group with anarchist involvement is the Israeli Committee Against House Demolitions. ICAHD focuses on preventing the demolition of Palestinian houses by the Israeli army both via legal methods and direct action. . . . Lastly, Salon Mazal is an anarchist infoshop in Tel Aviv, with a bookshop, library, vegetarian cafe and space for meetings, lectures and film screenings.[75]

Israeli anarchist Uri Gordon (author of the influential book *Anarchy Alive!*) observes that in Israel "anarchists are few in numbers. Though no hard data exist, on my own rough estimate there are up to three hundred Israelis who are politically active and who would not object to being called anarchists."[76] Gordon provides a deeper context for understanding their efforts:

In Palestine/Israel, anarchism has been a continuous undercurrent for decades, from the libertarian socialism of the early kibbutz movement to the Yiddish anarchist publishing and cultural clubs of the 1950s. Contemporary Israeli anarchism first emerged in the punk scene of the late 1980s, at a time of parallel growth in army refusal and evasion during the first intifada. The Israeli animal liberation movement emerged from the same milieu, and many Israeli anarchists have been part of both movements. The major boost arrived in the late 1990s with the wave of resistance to capitalist globalization.[77]

Of the explicitly anarchist projects in the region, Anarchists Against the Wall (AATW) is perhaps the most prominent. Established in 2003 as a direct action group opposed to the construction of the wall being built by Israel in the West Bank, AATW has worked in cooperation with Palestinians in a joint struggle, regularly participating in demonstrations and direct actions against the wall in particular, and the occupation in general, across the West Bank. As Gordon observes: "Rejecting the appeal to governments to modify their behavior, and indeed the institution of the state itself, [AATW] calls instead for direct action—physical intervention against injustice—in forms that by themselves prefigure an alternative to present systems of domination and exploitation."[78] AATW asserts that it is "the duty of Israeli citizens to resist immoral policies and actions carried out in our name. We believe that it is possible to do more than demonstrate inside Israel or participate in humanitarian relief actions. Israeli apartheid and occupation isn't going to end by itself—it will end when it becomes ungovernable and unmanageable."[79] In this sense, AATW is more than merely a protest group; it is directly confronting the impetus of the nation-state as a locus of dehumanizing, expansionist, and militaristic policies. As their literature notes,

the mere presence of Israelis at Palestinian civilian actions offers some degree of protection against army violence. . . . Even though many Israeli activists have been wounded at the demonstrations, some of them seriously, it is the Palestinians who have paid the highest toll. . . . The army and the Israeli government try to put an end to Palestinian popular resistance using every form of repression, and to prevent Israeli activists from joining this struggle. Under the occupation's law it is possible to indict people for simply participating in a demonstration. In the course of the last several years, AATW activists have been arrested hundreds of times and dozens of indictments were filed against them. The legal repression by the Israeli authorities is just another front for the Israeli authorities to try and crack down on resistance.[80]

This ongoing repression of anarchists was confirmed in a report by *Haaretz*, which documented how the Israeli security force (Shin Bet) had put "anarchists in the crosshairs" through a variety of measures designed to foster intimidation through harassment and the monitoring of activists.[81] In response, Gordon laments that "it's pretty rough being an anarchist in Israel these days" even as he affirms that they "are demonized because their actions are coherent and bold."[82] Defiantly, Gordon openly rejects all forms of authoritarianism and imposed rule—both Israeli and Palestinian alike—and asserts that the success of Israeli anarchism in particular "is a question of starting to practice desertion, refusal, sabotage, attack against every violent authority, all coercive power, and every state." Indeed, this is not work for the faint of heart, and anarchists in the region have been coping with issues of burn-out, attrition, legal sanctions, and ostracism. As Gordon writes, there is an "uncommon degree of state violence faced by the Israeli and international anarchists" who participate in anti-occupation actions, and as a result many of them "experience not only physical wounds but also anxiety, guilt, depression, irritability and feelings of alienation and isolation."[83]

Still, there is strong motivation to continue the work, not in the least due to the fact that the Israel-Palestine conflict "is a linchpin of the Clash of Civilizations ideology—and, for the same reason, a unique acupuncture point for anarchist activity."[84] Gordon's incisive analysis, informed by his direct participation and scholarly acumen alike, grapples with the complex questions of nationalism and statehood involved in this seemingly intractable and globally central conflict. While anarchists reject the state as a desirable unit of human association, there is some tension in this blanket position when it comes to the national liberation struggles of oppressed peoples (as in Egypt)—and the question of what to do vis-à-vis stateless peoples, whose condition creates greater vulnerability, is even thornier for anarchists, as Gordon notes: "The overwhelming majority of Palestinians want a state of their own alongside Israel. So how can anarchists reconcile their support for Palestinian liberation with their anti-statist principles? How can they promote the creation of yet another state in the name of 'national liberation'?"[85]

A No-State Solution?

In addressing these central questions Gordon propounds a number of potential solutions, none of which are completely satisfactory, including that anarchists might: recognize the contradiction but stand in solidarity with the Palestinians' desire for statehood; comprehend that the addition of one more state does not significantly alter the Westphalian map of the world; support a Palestinian state as a strategic step toward liberalization of democratic possibilities; or shift the focus of the argument to the provision of solidarity and support "without reference to the question of statehood."[86] The intricate realities of the Israel-Palestine dilemma are such that any preconceived notions based on ideological purity (e.g., anarchists must reject all states) rapidly fall away in actual practice. For instance, Gordon analyzes the efforts of entities such as AATW through a lens of a bi-nationalism that seeks to foster a mobilization devolving upon

> manifestly different relations between Israelis and Palestinians—ones based on partnership, solidarity, and empathy rather than estrangement, separation, and fear. The joint campaign against the Segregation Barrier has thus become a protracted experiment in bi-nationalism, a face-to-face encounter at the barricades where Israelis and Palestinians can shed their stereotyped identities toward one another and create shared communities of struggle. . . . The practice of joint struggle takes place in full recognition of the inequalities between the Israeli and Palestinian participants—in terms of economic resources, freedom of movement, safety from arbitrary state violence, and so on. This recognition is partly made possible by the Israeli participants' anarchist perspective, which so distances them from the Zionist narrative as to render unnecessary the artificial neutrality maintained by the discourse of coexistence. Rather, the joint struggle remains infused with a spirit of shared antagonism toward the regime of occupation, and a refusal of false normalization.[87]

In the end, Gordon endorses a bioregional approach, which seeks to move the unit of analysis from the state to the geographical area itself, thus opening up a space for "personal and collective identities that can flourish within and alongside it," constituting a new view of the landscape that "is incompatible not only with war and occupation but also with capitalism, racial and religious bigotry, consumerism, patriarchy, and any number of other trenchant features of hierarchical society."[88]

This perspective is akin to what has been termed a "no-state solution," and, as James Horrox has observed, it reflects "a renewed move towards the kind of stateless commonwealth originally envisaged by many of the [kibbutz] movement's founders."[89] Such a provocative position has been articulated from a number of contemporary fronts, including by the American-Israeli anarchist Bill Templer, who wrote in 2003:

> Reinventing politics in Israel and Palestine means laying the groundwork now for a kind of Jewish-Palestinian Zapatismo, a grassroots movement to "reclaim the commons." This would mean moving towards direct democracy, participatory economy and genuine autonomy for the people; towards Martin Buber's vision of "an organic commonwealth … that is a community of communities." We might call it the "no-state solution." Forms of neoliberal governmentality do not work here, are unsustainable. At all spatial scales, Israelis and Palestinians have learnt they have no security from the bankruptcy of its iterations. … In a sense, this conflict is emblematic of the "perverse perseverance of sovereignty," its "vicious, security-based ontology." We need to turn that authoritarian ontology on its head.[90]

Ultimately, Templer envisions a process of "*staged transformation*: moving from two states (Stage One) to a unitary, bi-national state (Stage Two), and on to what we might call the 'Jerusalem Cooperative Commonwealth.' "[91]

Following Templer, James Herod seeks to circumvent the transition phases; he argues in terms that recall those deployed by anarchists in the classical milieu:

> Neither the two-state nor the one-state solution will solve the problem in Palestine. Only the no-state solution will. The no-state solution calls for dismantling the Israeli state and abandoning any attempt to establish a Palestinian state. Rather, the peoples living in the territory of historical Palestine will progress to the advanced decentralized social form of an association of autonomous self-governing communities based on direct democracy. … This beautiful anarchist proposal—an obvious solution—has unfortunately not even been on the agenda. … The capitalist-controlled nation-state system is so strong and entrenched that it is hard to think outside that framework, and hardly anyone has. Now, however, a few

innovative voices are being heard in favor of the idea, for example, those of Bill Templer or Uri Gordon.[92]

In mid-2011, I joined the discussion with a short piece exploring these themes, arguing that the widely preferred "two-state framework could deepen the conflict by further solidifying it, institutionalizing it, and rendering it susceptible to even greater outside influence"; I further posed this question: "Might the wall (both literally and culturally) between these two emergent nations grow even higher and the distance between them even greater when separateness becomes nationally reified?"[93] In the end, I opined that "starting with the planet's most intractable conflict as a linchpin for creating a nation-free world would be a powerful statement of historical import. Indeed, the 'road map to peace' in the Middle East (and elsewhere) shouldn't look merely like an atlas of states."[94] Acknowledging the utopian sensibilities of such a perspective, it nevertheless remains the case that the statist version of global order has not exactly been idyllic, nor has it yielded a more just, peaceful, or sustainable world.

Where to from Here?

In this chapter we have seen, once again, the uniquely anarchist tendency to both negate and construct, in the belief (as Bakunin once famously said) that "the passion for destruction is a creative passion, too." In today's interconnected yet multifarious world, however, anarchists bear a greater burden to articulate and implement a coherent alternative to the present set of arrangements promulgated by capital and the state. Corporate globalization and state militarization both possess unitary, monolithic qualities, and yet they have also shown themselves to be flexible, mutually supportive, and capable of absorbing even those episodes that at first glance appear as challenges to their legitimacy and sustainability. This sort of crisis-based capitalism has demonstrated an enveloping resiliency that keeps people and communities around the world firmly entrenched within its confines—sometimes by force, and sometimes by choice. The destruction of this system, even if it could somehow be accomplished, provides no guarantee that a better world will spontaneously emerge out of the sudden, widespread experience of human freedom. In fact, it is possible that the net result would be more authoritarianism instead, as the vestiges of the fallen order seek to reassert themselves in a world of tenuous sustenance.

Against this, anarchists everywhere (literally) have been working to develop a new model based on a liberatory, ecological, and visionary praxis that seeks to supplant the present system (and its apocalyptic sensibilities) through a combination of open contestation and alternative interrelation. Anarchists organize locally, link their efforts through networks, make collective decisions while preserving individual liberty and community autonomy, and steadily strive to manifest "a nascent global movement" (as promised at the outset of this chapter) that integrates the best of the anarchist tradition from the past, responds directly to the needs and desires of the present, and articulates the non-prescriptive contours of a dynamic and abundant future. Far from taking it on faith that this future will necessarily emerge following either a successful revolution or systemic collapse, anarchists and their allies instead strive tirelessly (and at times at great personal cost and/or risk) to help create a viable space for humankind within the larger workings of a planetary system that includes both nature and culture equally in its calculus. The question before us, then—one which is rarely broached in substantial detail—is whether these efforts have been, or are likely to be, successful. This is where we will venture in the next chapter.

CHAPTER 7

Assessing Anarchism's Impact

Up to this point we have looked at anarchism from a number of distinct yet interrelated perspectives: theories, practices, tactics/ethics, ecologies, communities, and global issues. Spanning this range of applications, it has become apparent that anarchism represents a complex balance of tensions, interventions, and ideals, greatly exceeding the base caricature of *anarchy* as mere chaos or uninformed naïveté. Still, key questions remain: Has anarchism's resurgence increased its concrete effectiveness? Is it a passing trend, or will anarchism be a potent presence for the foreseeable future? In some ways, anarchism's successes are also potential trouble spots, as indicated by the appearance of mainstream anarchist characterizations and commercial attempts at marketing "anarchist chic" as an apolitical style rather than a coherent force for change. Even more disconcerting has been the overt repression of anarchists and anarchist organizing in general, yet this ironically also may serve as an indication of anarchism's efficacy. The task in this chapter will be to frankly assess anarchism's effectiveness on a number of levels, including in the political, social, and cultural realms. Such an endeavor has yet to be undertaken systematically in the anarchist milieu, and while a comprehensive evaluation would be beyond the scope of this work, my intention here is to sketch the outlines of a framework that could be useful for analyzing anarchism's impact while pointing toward questions for the future.

At the outset, discussions of radical political theories or underground sub-cultures often omit any actual assessment of their efficacy and utility, instead either (a) strenuously arguing the case for the theory/movement, or (b) taking it as a given that it is valid and thus simply exploring its workings in philosophical and/or practical terms. In essence, this volume has been a combination of both, simultaneously assuming anarchism's basic tenability yet taking pains to articulate and illustrate for readers who are either uninitiated or unconvinced exactly why this is so. In this penultimate chapter, I will continue in this vein, specifically referring back to some of the guiding questions referenced in the Preface to this volume: Does anarchism work in theory and/or practice? What would an anarchist society look like in actuality, and how do anarchists manage the major issues of our time, from war to the economy? Does anarchism require at the outset that we alter our view of human nature, or would people living in anarchist societies simply change for the better over time? Throughout this volume, incipient answers to these queries have been offered; here, I will step back a bit and more directly assess anarchism's successes and failures, framing the discussion around the fundamental question that any sociopolitical movement eventually must confront, namely: *is it working?*

This issue of functionality is more than merely a tactical assessment. It requires a broader sense of what the goals are, who we are trying to reach, what the criteria are for effectiveness, how our movement compares to others, and whether one's aims are short- or long-term in nature. For instance, it could be argued that violent methods of change "work" in the sense of removing specific targets or imposing certain conditions on others; this is, in essence, the logic of warfare that has dominated much of human affairs for centuries. Yet the continuity of war and its enormous associated costs indicate that its utility for promoting peace is greatly delimited if not altogether impracticable, yielding a scenario in which warfare might work in terms of accomplishing "regime change" but not for achieving wider aims of democratization, liberation, and the like. Social movements (loosely defined as collective "sustained challenges to authorities") confront similar realities, and anarchism is no exception as it grapples with issues of tactics and ethics.[1] However, the uniquely diffuse nature of anarchism requires more nuanced treatment in order to fully understand its impact, since it generally lacks many of the formalities (e.g., structured organizations, leaders, political parties, financial instruments, representatives) that are commonly found within movements aiming to alter prevailing societal conditions.

Moreover, the claims advanced by anarchists, coupled with the inherently non-reformist nature of anarchism, likewise suggest that standard evaluative methods may not fully apply. Shall we count anarchism as a failure since authoritarian power still exists, and there has not been a worldwide revolutionary uprising to throw off the domination of nation-states and capital? Revolutions tend to reflect an "all or nothing" quality, such that they may appear to have failed right up until the time that they succeed; as Marco Giugni notes, "revolutionary movements are only rarely successful, but when they do succeed, the changes they bring about are fundamental and often long-lasting reversals of the existing social and political structures."[2] Anarchism further possesses the quality of not simply agitating for a revolution in which one set of leaders replaces another, but for a fundamental reorientation of values whereby there are no longer any "leaders" in the sense that they have come to exist. As argued in previous chapters, anarchism takes the view that notions of *equality* and *freedom* must be applied everywhere in order for them have meaning at all. But how can this be accomplished, without resort to decidedly un-anarchistic forms of persuasion, if not coercion? "An anarchist society, if ever realized, will be realized universally. But any attempt to create a worldwide organization for the specific purpose of achieving this society would be like building a house starting from the roof, and would defeat its purpose because it would claim a competence of interest that it has not."[3]

A further challenge to any attempt at systematic assessment is the processual, fluid, spontaneous, and open-ended nature of anarchism. As Rudolf Rocker has observed, anarchism "does not believe in any absolute truth, or in any definite final goals for human development, but in an unlimited perfectibility of social patterns and human living conditions which are always straining after higher forms of expression, and to which, for this reason, one cannot assign any definite terminus nor set any fixed goal."[4] Anarchism consists in large measure of a series of "fragile yet exceedingly beautiful experiments" that strive to create in the present "the lived practice of freely constituting one's community collectively" and simultaneously to "supply messages in bottles to future generations," as Cindy Milstein intones.[5] Still, it is equally the case that "anarchism cannot be filed away as an outburst of the romantic mood in politics [or] as an incoherent voice of protest."[6] As we have seen, anarchism may not constitute a "program" in the typical sense, but it clearly devolves upon certain loosely-shared values (e.g., autonomy, community, equality), and it likewise manifests those in a number of concrete scenarios (e.g., collectives, networks, blocs). These qualities provide sufficient grounds for assessment, remaining cognizant of the limits to applying standard evaluative criteria given anarchism's unique proclivities.

Measures of Success

As a general matter, sociological assessments of movement effectiveness often focus the inquiry around traditional benchmarks connoting "systemic gains," including "electoral success, greater representation within official institutions, [and] a larger share of collective resources."[7] Another common basis for evaluation is to "examine the written goals of organizations as well as interview or observe those in leadership positions," in order to determine how closely the movement's activities come to meeting its stated aims.[8] Movements can also be assessed in terms of how well they serve as a "vector for the democratization of society," oftentimes constructed in pluralistic terms such as the promotion of due process, economic opportunities, equal rights, or political participation.[9] In these formulations, we can already see the reliance upon numerous presuppositions that are wholly antithetical to anarchism; thus, an "anarchist politics does not need to hold itself against those dominant, and dominating, terms of a 'culture of evaluation,' " as Jamie Heckert asserts.[10] Instead, anarchism represents a "political logic that escapes the categories of traditional social movement theories," focusing not on "gradualist or reformist" pursuits but on *emergent* ones, measured simultaneously in the constructive "small steps of everyday life" and in "the amplitude of the paralysis of the economy, of normality."[11]

Fortunately, even among the classical strands of social movement analysis, a number of criteria have been developed that apply more directly to the workings of anarchism. These include: the utility of disruptive tactics; cultural changes rather than only political or economic ones; the directionality of change rather than just specific outcomes; the reclamation of space for movement activities; changing the salience of issues in the public debate; reframing the meanings of terms and interactions; focusing on the empowerment and identity constructions of movement actors; highlighting the worthiness and commitment of participants; the creation of a "credible threat" to established authorities; and the level of repression experienced by the movement, either overtly or covertly.[12] On a more basic level, the question could even be bluntly posed as Staughton Lynd does: "Are we winning?"[13] With due regard to anarchism's anti-authoritarianism and thus its implicit rejection of winners and losers, we might reframe the question as stated above ("Is it working?"), but the essential spirit remains intact. The task here will be to assess anarchism's impact, drawing upon the more organic criteria gleaned from the social movement literature and remaining mindful of the notion that "we should use methods appropriate to the form of our problem and to the character of the world we are studying"—always with the aim of discerning what is working, what is not, and how we might traverse the arduous path toward a world built upon the best virtues of anarchy.[14]

Sociopolitical Change

Anarchism resides in the fringes of the major political theories to emerge out of the Enlightenment, and even though it rejects most of the principles embedded in the dominant order—hierarchy, competition, profit, stratification, representation, and the like—it still remains within its linguistic parameters to a large extent; thus it remains within its ideological confines as well. In framing itself as anti-authoritarian, anti-capitalist, and anti-state, anarchism reflects an inherent impetus to reject all such appearances of *archy* (as the name itself counsels), yet this neglects to clearly convey anarchism's constructive sense of not simply doing away with these structures but replacing them with radically egalitarian alternatives. In this sense, as Edward Abbey has said, we might argue that "anarchy is democracy taken seriously."[15] Although it rejects the sense of democratic pluralism that devolves upon either proportional or republican forms of electoral process, in its fullest dimensions we come to see that "anarchism represents the condition in which the optimal state of external plurality can exist."[16]

Anarchism thus remains within the scope of many established sociopolitical notions but carries them to their logical extreme, arguing for a new social and political landscape that in some ways (as Abbey's famous quote suggests) takes seriously the sacrosanct values of the dominant culture—at least insofar as they are written, if not actually practiced. Anarchists believe deeply in autonomy and individualism, for example, but not the bourgeois conceptions that are bound up with legal rights and the privatization of wealth. Anarchism is a theory of maximal freedom, arguing that this is a precondition for a healthy social order based on voluntary association and mutual aid, and thus it transcends the narrow scope of constitutional liberties that are circumscribed by the coercive apparatus of the state and the capitalist profit motive. Anarchism offers no blueprint, maintaining instead that the liberation of humankind from its consumerist, compulsory shackles will restore relations to a base of true equality that more closely resembles the deeply rooted virtues of human communities from time immemorial. In this sense, anarchism does not seek to compete with dominant theories but to surmount them:

> Within political philosophy, anarchism is the position that we should let go and see what happens. This means that anarchism cannot be the rival of any theory of justice. Anarchism, rather, constitutes the realm that is as a whole the rival of the realm of theories of justice. It corresponds to a noninstrumental consciousness of our relations to

one another and the world. It is a sort of consciousness that does not set an ideal and then try to force the world into that configuration, but allows the world and ourselves to grow wild.[17]

As such, it is difficult to gauge whether anarchism has served to bring about sociopolitical change, since its aim is the replacement of the realm rather than a reassignment of values within it. Still, we can discern the presence of movements from the political left and right alike that have taken up the mantle of anarchism (again, in words if not deeds) and its penchant for political processes that begin with the primacy of the individual rather than the plenary powers of the state. The mainstream coding of this, of course, is largely negative; power holders and profiteers need do little more than throw the "A-word" around to conjure popular images of dangerous radicals with inimical aims in our midst. In so doing, however, an argument can be made that less overtly ominous entities—including some with agendas that embrace portions of the anarchist vision—may find greater space for public acceptance within the strictures of the existing political order. When anarchists break windows or set a police car on fire at a protest, it can sometimes tar the movement as a whole, but it can also serve to embolden mainstream players with a seat at the table who resonate (at least partly) with the radical critique of corporate globalization, for instance. Perhaps this is not quite "success," but it is not abject failure either.

Cultural Permeation

Beyond the political realm, there is the capacity to influence social mores and styles at a level that can have even greater potential impact in terms of arousing the populace to a new vision. Anarchism has been associated with various cultural forms (including punk rock, radical folk music, graffiti, raves), and it most notably has been at the forefront of the independent media movement since its inception. Anarchists have launched innumerable documentary filmmaking projects, publishing collectives, Web sites, "zines," bookstores, and artistic ventures in recent years. The circle-A symbol has been resurrected from the dustbin of history and can be found tagged on walls around the world, not to mention on t-shirts, stickers, pins, and tattooed body parts as well. Anarchist fiction, and science fiction in particular, has become a viable sub-genre in literature, and its contours have even found their way into a handful of feature films (e.g., *SLC Punk*, *Cecil B. DeMented*, *The Anarchist Cookbook*, *V for Vendetta*)—of course, not always with flattering representations.

Yet if we accept the theory that "there is no such thing as bad publicity," it certainly appears at the least that anarchism has inserted itself into popular culture in a way that seemed unlikely (if not impossible) only a few short decades ago.

In addition, the resurgence of anarchism in academia has been quite nearly phenomenal since the turn of the new millennium. A significant body of explicitly anarchist-themed works has appeared, covering topics ranging from protest to philosophy, steadily comprising an emerging field of "anarchist studies" complete with journals, professional societies, conferences, and the like. Despite concomitant processes of marginalization, it has become somewhat safer in recent years to identify as an anarchist, even to the point where it tends to attract intellectual and activist "tourists" to the milieu as well as genuine adherents. Indeed, this is the double-edged nature of cultural permeation, namely the potential watering-down of the concept as well as the tendency of marketing strategists to find ways of co-opting it. As with other radical movements and sub-cultures, anarchism sometimes suffers the dual process of repression and incorporation, which serves to further illuminate state/corporate synergy in its capacity to turn dissent into a commodity and excise from the cultural landscape those embracing the actual ideals rather than merely its stylistic appurtenances. The net result for evaluative purposes is another ambivalent one, but on balance there is no doubt that anarchism today is part of the cultural lexicon, and its intellectual and activist ranks have unquestionably seen a marked increase in the past decade—significantly, among young people in particular, which may pay further dividends in the future.

Resource Mobilization

The capacity to mobilize resources is a hallmark of social movement efficacy, which "emphasizes the interaction between resource availability, the preexisting organization of preference structures, and entrepreneurial attempts to meet preference demand."[18] Translating, the basic notion is that movements are essentially *demand-making* enterprises, and the degree to which they are successful depends upon (a) the level of resources they bring to bear on their efforts, (b) the resources they are able to procure from the system against which they are acting, and (c) how much their adherents are able to benefit from the resources thus procured. In a linear sense, a "resource" in this context is generally conceived as financial in nature, but more broadly we can also count as resources less tangible items including opportunities, spaces, empowerment of movement participants, and the capacity to influence public debate and increase the salience of issues through action. On another level, anarchists have served to draw away resources from the state and its security forces—in itself a tacit official admission of anarchism's efficacy—to a not-insignificant extent in recent years, yielding another way of thinking about "resource mobilization" for a movement. In particular, the resource of *space* (both in its physical and psychological senses) is a critical item for the success of any movement, since without it there are few opportunities to incubate ideas privately and/or to demonstrate them in a public manner.

While anarchists do not generally spend a great deal of time fundraising or lobbying, and in fact they widely reject the sort of "money fetishism" that underlies capitalism, oftentimes they do engage directly around issues of space. For instance, anarchists will squat in abandoned buildings, reclaim public space through direct interventions (e.g., Critical Mass, Reclaim the Streets, Food Not Bombs), set up infoshops and community centers, and grow food in "guerrilla gardens" scattered throughout urban centers. Anarchists organize to create greater space in their communities around issues of housing, economic and environmental justice, race relations, immigrants' rights, anti-gentrification, police brutality, and more.[19] Additionally, anarchists are often at the front lines (literally) of mass demonstrations in which both the physical space of the protest and the political space of claims-making are actively taken back (if only temporarily) from the forces of the prevailing order. Anarchists strive to promote safe spaces, free spaces, and other versions of *autonomous zones* that serve to provide loci for networking and movement-building and, perhaps more importantly, for people to gain a sense of what it might be like to live outside the strictures of the existing society—that is, to experience anarchy. The production of such liberated spaces may be the primary resource promulgated by anarchist movements; other important resources mobilized in the milieu include the literature base distributed through publishers and alternative media outlets, as well as the personal accoutrements of style.

Anarchists sometimes possess a fairly remarkable entrepreneurial spirit that makes the production of these resources possible on a do-it-yourself, small-scale basis. The proliferation of anarchist resources—from garb and music to literature and infoshops—does not necessarily correlate with wider forms of sociopolitical success, as Joel Olson pointedly contends:

> Surprisingly much of the contemporary anarchist milieu has abandoned movement building. . . . Divorced from a social movement,

the strategy of building autonomous zones or engaging in direct action with small affinity groups assumes that radicals can start the revolution. But revolutionaries don't make revolutions. Millions of ordinary and oppressed people do. Anarchist theory and practice today provides little sense of how these people are going to be part of the process, other than to create their own "free spaces" or to spontaneously join the festivals of upheaval. This is an idealistic, ahistorical, and, ironically, an elitist approach to politics, one that is curiously separated from the struggles of the oppressed themselves.[20]

In this sense, analyzing anarchism as an effective movement is problematic, insofar as the dominant modes of anarchist organizing (protest and autonomy) are not necessarily constitutive of what might properly be termed a *social movement* in the first instance. Even taking the broader view of a movement as simply a sustained, collective challenge to authority, today's anarchism still leaves much to be desired in terms of whether the resources it has thus far mobilized actually constitute a serious threat to the dominant forces in society. Still, there are some formulations suggesting that anarchism may not be completely off-track in this regard.

Credible Threat

Olson's critique raises an important point of reflection for anarchists, namely whether our efforts are building toward a bona fide movement at all, let alone a revolutionary one. Charles Tilly has further counseled that we must take care not to confuse "all relevant popular collective action" with an actual social movement, that we do not conflate organizations or networks with the movement itself, and that we do not reduce complex "interactions among activists" into a single unitary "movement" that undermines a more pluralistic sense of understanding social change.[21] Tilly's formulation takes a broad view of viable movement tactics, including demonstrations, direct action, and occupations, but he also notes that social movement activists generally concentrate their public efforts on more ameliorative actions that involve lobbying, broadcasting, or moving authorities to take action through legal means.[22] Tilly further posits a framework called "WUNC" for analyzing the potential impact of a given movement, which considers *worthiness, unity, numbers*, and *commitment* as bases for gauging effect; for instance, a small number of movement participants who undertake actions with "simultaneous risk or sacrifice often have as large an impact as a large number of people who sign a petition, wear a badge, or march through the streets on a sunny afternoon."[23]

In the end, Tilly suggests that the critical factor for a movement is the degree to which it represents a "credible threat" to entrenched powers: "The general effectiveness of social movement organizing as a way of making public claims depends on the constitution of credible collective actors that could disrupt existing political arrangements."[24] In order to accomplish this without turning into either a cliché or a terrorist cell, Tilly argues that movements should pay attention to attributes including continual innovation, expanding their repertoires of action, dramatizing their claims, and highlighting the intelligibility of their messages.[25] In this vein, a number of analyses have indicated that "the use of force or disruptive tactics by social movements improves their chances of reaching their goals," and that "disruption is the most powerful resource that movements have at their disposal to reach their goals, since they lack the institutional resources possessed by other actors, such as political parties and interest groups."[26] The classical formulation of the utility of disruptive tactics was offered by William A. Gamson:

> Groups that were active and disruptive have fared better than those that were passive when attacked and that never used constraints as a means of influence. … It is more accurate to interpret the[se] results as "feistiness works" rather than "violence works." Feistiness includes the willingness to break rules and use noninstitutionalized means—to use disruption as a strategy of influence. … We do not know if these unruly challengers really had a higher success rate than those who stuck to election campaigns, lawsuits, and lobbying, but the spread of such unruly tactics from one movement to another suggests that challengers, at least, were convinced of their usefulness.[27]

Another way of getting at these issues has been suggested by Olson, who looks at patterns of *extremism* through a lens of historical utility and political efficacy:

> What is needed, then, is a theory of zealotry that does not defer to the pejorative tradition. Such a theory must recognize zealotry as a form of collective action rather than simply an individual affliction. It must not automatically presume that fanatical activity is undemocratic, yet it must acknowledge the antagonistic, us/them character of extremism. Zealotry is an activity practiced not so much by disturbed temperaments as by collectivities working to transform relations of power by creating an "us" in struggle against a "them," and

by pressuring those in between to choose sides. Accordingly, zeal-otry is *political activity, driven by an ardent devotion to a cause, which seeks to draw clear lines along a friends/enemies dichotomy in order to mobilize friends and moderates in the service of that cause.*[28]

In his "Letter from a Birmingham Jail," Martin Luther King, Jr., similarly inquired: "The question is not whether we will be extremists, but what kind of extremists we will be. Will we be extremists for hate or for love? Will we be extremists for the preservation of injustice or for the extension of justice? . . . Perhaps the South, the nation and the world are in dire need of creative extremists."[29] With the stakes for humankind escalating every day, it can plausibly be argued that extremism is preferable to complicity, and that the latter is far more dangerous than the former.

The upshot here for anarchism is that a movement's effectiveness is at times keyed to how well it defies authority and contests the workings of established power. Among movement actors, both historical and contemporary, anarchists certainly score well on this front. Through dramatic demonstrations of direct action, militant protest, property destruction, and even at times the use of violence, anarchists have sought to awaken the popular conscience from its doldrums of co-optation and complacency. At times, however, the message is in jeopardy of getting lost amidst the media's sanitizing gaze, and tactics that were once provocative (e.g., smashing corporate windows) can become routinized and stale when regularly repeated. Anarchists have successfully learned how to be disruptive; the challenge now is to continue doing so in creative and evolutionary ways that continue to pose a credible threat to established authority while communicating a coherent narrative in the process. Ironically, a primary method for accomplishing this is located within the seat of power itself and its tendency toward repression.

Delegitimation

One of the patterns we have seen throughout this volume is that authorities will go to great lengths to reinforce the image of the "violent anarchist," particularly through mediated representations of anarchists as thugs, rioters, criminals, and the like. Moreover, such invocations will often be cited as justifications for official repression of anarchists in particular and wider movements in general. Anarchists sometimes court this demonization process by choosing disruptive tactics for change, raising the prospect of a double-edged quality to disruption in which the use of force (or even the suggestion of it) works in both directions: activists can use confrontational tactics to increase their effectiveness, but the state can also gain greater latitude in employing force against them in return. As Gamson has observed, "when authorities have used violence and arrests to control [disruptive challengers], such means did not backfire on them. ... Furthermore, the more feisty the challenger ... the easier it is to frame the challengers as 'asking for it'. With the help of cooperating journalists, the most provocative expressions of the challengers will draw the media spotlight and will help frame it for the general audience—regardless of how typical or isolated they might be."[30] On the other hand, "challengers who link their actions to the nonviolent tradition get an extra measure of protection from the media spotlight [and] overt repression of such challengers becomes an especially risky tactic."[31] At the end of the day, Gamson counsels movement actors to "be ready to use disruptive, extrainstitutional means of influence since you may well need them to succeed, but do not be surprised if you become the target of covert and disruptive means of social control."[32]

These insights are influential and important to consider, but they also reflect something of an outmoded view in the post-9/11 era. Today, technologies of overt and covert social control have become commonplace and almost blithely accepted by a large portion of the population, especially in the United States. Security scans, warrantless wiretapping, and the pervasive presence of video cameras have become part of the fabric of life in modern society, and activists in particular routinely anticipate heightened scrutiny, infiltration of their organizations, and even the denial of travel and other basic rights of expression and association.[33] Authorities have not shown the sort of restraint toward non-violent activists that Gamson posits, given the overarching justification of "combating terrorism" that is regularly plied. Anarchists have been painted with this broad brush, from being declared a leading domestic terrorist threat in the United States to police in England asking citizens to provide them with any available information on known anarchists in their midst. Anarchists have been killed at mass demonstrations and have been special targets for official beatings, gassings, and mass arrests in recent years. While these incidences of repression perhaps do not quite rise to the levels experienced in past eras—which included executions, mass deportations, and other forms of official brutality—they nonetheless constitute an important basis for understanding the impacts of "social movement performances."[34]

Scholars often explore the intentional actions of movements, as well as the unintended consequences that "are not always related to their demands."[35] For anarchists, one example of an unintentional effect might be the police using teargas or effecting mass arrests on peaceful demonstrators in an action where the Black Bloc (discussed in more detail in Chapter Two) has engaged in direct action somewhere away from the site of the larger protest. This can have (and has had) the effect of polarizing activists, creating antipathies, and undermining solidarity—all of which might be viewed as intentional effects on the part of authorities. But such actions have also served to delegitimize the state, which has increasingly resorted to extralegal measures, denials of due process, and the use of direct force against non-violent protestors, including even members of the media who are ostensibly there as observers and chroniclers.[36] "Delegitimation," as Uri Gordon discerns, "refers to the sum total of anarchist interventions in public discourse, verbal or symbolic, whose message is to deny the basic legitimacy of dominant social institutions and eat away at the premises of representative politics, class society, patriarchy and so on."[37] To take another example, the technicians of global capitalism have lost legitimacy as the use of force to protect their meetings has expanded, and as they have increasingly retreated to more remote (and thus less transparent) venues to conduct the business of the corporate economy.[38] In this sense, anarchist activities have weakened the legitimacy of the state and capital by showing that they do not even follow their own rules and that their power is not exercised justly.

Power Relations

Thus, another key feature of social movements is how they transform power relations in society. Anarchism advocates an egalitarian, horizontal mode of power distribution, and while this has not yet permeated the larger culture, it has undoubtedly infused activist circles around the world, from small-group and community-based processes to global networks. As we have seen throughout this volume, anarchists seek to balance power among individuals, between individuals and social structures, between local units as they affiliate and/or federate, and among the peoples of the world across geopolitical and economic divides. To an extent, we can fairly say that these methods have been successful within the locales in which they have been applied, but their circumscription largely within the activist milieu has prevented further reformation of overall power relations in the larger society. Indeed, this is one of those qualities that renders anarchism as inherently revolutionary, and its failure to as yet be realized is part of the ongoing process of remaking the map of the world in which anarchists are regularly engaged.

A relevant conundrum that has plagued revolutions throughout history is sometimes referred to as *antipower*, or the tendency of any force to produce "an equal and opposite reaction," as Isaac Newton surmised. Sometimes this opposing force takes the form of repression, but it also at times comes about within the very source of the initial force itself. "Antipower is the motive force of genuine revolutions [and often] becomes power as soon as it is triumphant," as Giovanni Baldelli has observed.[39] What is unique about anarchism, in theory at least, is its refusal to exercise power in the triumphalist sense; just as one cannot be forced to free, by definition, neither can anarchism be imposed by coercive means. "You can impose authority but you cannot impose freedom," as Colin Ward notes.[40] Still, some in the milieu advocate tactics—either physical or moralistic—that possess a coercive quality, raising the question of whether anarchism at times runs the risk of becoming the very thing that it is struggling against: "That movement and those organizations will show themselves truly anarchist that will not practice, and will not structure themselves according to, the very methods they condemn in others. Power is power under any name. A revolutionary power, wanting the end of one system of oppression, is no guarantee against itself embodying another such system."[41]

Similarly, social scientists sometimes refer to a process of *reification*, in which an abstract notion is brought into being, oftentimes through processes ostensibly intended to contest it. Thus, in directly confronting the state, anarchists run the risk of further concretizing it as a thing worthy of such contestation, thereby elevating its posture. The same is true in reverse, of course, so that anarchists can gain stature as the state persecutes them as well. The difference, however, is that the state has far greater control over representations of power (particularly vis-à-vis its sway over the mainstream media), such that in the public's mind anarchist actions might serve to reify the state as a bastion of order and protection, whereas anarchists are often reified as hooligans or terrorist threats. This was true even in the propaganda put forth as far back as a century ago: "Thus, in the name of the revolution, the Anarchists serve the cause of reaction; in the name of morality they approve the most immoral acts; in the name of individual liberty they trample under foot all the rights of their fellows."[42] Now, this sort of hysterical pronouncement is certainly overblown, and anarchists are hardly alone among movement actors who confront potential hypocrisies in navigating an oppositional stance within such a totalizing society. But the implicit cautionary tale is valid, and anarchists would do well to continue heeding it.

Identity Construction

Perhaps the greatest success for which anarchism can claim at least partial credit—and likewise comprising a platform for anarchist power relations coming into greater clarity—is the theory's position of maximal equality and how it has endeavored to span identity attributes including race, class, gender, sexual orientation, ability, and more. Anarchists believe in the innate equality and the capacity for productive empowerment of every individual, at least in principle. This becomes more challenging to maintain in the face of viewing political adversaries (e.g., coercive state officials, corporate profit-eers, hate groups, and supremacists) as "the enemy" within a movement context, and anarchists have not always been especially tolerant of or respectful toward those among the power elite in particular. But by and large, anarchists are busier building communities and facilitating movements than they are engaging in direct (and potentially dehumanizing) confrontations with adversaries. Indeed, anarchism focuses on the "cop in your head" as well as the one on the street, indicating that the true test of overcoming hierarchy is to confront the roots of it that we unconsciously embrace and enact in our lives. In this sense, anarchism is about individual character development as much as institutional challenge; "it is not a program for political change but an act of social self-determination."[43]

Despite the fact that "anarchism remains a largely white ideology in the U.S.," as Olson observes, it is also the case that "American anarchist thought and practice can provide a powerful analysis of race."[44] Extending the point, Olson concludes that a thoroughgoing deconstruction of hierarchy "has broadened contemporary anarchism into a critique of all forms of oppression, including capitalism, the state, and organized religion but also patriarchy, heterosexism, anthropocentrism, racism, and more."[45] Anarchism is unique among political theories in its attempt to "attack all forms of oppression, not just a 'main' one, because without an attack on hierarchy itself, other forms of oppression will not necessarily wither away after capitalism (or patriarchy, or colonialism) is destroyed."[46] Similar themes have been sounded by anarcha-feminists, who assert that "anarchists challenge any form of organization or relationship which fosters the exercise of power and domination," likewise that "anarchism understands that all oppressions are mutually reinforcing."[47] As L. Susan Brown articulates,

> not only is anarchism inherently feminist, but also it goes beyond feminism in its fundamental opposition to all forms of power, hierarchy, and domination. . . . While race, class, age, gender, sexuality, or ability, for instance, may pose analytical problems for other

movements, anarchism is capable of dealing with all these issues as legitimate because of its fundamental commitment to freedom for *all* people. No one oppression is given special status in anarchism—*all* oppression is equally undesirable. Anarchists fight for human freedom against each and every form of power and domination, not just a particular historical manifestation of power.[48]

Social movement analysts have begun to embrace the tenor of these insights, noting that there has been a "shift to identity construction" along with a redefinition of movements in part as "identity-creating structures."[49] These analyses further indicate the interlinked nature of personal transformation and political change, thus connecting the development of identities and societies.

In addition to race and gender issues, anarchism directly and critically engages matters of sexuality, as well as confronting disability issues by positing new rubrics such as "alter-ability" that seek to "encourage the less able to build their own alternative structures of useful activity integrated within a cooperative framework."[50] In recent years, anarchism has found productive intersections with fields including "postcolonial thought, queer studies, black and Chicano studies, cultural studies, and feminism," among other schools of thought and practice.[51] Anarchism has had a long tradition of confronting issues of class, economic justice, and the conditions of labor; more recently, it has found application in critical investigations of homelessness, marginalization, and forms of underground economics that exist beneath the veneer of capitalist society.[52] Anarchists wade into areas often neglected by other movements, such as parenting and family roles, likewise including an ethical orientation that asks us to fully consider the impact of all of our interpersonal relationships—from families and friendships to neighborhoods and workplaces—as sites for collective construction.[53] The contemporary anarchist milieu is thoroughly global and includes voices from both majoritarian and subaltern perspectives, representing the full range of identity constructions found across human cultures. Still, the actual practice of a fully non-hierarchical world remains a work in progress, and anarchism must continue to grapple with its own imbrications within structures of oppression that reflect outmoded ways of thinking about personal relations and social locations alike.

Building Alternatives

Ultimately, the primary evaluative measure for social movements—whatever definition we ascribe, and regardless of their level of organization—is how well they build alternatives and construct new narratives that challenge prevailing arrangements and point the way forward. Throughout this volume, I have attempted to depict a productive, proactive, and positive view of anarchism that indicates its simultaneous capacities for contestation and construction. Taken together, the examples cited and theories analyzed throughout the foregoing chapters present a vision of anarchism that is grounded in the autonomous actions of individuals, communities, and wider networks in managing the conditions of their lives within the context of cooperative, mutually beneficial endeavors. As previously noted, anarchism eschews concrete blueprints or formulas in favor of an organic and evolutionary approach to social organization, on the theory that challenges and conflicts are best handled in real time by the people closest to them, oftentimes spontaneously but also informed by the lessons of the past. Indeed, human history from its earliest underpinnings reflects the inherent ability of individuals and communities to navigate crises, promote just relations, federate and exchange with others, and live within the carrying capacity of the planet—all without imposing rigid hierarchies and regimes of control that by now appear increasingly like a slippery slope to technocratic totalitarianism. As Peter Marshall concludes, "for most of human evolution and history people have lived peaceful, cooperative lives without rulers, leaders, politicians, soldiers, policemen and taxmen."[54]

This is not to say that every pre-existing culture has been anarchistic, or that we want to return to some earlier "golden age" (even if it was possible) when people lived in perfect harmony. Quite likely, such a state of affairs was never truly evident, and history reflects a complex range of societal forms among the many cultures that have existed. Whatever we make of the past, it is the challenge of the present that we must confront if the human experiment is to continue. Like many others, anarchists struggle to cope with the rapid changes in technologies of surveillance and control, the destabilization of the environment, widening gaps of wealth and opportunity, the waste and destruction of a permanent war economy, the linearizing and privatizing influence of global capital, increasing vulnerabilities as to essentials including food and water, media hegemony, toxification and declining health, the centralization of political power, and all of the myriad crises presented by the world as it is currently configured. Anarchists have been steadily building alternative arrangements to tackle these crises—including intentional communities, anti-capitalist economies, free schools, seed banks, and independent media centers. One intriguing example is that of the Rainbow Family of Living Light, which has held regular "gatherings" on public lands (attracting tens of thousands) for over four decades, approximating the complex range of initiatives that define human communities.[55]

Still, to somehow overcome (or even address) all of the challenges presently confronting humankind would be well beyond the capacity of any single movement or theory. The totality of these crises—knowledge of which is in fact widely known—promotes a sense of detachment, despair, and disempowerment that only serves to feed back into the downward spiral. Some may be hoping that the "powers that be" will step in and save us, and indeed there may well be technological innovations on the horizon that appear to promise abundant energy and resources, as well as greater control over the variables that contribute to destabilization. But without a concomitant change in values, from a mindset of domination and competition to one of equality and mutualism, we are likely to find ourselves back in a place of dependency and subjugation. Perhaps some would opt for a gilded cage that obscures their view of the world outside the bars; anarchists emphatically reject such resignations and urge people everywhere to rattle those cages until a resonance frequency is found that breaks them down once and for all. This may well be the central anarchist value and vision, namely that we still have the ability and opportunity to turn the Titanic around and avert the cataclysm ahead. Indeed, we can even dismantle it altogether and creatively use the pieces to build a new ship right now.

Metaphors aside, anarchists have actually come a long way in terms of delineating a non-prescriptive vision for alternative societies as against the hegemony of the dominant order. Again, the essence is contained more in the process than the result, more about what an anarchist society *does* than what it *is*. In this regard, we have examined processes including self-management, mutual aid, solidarity, direct action, prefiguring, consensus decision making, restorative justice, liberatory education, participatory governance, egalitarian distribution, networking, and more. None of these in itself tells us exactly what an anarchist society will look like, and indeed different communities may apply these processes in divergent ways. The basic unifying premise, however, is that in doing so they will at least leave open the prospect of healthy social evolution, rather than the apparently destructive path we are on today. Anarchism cannot solve all of our problems, but it does offer a way of looking at the world—and the people in it—as a complex system comprised of self-actualized units that are equally entitled to define the conditions of life and the course of history. Capitalists and statists have already pronounced the "end of history" with the purported triumph of their paradigm, but anarchists maintain through their words and deeds that the future is yet to be written. That may be as good as it gets.

Buying Time

In this chapter, I have sought to assess the relative impact and effectiveness of anarchism in theory and practice, tracing the broad outlines of an evaluative framework for anti-systemic and revolutionary pursuits that often defy the terms of traditional sociological measuring devices. Overall, it appears that anarchism today has actually progressed quite well in terms of expanding its scope, refining its points of tension, and promoting its vision. Nonetheless, much remains to be done, and there probably is not a single anarchist who believes that the revolution is won and the task accomplished. Indeed, anarchists in general accept the basic facts that the work will *never* be done, that the maintenance of freedom and equality will *always* be unfolding, and that humankind will be engaged in an *eternal* process of learning how to live in balance with one another and the rest of non-human nature; as Harold Barclay observes, "even if anarchy were to be achieved, eternal vigilance would be the bare minimum price for even a modicum of success."[56] In this sense, the ultimate aim of anarchism is to continue this process, holding open the window of opportunity in which to invent and implement new visions for as long as possible, even in the face of escalating crises and long odds. The totality of anarchist praxis, in conjunction with movement actors from many other fronts, has at least served to "buy time" (ironically, a capitalist construct if ever there was one) and liberate space for the creation of alternatives. This quest for the future is perhaps the defining task before us, and its exploration will fittingly serve as a tentative conclusion to this volume.

Anarchism as Future Vision

Anarchism possesses an intriguing temporal perspective that equally credits the past, present, and future in its analyses and actions. Sometimes anarchists embrace the notion of "primitivism" as an expression of longing for a bygone day, at times explicitly calling for a return to the Paleolithic "hunter-gatherer" age in which humans are said to have lived without rigid social hierarchies and within the carrying capacities of the habitat. Even those that do not issue such a call still oftentimes draw lessons from the stateless societies that predominated our shared past, as well as from more recent historical examples of "anarchy in action" such as the Spanish Civil War. At the same time, anarchists deploy a wide spectrum of "direct action" tactics in the present that seek to undermine and alter the prevailing order, carve out spaces of autonomy and resistance, and build a set of sustainable alternatives to meet the needs of individuals and communities while forestalling the ongoing degradation of the environment. And anarchists also have one eye on the future, not in a prescriptive sense but more so in the practice of "prefiguring"—that is, in the recognition that actions taken in the present will (and should) model the new society in the making, serving not only to contest power but to create the basis for tomorrow's anarchism. Interestingly, sometimes this imagined future looks a bit like the past.

In this deep-seated temporal linkage, anarchism reflects a crucial sensibility that often goes unacknowledged in social theory, namely that we are *all* futurists all the time—for good, bad, or otherwise. As Noam Chomsky points out, through the choices we make today we are continually asserting "our control over the fate of future generations," creating a "basic moral imperative" that underscores much of environmentalism and anarchism alike.[1] Colin Ward further asserts that "a society advanced enough to accept the environmental imperatives of the 21st century will be obliged to reinvent anarchism as a response to them," indicating that "anarchism is the only political ideology capable of addressing the challenges posed by our new green consciousness to the accepted range of political ideas."[2] Uri Gordon concurs that "in a future plagued by energy scarcity, climate instability and financial meltdown, anarchist values and forms of organizing will become increasingly important. . . . The challenge anarchists and their allies face today is to disseminate their skills and ideas, creating a better chance that the move through industrial collapse will lead to a truly liberated world."[3] Continuing in this vein, Peter Marshall concludes that anarchism "is more urgent than ever if we are to survive the ecological crises and reverse the growing injustice and inequality in the world. We need to imagine and realize an alternative future and social reality, one based on autonomy, individuality, community, solidarity and a deep concern for the natural world."[4]

Indeed, the problems confronting humankind are manifold, and they have potentially dire implications for the future. At the same time, anarchists (and other dedicated activists) have been steadily articulating and implementing the seeds of a new vision. Given its inherently revolutionary posture and its comprehensive critique of power, domination, and hierarchy, anarchism holds great promise for accomplishing the task of "building independent, sustainable alternatives and community self-sufficiency" and likewise "displaying attractive models that people can implement."[5] Uncompromising in its rejection of technocratic rule, anarchism possesses the capacity to directly engage "today's most pressing issues, including: food shortages, the distribution of resources, the role of technology, access to political power, the roots and sources of conflict, the origins of oppression and marginalization, and the potentially irreparable harm being done to the biosphere."[6] To cope with this ever-expanding list of crises, anarchism itself has continued to evolve new forms, such as "insurrectionalism, primitivism, anarcha-feminism, Situationist anarchisms, especifismo, and platformism," plus establishing productive intersections with areas of inquiry including "radical anti-racist politics such as 'Race Traitor,' radical queer theories, environmentalism(s), and animal liberationism, as well as anarchist practices emerging from post-colonial states and indigenous populations."[7]

Increasingly, a sense of impending collapse looms large in the modern psyche. Anarchists are among the relatively few (within the privileged nations, in particular) who choose neither to ignore this through self-medication and functional distraction, nor to pretend that it is simply part of business as usual with no cause for alarm. "We have taken a monstrously wrong turn," as John Zerzan pointedly asserts, "from a place of enchantment, understanding and wholeness to the absence we find at the heart of the doctrine of progress. Empty and emptying, the logic of domestication, with its demand to control everything, now shows us the ruin of the civilization that ruins the rest."[8] Even against this stark realization that the facade of progress and plenty has steadily pushed the world to the brink, perhaps irreversibly so by some ecological measures, anarchists refuse to "go gentle into that good night" and instead consciously choose to "rage, rage against the dying of the light," as the oft-quoted lines by the poet Dylan Thomas suggest. Writing on "The Transformation of the Future," anarcha-feminist Peggy Kornegger thus intones:

> I used to think that if the revolution didn't happen tomorrow, we would all be doomed to a catastrophic (or at least catatonic) fate. I don't believe anymore that that is necessarily true. In fact, I don't even believe in that kind of before-and-after revolution, and I think we set ourselves up for failure and despair by thinking of it in those terms. I do believe that what we all need, what we absolutely require in order to continue struggling (in spite of the oppression of our daily lives), is hope, that is, a vision of the future so beautiful and so powerful that it pulls us steadily forward in a bottom-up creation of an inner and outer world both habitable and self-fulfilling for *all. . . .*
>
> . . . Nothing we can do is enough, but on the other hand, those "small changes" we make in our minds, in our lives, in one another's lives, are not totally futile and ineffectual. It takes a long time to make a revolution: it is something that one both prepares for and lives now. The transformation of the future will not be instantaneous, but it can be total . . . a continuum of thought and action, individuality and collectivity, spontaneity and organization, stretching from what is to what can be. Anarchism provides a framework for this transformation. It is a vision, a dream, a possibility which becomes "real" as we live it.[9]

Holding a Vision

The central question before us, then, might simply be stated as: "Where do we go from here?"[10] From Starhawk to Peter Gelderloos—who can be taken to represent the poles of a spectrum of anarchism from prefigurative paganism to militant mobilizations—there is actually a nascent convergence of future visions in the anarchist milieu. For her part, Starhawk begins from the premise that *revolution* is "what we are, not what we will become; what we do, not what we will do someday … a living process happening now"; in this view, the simultaneous task of *evolution* is equally crucial, entailing an effort to "provide the alternatives, build the models, invent the new life-friendly technologies, and demonstrate that ecological sanity is actually more profitable."[11] Her ultimate vision for both today and tomorrow includes: protecting the life-sustaining systems of the planet; resisting commodification and reclaiming the sacred; restoring communities' control over their resources and destinies; respecting and learning from indigenous cultures; conducting our business with due regard for future generations; promoting opportunities for all people to meet their needs and fulfill their dreams; treating labor and laborers justly and with dignity; ensuring the basic means of life for all; and creating participatory structures in which people have a voice in all decisions that affect them.[12]

This is a thoroughly anarchist vision, though it need not be called that to appreciate its innate logic and desirability. Gelderloos approaches similar themes from a revolutionary starting point that "visions make us stronger, and we will all need the courage to break once and for all with the existing institutions and the false solutions they offer," segueing into the evolutionary task of describing "how an ecological, anti-authoritarian society could manifest itself."[13] Articulating his vision, Gelderloos focuses on attributes including: bringing about an end to fossil fuel extraction; replacing industrial food production with sustainable growing at local levels; rejecting the exploitative mentality of the market; abandoning some cities and greening others; producing energy and other essential resources locally; convening neighborhood assemblies and other forms of decentralized decision making; returning control of daily life to individuals and small groups; establishing a gift economy; removing the compulsion of work and instead making it enjoyable; abolishing the police and other forms of coercive force; maintaining viable transportation and communication between local units; and healing the world from the ravages of capitalism through permaculture and sustainable social and ecological practices.[14]

We can see immediately how much synergy exists between these visions, which again come from fairly disparate sources within contemporary anarchism—and additional affirming visions abound in the milieu. Marshall, for instance, sees a world in which people can run free, link with neighbors, become rooted in their bioregion, cooperate routinely, decentralize communications, and establish horizontal modes of social organization—taking the broad view that, ultimately, "no one path is paramount: there are many different ways up a mountain."[15] Crispin Sartwell aspires to an anarchism that devolves upon self-sovereignty and individual responsibility, loosely formed collectives and associations, deeper connections to one another and nature, greater complexity in human identities beyond mere capitalist forms, conscience and self-discipline, and non-prescriptive voluntaristic forms of social association.[16] Carissa Honeywell discerns a British tradition of anarchism that encompasses "virulent rejections of war, universal opportunities for aesthetic expression, experimental student-led techniques in education, the devolution of political and economic control to the lowest possible community level in various spheres, popular control over the use of technology and land, and the re-evaluation of social mores according to their individual and social benefit and authenticity," with the combined effect of "encouraging voluntarism, empowering communities, building social relationships, [and] supporting liberating opportunities for self-help."[17] And Donald Black subtly projects the rise of a "new anarchy [that is] neither communal nor situational, yet both at once."[18]

These burgeoning visions are representative of the anarchist tendency to focus on pragmatic possibilities and ideal alternatives at the same time. All of the notions mentioned above are practicable (at least in part) in the present, and yet each points toward a potential future that remains a gleam in the visionary's eye. This is the essence of prefiguring and of anarchism as well, namely that we desire a world that is always in the making, that eschews total or final visions for the sake of ongoing experimentation, that remains open to rethinking its own basic premises, that restores the capacity to make any such decisions to individuals and communities that are locally rooted yet working in concert, that respects the singular and the whole simultaneously as necessary reflections of one another. As P. M. observes in articulating the complex, evolutionary vision of a global network of autonomous communities contained in the landmark work *bolo'bolo*, what we seek is "not a system, but a patchwork of micro-systems."[19] As such, Cindy Milstein observes, "anarchism asks that people 'build the road as they travel.' "[20]

Thus, as Milstein counsels, "the 'end' of anarchism is not a final destination . . . nor a revolution after which all becomes and remains perfect."[21] Anarchism is not a "blueprint or rigid plan," rather taking the view that "no one can dictate the exact shape of the future"; unlike thinkers from other traditions, "anarchists exercise extreme caution when discussing 'blueprints' of future social relations since they believe that it is always up to those seeking freedom to decide how they desire to live."[22]

As Chomsky concurs, "though our visions can and should be a guide, they are at best a very partial one. They are not clear, nor are they stable, at least for people who care about the consequences of their acts. Sensible people will look forward to a clearer articulation of their animating visions and to the critical evaluation of them in the light of reason and experience."[23] Ultimately, then, "we should be cautious in trying to sketch out the nature of the future society in too much detail" and instead "try and experiment and chip away at existing structures."[24] Perhaps nowhere is this "experimental futurism" more evident than in the ongoing debate about what role technology is to play in any anarchist vision for today, or tomorrow.

Techno-topia, or Future Primitive?

In Chapter Four we looked in detail at primitivism, critiques of civilization, and competing views over technology. I will not rehash that analysis here, except insofar as to note that anarchism (as in many other contexts) reflects a curious dual tendency to embrace Luddism *and* high technology, to both ignore and infiltrate modern machinery, to "get back to the garden" and "boldly go where no one has gone before" all at once. Even anarchists who utilize modern technologies of communication and conveyance—which is nearly everyone—often express ambivalence about the efficacy and ethicality of such devices. The objections are over the economic arrangements in which these technologies are produced, the inherent anti-environmentalism contained within their workings, their dehumanizing aspects of automation and mediation, the capacities for greater social control embedded in their use, and the mechanistic worldview they reflect. Above all, anarchists reject the specialized, centralized knowledge necessary to maintain a technological society, as well as the concomitant dependency it fosters among a populace increasingly reliant upon remote machinery to run our daily lives, largely immune from accountability and beyond our capacity to either regulate or even fully understand it. Zerzan laments: "As we have become more alien from our own experiences, which are processed, standardized, labeled, and subjected to hierarchical control, technology emerges as the power behind our misery and the main form of ideological domination."[25]

Still, Zerzan's *future primitive* worldview is by no means fully accepted by anarchists. Historically, in the more halcyon early days of industrialism, agrarian and ecological anarchists (including Peter Kropotkin and Elisée Reclus, among others) actually saw great hope in technology to alleviate the toils of labor and enable greater self-sufficient production of food. Graham Purchase observes, for instance, that Reclus "was much more willing to enthusiastically endorse developments in technology than perhaps he might have been, had he been living today; believing that the intelligent and ecologically informed use of science and technology could produce harmony, beauty, and abundance for all."[26] Even today, many still place great faith in technology to solve the myriad crises before us, perhaps more out of a sense of necessity than desire, but the result is the same. How are we to feed seven billion people without agribusiness and industrial food production methods? Can we reverse the threshold-crossing processes driving climate change without employing technological fixes? Will the global economy be able to function without the internet infrastructure? What would become of the ability to travel and stay connected to others if mass technologies were to disappear? Can we survive sans machinery?

These sorts of queries indicate at least partly why technology enjoys such wide acceptance in society, to the degree of fetishism by now, and why so many seem willing to accept even greater technological interventions in order to try and fix the problems already caused by it. This sort of "doubling down" perspective is potentially disastrous, both for personal freedom and ecological survival alike. The proposed "solutions" to today's crises read like a Pandora's box of science-fiction scenarios that portend further potential destabilization of the biosphere, increased centralization of state-corporate power, and deeper incursions into human integrity. Nuclear power is by now an obvious "false solution," as is biotechnology, but right around the corner are even more disconcerting developments like the geoengineering of the environment (i.e., altering the planet's basic cycles) and nanotechnology (i.e., manipulation of matter at the molecular level). Anarchists are, by and large, as future-oriented as anyone, and there are even celebratory invocations to be found in the milieu, such as the assertion that "technological society may serve as an appropriate model of anarchist utopia" by producing a "positive chaos" or "Techno-verse" that challenges the totalizing view of order and control.[27]

Fortunately, as Richard J. F. Day describes, "the basic principles of engineering work against the fantasy of a totally integrated world. As any computer user knows, the more complex a system becomes the more difficult it is to maintain, the more often and catastrophically it fails."[28] The internet may be the quintessential example of this phenomenon: in order to sustain its utility, it has been increasingly brought under central control and regulation (in fact, it originates from the military-security apparatus), making it a more attractive target for hackers, black marketers, and other high-tech pirates who are able to impinge upon this expanding monolith from literally anywhere in the world. Decentralization and diversification are actually far more stable methods of organization, as anarchists have been asserting for centuries, but these values do not serve the interests of state and corporate hegemony. Gordon thus concludes that, despite appearances of decentralized openness, the internet's "enabling infrastructures have the more usual characteristics of modern technological systems," including not only the resource-intensive creation of computer hardware but also the "enormous level of precision and authoritative coordination" required for both production and reproduction of the system.[29]

In answer to such eventualities, Hakim Bey offers a creative response that celebrates chaos and rejects both "anti-Tech anarchism [and] the concept of the Technological fix as well," asserting bluntly that "if a given technology, no matter how admirable *in potential* (in the future), is used to oppress me here and now, then I must either wield the weapon of sabotage or else seize the means of production."[30] Indeed, the stakes are high, and anarchists—even with their complex love-hate relationship with technology—stand increasingly isolated among social movement groups in offering resistance to and a critique of expanding technocratic control. Gordon urges us to grasp the basic dilemma of our time: "No amount of financial speculation or high-tech intervention will buy the system out of its inevitable crash. The time of the turning has come, and we are the generation with the dubious fortune to live and die in its throes."[31] As such, "anarchists and their allies are now required to project themselves into a future of growing instability and deterioration, and to re-imagine their tactics and strategies in view of the converging crises that will define the twenty-first century."[32]

Still, amid the decaying fabric, there remain opportunities for "low-tech innovation in areas like energy, building and food production," and perhaps this is what figures like Kropotkin and Reclus had in mind over a century ago.[33] Maybe we cannot go back—there is "no escape backward in time," as Bey notes—but we can certainly go forward by reviving the traditional knowledge of the past, selecting human-scaled technologies that can be crafted and serviced by a wide range of users, letting local communities decide the appropriate tools for their needs, and ultimately turning today's mounting technology-driven crises into new opportunities for "creativity, conviviality and cooperation."[34] In the end, as Gordon advises, "there are no guarantees," and anarchists will need to remain engaged, vigilant, critical, and constructive to help surmount the unfolding cataclysms.[35] Anarchism is uniquely situated to foster the growth of communities that embrace realistic strategies—not merely for survival, but toward a renaissance of new ideas and practices that possess a long historical pedigree. This may sound a bit like the plot of a science fiction tale, and indeed it has been recorded as such on more than one occasion.

Science Friction

In working out its future visions, anarchism has found a willing venue in the annals of science fiction.[36] Explorations of anarchistic themes have appeared in the "cyberpunk" writings of William Gibson, Bruce Sterling, and Rudy Rucker; the technolibertarian visions of Robert A. Heinlein, Ken MacLeod, and Vernor Vinge; and the sociopolitical works of Michael Moorcock, Iain M. Banks, and Norman Spinrad. Some of the most instructive anarchist futures have been developed by science fiction writers, helping to popularize anarchism for a wide readership in the process. The best known of these works is likely Ursula K. Le Guin's *The Dispossessed: An Ambiguous Utopia* (1974), which explores the development of a lunar anarchist society as it compares with its capitalist-authoritarian parent planet; her work further considers the ways in which centralization and bureaucratization can become entrenched even in an ostensible anarchist society when eternal vigilance is abandoned in favor of a static utopianism. Similar themes are found in James P. Hogan's *Voyage from Yesteryear* (1982), where a renegade anarchist colony is invaded by capitalist-autocratic forces attempting to reclaim it—with the latter being confronted by mass non-violence and eventually becoming subsumed within the decentralized, cooperative society. Eric Frank Russell's *The Great Explosion* (1962) likewise features the classless, gift-economy society of the "Gands" (after Gandhi) using passive resistance against invading military authoritarians.

The theme of contrasting futures is further explored in Marge Piercy's *Woman on the Edge of Time* (1976), in which a young woman trapped in a brutal, repressive society travels to the future where two competing "realities" are on the verge of war: an elitist autocracy versus a culture based on enchantment, androgyny, human-scaled technology, and ecological balance. Adopting a revolutionary posture in her own time, the young woman's actions become a pivotal point in history for the realization of a future world based on equality, harmony, and sanity. Pat Murphy's brilliant *The City, Not Long After* (1989) depicts a band of post-cataclysm survivors in San Francisco successfully deploying a wide-ranging campaign of resistance (mainly utilizing non-compliance and monkeywrenching tactics) against a military unit bent on restoring "law and order" in the aftermath of collapse. "We don't have a representative form of government," the resisters tell one of the military commanders. "We follow more of a town council model. When we want to decide something, we all get together and discuss it. But you'd be surprised how few things really affect everyone. Most decisions can be made in smaller groups."[37] In Starhawk's *The Fifth Sacred Thing* (1993), a similar post-apocalyptic battle ensues between egalitarian eco-topian survivors and authoritarian militaristic aggressors. The book notably opens with a "Declaration of the Four Sacred Things" ("air, fire, water, and earth"), which proclaims in part: "No one has the right to appropriate them or profit from them at the expense of others. Any government that fails to protect them forfeits its legitimacy."[38]

These are merely glimpses from an expanding genre, intended to provide another perspective from which to consider the potential realization of an anarchist future. Taken together, the combined lesson of these scholarly and literary works is that if we fail to take steps to actualize that vision right here in the present, the notion of having any future at all is speculative at best. This is not alarmism but merely extrapolation; the insights of these authors are intended to push us out of our comfort zones, creating a sense of friction as we move through the confines of our daily routines, one that could serve to mobilize our untapped capacities for action. Kim Stanley Robinson (himself an anarchist science fiction author, noted for his Mars series among other works) writes in the introduction to *Future Primitive* that the "consensus vision of our future" is marketed back to us "in great industrial city-machines, with people as the last organic units in a denatured, metallic, clean, and artificial world."[39] Robinson continues:

> We are beginning to understand that this imagined future is impossible to enact. . . . Industrial existence cannot save us from the coming environmental crisis; indeed, it is part of the problem. In all likelihood we have already overshot our environment's carrying capacity. . . . We are in a race to invent and practice a sustainable mode of life before catastrophe strikes us. So we are in the process of rethinking the future, of inventing a new consensus vision of what it might be. . . . All manner of alternative futures are now being imagined, and many of them invoke the wilderness, and moments of our distant past, envisioning futures that from the point of view of the industrial model look 'primitive.' . . . These science fictions reject the inevitability of the machine future. . . . These visions are

utopian statements of desire, full of joy and hope and danger, re-opening our notion of the future to a whole range of wild possibilities.[40]

Back to the Future

As we move toward our destination, new paths also appear just ahead. This is the essence of the anarchist reading of the *future*, namely that it is the moment where the present—always contested, never perfected—opens onto fresh vistas in which to continue the experiment. The anarchist utopia is one of process and not place, open-ended, defined by its practices rather than a program. Throughout this work, I have attempted to give voice to this ever-changing anarchist vision, highlighting its points of tension and convergence alike, depicting it concretely but on perpetually wet cement that can be rewritten over and over again. Anarchy is ordered chaos, the resiliency of diversity, the stability of change. It harks back to the best virtues of human history and development, projecting ahead to a world where the wisdom of the past is integrated with the knowledge of the present. *Anarchism*: the infinitude of the cosmos; the solitude of the self. In the end, there is less separating the one from the many than it otherwise appears. Being and becoming, locked in an eternal dance; free spirits in the presence of fate, never resting yet always at peace; gazing upon the limitless horizon in the recognition that the road ahead will be arduous, adventurous, and, ultimately, will lead us back again to the place from which we embarked.

Notes

Foreword

1. Rebecca Solnit, *A Paradise Built in Hell: The Extraordinary Communities That Arise in Disaster* (New York: Viking Press, 2009).
2. Alex Martin, "On a Street Named Desire," *Newsday*, September 26, 2005.
3. Michael Tomasello, *Why We Cooperate* (Cambridge, MA: MIT Press, 2009).

Introduction

1. Alex Prichard, "Introduction: Anarchism and World Politics," *Millennium: Journal of International Studies* 39, no. 2 (2010): 373.
2. Kenneth C. Wenzer, "Godwin's Place in the Anarchist Tradition—A Bicentennial Tribute," *Social Anarchism: A Journal of Theory and Practice* 20 (2006), http://www.socialanarchism.org/mod/magazine/display/27/index.php.
3. Ibid.
4. For example, see George Woodcock, *Anarchism: A History of Libertarian Ideas and Movements* (New York: Meridian Books, 1962); George Crowder, *Classical Anarchism: The Political Thought of Godwin, Proudhon, Bakunin, and Kropotkin* (Oxford, UK: Clarendon Press, 1991); Peter Marshall, *Demanding the Impossible: A History of Anarchism* (New York: Harper Perennial, 2008).
5. Peter Kropotkin, *The Conquest of Bread and Other Writings*, ed. Marshall Shatz (Cambridge, UK: Cambridge University Press, 1995), 233–34.
6. Ibid., 235.
7. Emma Goldman, *Anarchism and Other Essays* (Port Washington, NY: Kennikat Press, 1969), 68–71.

8. Uri Gordon, "Anarchism: The A Word," *New Internationalist*, June 1, 2011, http://www.newint.org/features/2011/06/01/anarchism-explained; Marshall, *Demanding the Impossible*, xi.

9. Staughton Lynd and Andrej Grubacic, *Wobblies & Zapatistas: Conversations on Anarchism, Marxism and Radical History* (Oakland, CA: PM Press, 2008).

10. Sam Mbah and I. E. Igariwey, *African Anarchism: The History of a Movement* (Tucson, AZ: See Sharp Press, 1997), 27–35.

11. Luis A. Fernandez, *Policing Dissent: Social Control and the Anti-Globalization Movement* (Brunswick, NJ: Rutgers University Press, 2008), 51; Süreyyya Evren, "Introduction: How New Anarchism Changed the World (of Opposition) after Seattle and Gave Birth to Post-Anarchism," in *Post-Anarchism: A Reader*, ed. Duane Rousselle and Süreyyya Evren (London: Pluto Press, 2011), 1.

12. Uri Gordon, *Anarchy Alive! Anti-Authoritarian Politics from Practice to Theory* (Ann Arbor, MI: Pluto Press, 2008), 5; Crispin Sartwell, *Against the State: An Introduction to Anarchist Political Theory* (Albany, NY: SUNY Press, 2008), 14.

13. Starhawk, *Webs of Power: Notes from the Global Uprising* (Gabriola Island, BC: New Society Publishers, 2002), 15.

14. Janet Thomas, *The Battle in Seattle: The Story Behind and Beyond the WTO Demonstrations* (Golden, CO: Fulcrum Publishing, 2000), 10.

15. Ibid., 209.

16. Ibid., 46.

17. Teoman Gee, " 'New Anarchism': Some Thoughts," *Alpine Anarchist Productions*, January 2003, 5.

18. David Graeber, "The New Anarchists," *New Left Review* 13 (January–February 2002), http://www.newleftreview.org/A2368.

19. Starhawk, *Webs of Power*, 208.

20. Jeff Ferrell, *Tearing Down the Streets: Adventures in Urban Anarchy* (New York: Palgrave, 2001), 234.

21. Ibid., 20.

22. Ibid., 34.

23. Graeber, "The New Anarchists."

24. Ibid.

25. Ferrell, *Tearing Down the Streets*, 243.

26. Gee, "New Anarchism," 4.

27. Franklin Foer, "Protest Too Much," *New Republic*, May 1, 2000, http://greenspun.com/bboard/q-and-a-fetch-msg.tcl?msg_id=0033Wy

28. Cindy Milstein, *Anarchism and Its Aspirations* (Oakland, CA: AK Press, 2010), 4.

29. Chris Dodge, "Anarchism 101," *Utne Reader*, May–June 2001.

30. Gee, "New Anarchism," 4.

31. Fernandez, *Policing Dissent*, 157–61.

32. Sean Robinson, "The Elusive Face of Anarchism," *The News Tribune*, July 10, 2011, http://www.thenewstribune.com/2011/07/10/1739559/the -elusive-face-of-anarchism.html.

33. Randall Amster et al., eds., *Contemporary Anarchist Studies: An Introductory Anthology of Anarchy in the Academy* (New York: Routledge, 2009), 5.

34. Milstein, *Anarchism and Its Aspirations*, 5.

35. David Graeber and Andrej Grubacic, "Anarchism, or the Revolutionary Movement of the 21st Century," *Irvine Infoshop*, n.d., http://irvineinfoshop .files.wordpress.com/2009/01/anarchism-graebergrubacic.pdf.

36. Gordon, "Anarchism: The A Word."

37. Gee, "New Anarchism," 4.

38. See, for example, Starhawk, *Webs of Power*; and David Graeber, *Direct Action: An Ethnography* (Oakland, CA: AK Press, 2009). An impressive compendium on Canadian anarchism in particular highlights the post-Seattle actions there as well as the roots to which it owes its existence, in part: Alan Antliff, ed., *Only 'A' Beginning: An Anarchist Anthology* (Vancouver, BC: Arsenal Pulp Press, 2004).

39. Gordon, *Anarchy Alive!* 5.

40. Abe Greenwald, "The Return of Anarchism," *Commentary*, March 2011, http://www.commentarymagazine.com/article/the-return-of -anarchism/.

41. Ibid.

42. Ezra Klein, "'You're Creating a Vision of the Sort of Society You Want to Have in Miniature'," *Washington Post*, October 3, 2011, http://www.washing tonpost.com/blogs/ezra-klein/post/youre-creating-a-vision-of-the-sort-of-society-you -want-to-have-in-miniature/2011/08/25/gIQAXVg7HL_blog.html.

43. Zach Williams, "O.W.S. Through the Lens of Anarchy," *Downtown Express*, November 23, 2011, http://www.downtownexpress.com/?p=4864.

44. David Graeber, "Occupy and Anarchism's Gift of Democracy," *The Guardian*, November 15, 2011, http://www.guardian.co.uk/commentisfree/ cifamerica/2011/nov/15/occupy-anarchism-gift-democracy.

45. Colin Ward, *Anarchism: A Very Short Introduction* (Oxford, U.K.: Oxford University Press, 2004), 10.

46. Gee, "New Anarchism," 1.

47. See CrimethInc., *Recipes for Disaster: An Anarchist Cookbook* (Olympia, WA: CrimethInc. Ex-Workers' Collective, 2004); Gabriel Kuhn, ed., *Neuer Anarchismus in den U.S.: Seattle und die Folgen* (Münster, Germany: Unrast-Verlag, 2008).

Chapter 1

1. Brian Morris, "Anthropology and Anarchism," *Anarchy: A Journal of Desire Armed*, Spring/Summer 1998, 41; Harold Barclay, *People Without*

Government: An Anthropology of Anarchy (Seattle, WA: Left Bank Books, 1990), 12.

2. CrimethInc., "Fighting for Our Lives: An Anarchist Primer," n.d.

3. Ibid.

4. Royce Logan Turner, "Anarchism—A Political Philosophy for the Age?" *Contemporary Review*, n.d.

5. Graeber and Grubacic, "Anarchism"; Milstein, *Anarchism and Its Aspirations*, 11.

6. Ibid. (quoting Malatesta).

7. Goldman, *Anarchism and Other Essays*, 69–73.

8. Leo Tolstoy, *Government Is Violence: Essays on Anarchism and Pacifism*, ed. David Stephens (London: Phoenix Press, 1990), 15.

9. Lisa Kemmerer, "Anarchy: Foundations in Faith," in *Contemporary Anarchist Studies: An Introductory Anthology of Anarchy in the Academy*, ed. Randall Amster et al. (New York: Routledge, 2009), 210; Gordon, *Anarchy Alive!* 19.

10. Peter Kropotkin, *Kropotkin's Revolutionary Pamphlets*, ed. Roger N. Baldwin (New York: Benjamin Blom, 1927/1968), 39–41.

11. Peter Kropotkin, *Fugitive Writings*, ed. George Woodcock (New York: Black Rose Books, 1993), 149.

12. Peter Kropotkin, *Mutual Aid: A Factor of Evolution*, ed. Paul Avrich (New York: New York University Press, 1972), 20.

13. Hakim Bey, *T.A.Z.: The Temporary Autonomous Zone, Ontological Anarchy, Poetic Terrorism* (Brooklyn, NY: Autonomedia, 1991), 10.

14. John P. Clark and Camille Martin, eds., *Anarchy, Geography, Modernity: The Radical Social Thought of Elisée Reclus* (New York: Lexington Books, 2004), 23–24.

15. Murray Bookchin, "What Is Social Ecology?" in *Environmental Philosophy: From Animal Rights to Radical Ecology*, 2nd ed., ed. Michael E. Zimmerman et al. (Englewood Cliffs, NJ: Prentice Hall, 1993), 355 (emphasis in original).

16. Todd May, "Is Post-Structuralist Political Theory Anarchist?" *Philosophy and Social Criticism* 15, no. 2 (1989): 171.

17. CrimethInc., "Fighting for Our Lives."

18. Colin Ward, *Anarchy in Action* (New York: Harper Torchbooks, 1973), 12.

19. Gee, "New Anarchism," 11–12.

20. Starhawk, *Webs of Power*, 141.

21. Quoted in Gordon, *Anarchy Alive!* 27.

22. See Todd May, *The Political Philosophy of Poststructuralist Anarchism* (University Park, PA: The Pennsylvania State University Press, 1994), 66.

23. Ward, *Anarchy in Action*, 11.

24. Marshall, *Demanding the Impossible*, 43.

25. Michael Bakunin, *God and the State* (New York: Dover Publications, 1970), 33.

26. Herbert Read, *Anarchy and Order: Essays in Politics* (Boston, MA: Beacon Press, 1954), 155.

27. Gustav Landauer, *Revolution and Other Writings: A Political Reader*, ed. and trans. Gabriel Kuhn (Oakland, CA: PM Press, 2010), 214 (emphasis in original).

28. James Horrox, *A Living Revolution: Anarchism in the Kibbutz Movement* (Oakland, CA: AK Press, 2009), 2.

29. CrimethInc., "Fighting for Our Lives" (emphasis in original).

30. P. M., *bolo'bolo* (Brooklyn, NY: Semiotext(e), 1995), 19.

31. Goldman, *Anarchism and Other Essays*, 64.

32. Ibid., 68.

33. Gordon, *Anarchy Alive!* 5.

34. Noam Chomsky, *Chomsky on Anarchism*, ed. Barry Pateman (Oakland, CA: AK Press, 2005), 123.

35. Jean-Jacques Rousseau, *The Social Contract and the Discourses* (London: Everyman's Library, 1973), 84.

36. Daniel Guérin, *Anarchism: From Theory to Practice*, trans. Mary Klopper (New York: Monthly Review Press, 1970), 13.

37. Ward, *Anarchy in Action*, 28.

38. Milstein, *Anarchism and Its Aspirations*, 25.

39. Ibid., 73.

40. Peter Kropotkin, *The Conquest of Bread*, ed. Charles Weigl (London: Taylor and Francis, 2006), 70.

41. See Randall Amster, "Anarchy, Utopia, and the State of Things to Come," in *Contemporary Anarchist Studies: An Introductory Anthology of Anarchy in the Academy*, ed. Randall Amster et al. (New York: Routledge, 2009), 290–301.

42. Chomsky, *Chomsky on Anarchism*, 178.

43. Ibid., 222.

44. Rudolf Rocker, *Anarchism and Anarcho-Syndicalism* (London: Freedom Press, 2001), 33.

45. Ward, *Anarchy in Action*, 52.

46. See Duane Rousselle and Süreyyya Evren, eds., *Post-Anarchism: A Reader* (London: Pluto Press, 2011).

47. Andrew M. Koch, "Poststructuralism and the Epistemological Basis of Anarchism," *Philosophy of the Social Sciences* 23, no. 3 (September 1993): 341.

48. Todd May, "Post-Structuralist Political Theory," 177.

49. Rocker, *Anarchism and Anarcho-Syndicalism*, 14.

50. Randall Amster, "Anarchism as Moral Theory: Praxis, Property, and the Postmodern," *Anarchist Studies* 6, no. 2 (October 1998): 109.

Chapter 2

1. William Powell, "From the Author," regarding *The Anarchist Cookbook*, http://www.amazon.com/dp/0974458902.

2. Starhawk, *Webs of Power*, 79, 96.

3. Quoted in Ferrell, *Tearing Down the Streets*, 94.

4. Howard Zinn, "Introduction: The Art of Revolution," in Read, *Anarchy and Order*, xi.

5. Ibid., xviii.

6. Ibid.

7. Starhawk, *Webs of Power*, 260.

8. Read, *Anarchy and Order*, 51.

9. Ghaith Abdul-Ahad et al., "The Fight to Rescue the Arab Spring," *The Guardian*, July 15, 2011, http://www.guardian.co.uk/world/2011/jul/15/arab-spring-rescue-renewed-protesters.

10. Errico Malatesta, "The Anarchist Revolution," *Anarchy Archives* (c. 1925), http://dwardmac.pitzer.edu/anarchist_archives/malatesta/tar.html.

11. Alexander Berkman, "What Is Communist Anarchism?" *The Anarchist Library* (1929), http://theanarchistlibrary.org/HTML/Alexander_Berkman__What_Is_Communist_Anarchism_.html.

12. David Graeber, "Revolution in Reverse," *Infoshop News*, October 16, 2007, http://news.infoshop.org/article.php?story=2007graeber-revolution-reverse.

13. Gordon, "Anarchism: The A Word."

14. Goldman, *Anarchism and Other Essays*, 71.

15. Voltairine de Cleyre, "Direct Action," *Anarchy Archives* (1912), http://dwardmac.pitzer.edu/Anarchist_Archives/bright/cleyre/direct.html.

16. Ibid.

17. Ibid.

18. Gordon, "Anarchism: The A Word."

19. Graeber, *Direct Action*, 203.

20. Ibid., 204–5.

21. Fernandez, *Policing Dissent*, 53.

22. Ibid.

23. De Cleyre, "Direct Action."

24. Starhawk, *Webs of Power*, 228.

25. Gordon, "Anarchism: The A Word"; Graeber, *Direct Action*, 210–11.

26. Graeber, *Direct Action*, 210.

27. Rob Sparrow, "Anarchist Politics and Direct Action," *Spunk Library* (n.d.), http://www.spunk.org/texts/intro/sp001641.html.

28. Graeber, *Direct Action*, 208.

29. Starhawk, *Webs of Power*, 208.

30. Francis Dupuis-Déri, "The Black Blocs Ten Years after Seattle," *Journal for the Study of Radicalism* 4, no. 2 (2010): 47, 53.

31. Ibid., 47–49.

32. Ibid., 47.

33. Ibid., 57.

34. Graeber, *Direct Action*, 407; Dupuis-Déri, "The Black Blocs," 56.

35. Dupuis-Déri, "The Black Blocs," 60.

36. Graeber, *Direct Action*, 288, 352.

37. Dupuis-Déri, "The Black Blocs," 60–61.

38. Graeber, *Direct Action*, 407.

39. Ibid.

40. Dupuis-Déri, "The Black Blocs," 49.

41. Starhawk, *Webs of Power*, 122–23.

42. Ibid.

43. Mike Kaulbars, "Diversity of Tactics: The Noise before Defeat," *News Junkie Post*, July 26, 2010, http://newsjunkiepost.com/2010/07/26/diversity-of-tactics-the-noise-before-defeat/.

44. Dupuis-Déri, "The Black Blocs," 73.

45. Starhawk, *Webs of Power*, 122.

46. Teoman Gee, "Militancy beyond Black Blocs: An Essay," *Alpine Anarchist Productions*, December 2001, 7.

47. Ibid., 10.

48. Ibid.

49. Starhawk, *Webs of Power*, 127.

50. Ibid., 95.

51. Kaulbars, "Diversity of Tactics."

52. Goldman, *Anarchism and Other Essays*, 69.

53. Michael Schmidt and Lucien van der Walt, *Black Flame: The Revolutionary Class Politics of Anarchism and Syndicalism* (Oakland, CA: AK Press, 2009), 19 (emphasis in original).

54. Ibid., 6.

55. Ibid., 134.

56. Edward Abbey, "Theory of Anarchy," in *One Life at a Time, Please* (New York: Macmillan, 1988), 26.

57. Graeber and Grubacic, "Anarchism."

58. Starhawk, *Webs of Power*, 236.

59. Ferrell, *Tearing Down the Streets*, 105, 154.

60. CrimethInc., *Recipes for Disaster*, 11.

61. Graeber, *Direct Action*, 10–11 (emphasis in original).

62. Richard J. F. Day, "Hegemony, Affinity and the Newest Social Movements: At the End of the 00s," in *Post-Anarchism: A Reader*, ed. Duane Rousselle and Süreyyya Evren, 107.

63. Landauer, *Revolution and Other Writings*, 214.

64. Jarret S. Lovell, *Crimes of Dissent: Civil Disobedience, Criminal Justice and the Politics of Conscience* (New York: New York University Press, 2009), 14; CrimethInc., "Fighting for Our Lives."

65. Graeber, *Direct Action*, 527 (quoting CrimethInc.).

66. Howard J. Ehrlich, "How to Get from Here to There: Building Revolutionary Transfer Culture," in *Reinventing Anarchy, Again*, ed. Howard J. Ehrlich (San Francisco, CA: AK Press, 1996), 349.

67. Milstein, *Anarchism and Its Aspirations*, 43.

68. Jeff Shantz, *Constructive Anarchy: Building Infrastructures of Resistance* (Burlington, VT: Ashgate, 2010), 4.

69. Gordon, *Anarchy Alive!* 35.

70. Ibid., 38.

71. Malatesta, "The Anarchist Revolution."

72. Graeber and Grubacic, "Anarchism."

73. Graeber, *Direct Action*, 218, 236.

74. Ward, *Anarchy in Action*, 87.

75. Amster, "Anarchy, Utopia," 298.

76. Curious George Brigade, "The End of Arrogance: Decentralization and Anarchist Organizing," *Infoshop News*, August 8, 2002, http://news.infoshop .org/article.php?story=02/08/08/4834233.

77. Wikipedia, "List of Anarchist Organizations," http://en.wikipedia.org/ wiki/List_of_anarchist_organizations.

78. Food Not Bombs, "Frequently Asked Questions," http://www.food notbombs.net/faq.html.

79. Ibid.

80. Wikipedia, "Food Not Bombs," http://en.wikipedia.org/wiki/Food_Not _Bombs.

81. Lovell, *Crimes of Dissent*, 13.

82. Ferrell, *Tearing Down the Streets*, 44.

83. Graeber, *Direct Action*, 236.

84. Amster, "Anarchy, Utopia," 298.

85. CrimethInc., "Frequently Asked Questions," http://crimethinc.com/ about/faq.html.

86. Ibid.

87. CrimethInc., *Recipes for Disaster*, 4.

88. Wikipedia, "CrimethInc.," http://en.wikipedia.org/wiki/CrimethInc.

89. Ibid., see also Graeber and Grubacic, "Anarchism."

90. Wikipedia, "CrimethInc."

91. Graeber, *Direct Action*, 527.

92. Indymedia, "About Indymedia," http://www.indymedia.org/en/static/ about.shtml.

93. Wikipedia, "Independent Media Center," http://en.wikipedia.org/wiki/ Indymedia.

94. Ibid.

95. Graeber, *Direct Action*, 184.

96. Ibid., 237.

97. Ibid., 472.

Chapter 3

1. Sartwell, *Against the State*, 66–67.

2. Berkman, "What Is Communist Anarchism?" 171.

3. Martin Luther King, Jr., "Beyond Vietnam: A Time to Break the Silence" (Riverside Church, New York, New York, April 4, 1967), http://www.american rhetoric.com/speeches/mlkatimetobreaksilence.htm.

4. Berkman, "What Is Communist Anarchism?" 171.

5. Ibid.

6. Ibid., 169.

7. Graeber, *Direct Action*, 282.

8. Dupuis-Déri, "The Black Blocs," 73.

9. Starhawk, *Webs of Power*, 58–59.

10. Berkman, "What Is Communist Anarchism?" 168.

11. Anthony Parel, *Gandhi, Freedom, and Self-Rule* (Lanham, MD: Lexington Books, 2000), 69.

12. Emma Goldman, "My Further Disillusionment with Russia," 1924, http://www.panarchy.org/goldman/russia.1924.html.

13. Ibid.

14. Emma Goldman, *Red Emma Speaks: An Emma Goldman Reader*, ed. Alix Kates Shulman (Atlantic Highlands, NJ: Humanities Press, 1996).

15. Ira Chernus, *American Nonviolence: The History of an Idea* (Maryknoll, NY: Orbis Books, 2004), http://spot.colorado.edu/~chernus/NonviolenceBook/.

16. Berkman, "What Is Communist Anarchism?" 165, 168; Read, *Anarchy and Order*, 121.

17. Errico Malatesta, "Anarchism and Violence," *Zabalaza Books*, n.d., 1, 4, http://zinelibrary.info/files/Anarchism_and_Violence.pdf.

18. Adam Gabbatt, "Student Protests: After the March," *The Guardian*, November 11, 2010, http://www.guardian.co.uk/commentisfree/2010/nov/11/ student-protests-tuition-fees-london.

19. Scott Kennedy, "Violence and Anarchists: The Two Don't Go Together," *Santa Cruz Sentinel*, January 16, 2011, http://www.santacruzsentinel.com/ opinion/ci_17109835.

20. Kaulbars, "Diversity of Tactics."

21. Sartwell, *Against the State*, 13.

22. Starhawk, *Webs of Power*, 94.

23. William T. Hathaway, "Anarchists for Peace," *Dissident Voice*, February 2, 2011, http://dissidentvoice.org/2011/02/anarchists-for-peace/.

24. Starhawk, *Webs of Power*, 224.

25. Gordon, *Anarchy Alive!* 93.

26. April Carter, "Anarchism and Violence," in *Anarchism (Nomos XIX)*, ed. J. Roland Pennock and John W. Chapman (New York: New York University Press, 1978), 327.

27. Malatesta, "Anarchism and Violence," 3; Goldman, "My Further Disillusionment with Russia."

28. Bart de Ligt, *The Conquest of Violence: An Essay on War and Revolution* (London: Pluto Press, 1989), 75.

29. Landauer, *Revolution and Other Writings*, 214.

30. Bryan Farrell, "Vandalism, a Dead-End Tactic at Toronto G20 Demonstrations," *Waging Nonviolence*, June 28, 2010, http://wagingnonviolence .org/2010/06/vandalism-a-dead-end-tactic-at-toronto-g20-demonstrations/.

31. Maria L. La Ganga, "Oakland Officials Praise Response to Violence after BART Shooting Verdict," *Los Angeles Times*, July 10, 2010, http://articles .latimes.com/2010/jul/10/local/la-me-0710-oakland-20100710. See also Andy Chan, "Anarchists, Violence and Social Change: Perspectives from Today's Grassroots," *Anarchist Studies* 3, no. 1 (Spring 1999): 45: "Police and senior figures in government attribute (publicly at least) many commotions to anarchists . . . and you will find regular allusions to the provocations of 'outside anarchist agitators.' "

32. Ali Winston, "Anarchists, the FBI and the Aftermath of the Oscar Grant Murder Trial," *KALW News*, January 26, 2011, http://kalwnews.org/audio/ 2011/01/26/anarchists-fbi-and-aftermath-oscar-grant-murder-trial_811029 .html.

33. Ibid.

34. Fernandez, *Policing Dissent*, 157.

35. Ibid., 157–60.

36. Gabbatt, "Student Protests"; Kaulbars, "Diversity of Tactics."

37. Carter, "Anarchism and Violence," 326, 330.

38. Max Harrold, "New Police Unit Targeting Anarchists Comes Under Fire," *Vancouver Sun*, July 16, 2011, http://www.vancouversun.com/news/ police+unit+targeting+anarchists+comes+under+fire/5112795/story.html.

39. Ian Dunt, "Police Call for Information on Anarchists," *Politics.co.uk*, July 31, 2011, http://www.politics.co.uk/news/2011/07/31/police-call-for -information-on-anarchists.

40. Craig Rosebraugh, "Hit 'Em Where It Hurts," *The Anarchist Library*, Summer 2003, http://theanarchistlibrary.org/HTML/Craig_Rosebraugh__Hit__Em _Where_it_Hurts.html.

41. Gordon, *Anarchy Alive!* 84; Graeber, *Direct Action*, 224.

42. The Anarchist Studies Network, "What Anarchism Really Means," *The Guardian*, November 18, 2010, http://www.guardian.co.uk/commentisfree/ 2010/nov/18/anarchism-direct-action-student-protests.

43. Ibid.

44. Associated Press, "European Anarchists Grow More Violent, Coordinated," *USA Today*, December 28, 2010, http://www.usatoday.com/ news/world/2010-12-28-european-anarchists_N.htm.

45. Stephan Faris, "Who Are the Anarchists behind the Rome Embassy Bombs?" *Time*, December 24, 2010, http://www.time.com/time/world/article/ 0,8599,2039647,00.html.

46. Associated Press, "European Anarchists."

47. Libertäre Aktion Winterthur (Anarchist Action), "No Solidarity with 'Anarchist' Letter Bombers," *Anarkismo*, January 6, 2011, http://www .anarkismo.net/article/18439.

48. Ward Churchill, *Pacifism as Pathology: Reflections on the Role of Armed Struggle in North America* (Winnipeg, MB: Arbeiter Ring, 1998); Peter Gelderloos, *How Nonviolence Protects the State* (Cambridge, MA: South End Press, 2007).

49. Derrick Jensen, "Actions Speak Louder Than Words," *The Earth First! Journal* (September/October 1998), http://www.derrickjensen.org/work/published/essays-interviews/actions-speak-louder-than-words/.

50. Barclay, *People Without Government*, 143–44.

51. Goldman, *Red Emma Speaks*, 207.

52. De Ligt, *The Conquest of Violence*, 72.

53. Ibid., 81.

54. Graeber, *Direct Action*, 225.

55. Ibid., 408.

56. Gordon, *Anarchy Alive!* 80, 107–8.

57. Chaz Bufe, "Anarchism: What It Is & What It Isn't," *See Sharp Press*, 2003, Tucson, AZ http://www.seesharppress.com/anarchismwhatis.html.

58. Libertarian Socialist Organization, "You Can't Blow Up a Social Relationship—The Anarchist Case against Terrorism," Anarres Book Collective, 1979, http://libcom.org/book/export/html/122.

59. Judi Bari, "Earth First! and the FBI," in *States of Confinement: Policing, Detention, and Prisons*, ed. Joy James (New York: Palgrave Macmillan, 2000), 330.

60. Churchill, *Pacifism as Pathology*, 45 (emphasis in original).

61. Ibid., 103.

62. Gelderloos, *Nonviolence Protects the State*, 87, 96–97.

63. Ibid., 96.

64. De Ligt, *The Conquest of Violence*, 75.

65. Read, *Anarchy and Order*, 116.

66. Carter, "Anarchism and Violence," 324.

67. Carissa Honeywell, *The British Anarchist Tradition: Herbert Read, Alex Comfort, and Colin Ward* (London: Continuum, 2011), 5, 12.

68. Berkman, "What Is Communist Anarchism?" 205.

69. Carter, "Anarchism and Violence," 334, 336.

70. Quoted in Dupuis-Déri, "The Black Blocs," 58.

71. Graeber, *Direct Action*, 285.

72. Read, *Anarchy and Order*, 129.

73. See Andrew Cornell, "Anarchism and the Movement for a New Society: Direct Action and Prefigurative Community in the 1970s and 80s," *Perspectives on Anarchist Theory*, 2009, http://www.anarchiststudies.org/node/292; Morris, "Anthropology and Anarchism," 39.

74. Starhawk, *Webs of Power*, 211–12.

75. Graeber, *Direct Action*, 224.

76. Ibid., 225.

77. Marshall, *Demanding the Impossible*, 374.

78. Tolstoy, *Government Is Violence*, 8.

79. Ibid., 12–13.

80. Ibid., 15.

81. Ibid., 10–11.

82. Ibid., 10.

83. Ibid., 18.

84. Josh Fattal, "Was Gandhi an Anarchist?" *Peace Power: Berkeley's Journal of Principled Nonviolence and Conflict Transformation* 2, no.1 (Winter 2006): 4–5.

85. Srinivasa Murthy, *Mahatma Gandhi and Leo Tolstoy Letters* (Long Beach, CA: Long Beach Publications, 1987), 189.

86. Ibid.

87. Marshall, *Demanding the Impossible*, 422.

88. Mohandas Gandhi, Benares Hindu University Speech (Benares, India, [February 4, 1916]), http://www.emersonkent.com/speeches/benares_hindu _university_speech.htm.

89. Marshall, *Demanding the Impossible*, 423.

90. Ibid., 425.

91. Starhawk, *Webs of Power*, 95.

92. Dupuis-Déri, "The Black Blocs," 64.

93. Kaulbars, "Diversity of Tactics."

94. Jensen, "Actions Speak Louder"; Gelderloos, *Nonviolence Protects the State*, 59.

95. Libertarian Socialist Organization, "You Can't Blow Up."

96. Ibid.

Chapter 4

1. Andrew Flood, "Anarchism and the Environmental Movement," *Struggle* (April 1995), http://struggle.ws/talks/envir_anarchism.html.

2. Daniel Guérin, *Anarchism: From Theory to Practice*, trans. Mary Klopper (New York: Monthly Review Press, 1970).

3. Chernus, *American Nonviolence*.

4. David Watson, "Against the Megamachine: Empire and the Earth," in *Environmental Philosophy: From Animal Rights to Radical Ecology*, 4th ed., ed. Michael E. Zimmerman et al. (Upper Saddle River, NJ: Pearson Prentice Hall, 2005), 488.

5. For example, Vandana Shiva, *Earth Democracy: Justice, Sustainability, and Peace* (Cambridge, MA: South End Press, 2005); Joel Kovel, *The Enemy of Nature: The End of Capitalism or the End of the World?* 2nd ed. (London: Zed Books, 2007); John Bellamy Foster, Brett Clark, and Richard York, *The Ecological Rift: Capitalism's War on the Earth* (New York: Monthly Review Press, 2010).

6. Kovel, *The Enemy of Nature*.

7. Elisée Reclus, *Evolution and Revolution*, 7th ed. (London: W. Reeves, 1891), http://dwardmac.pitzer.edu/anarchist_archives/coldoffthepresses/evandrev.html.

8. Graham Purchase, *Anarchism & Environmental Survival* (Tucson, AZ: See Sharp Press, 1994), 53.

9. Ibid., 82.

10. Marshall, *Demanding the Impossible*, 340.

11. Goldman, *Anarchism and Other Essays*, 58, 64.

12. Kropotkin, *Mutual Aid*, 82.

13. Graham Purchase, "Anarchism and Ecology: The Historical Relationship," *Jura Media*, 1998, 13.

14. Green Anarchist International Association (GAIA), "The Ecoanarchist Manifesto," June 2008, http://www.anarchy.no/eam.html.

15. Brian Morris, *Ecology and Anarchism* (Malvern, UK: Images Publishing, 1996), 58.

16. Milstein, *Anarchism and Its Aspirations*, 59.

17. Chernus, *American Nonviolence*.

18. Purchase, *Anarchism & Environmental Survival*, 87.

19. GAIA, "The Ecoanarchist Manifesto."

20. David Orton, "My Path to Left Biocentrism, Part V: Deep Ecology and Anarchism," *Green Web Bulletin* 72 (2001), http://home.ca.inter.net/~greenweb/GW72-Path.html.

21. Alan Carter, "Saving Nature and Feeding People," *Environmental Ethics* 26, no. 4 (2004): 341.

22. Bookchin, "What Is Social Ecology?" 365 (emphasis in original).

23. John Clark, "What Is Social Ecology?" in *Renewing the Earth: The Promise of Social Ecology*, ed. John Clark (London: Green Print, 1990), 5–7 (emphasis in original).

24. Bill Devall and George Sessions, *Deep Ecology: Living as if Nature Mattered* (Salt Lake City, UT: Peregrine Smith Books, 1985).

25. John Clark, "Political Ecology: Introduction," in *Environmental Philosophy: From Animal Rights to Radical Ecology*, 4th ed., ed. Michael E. Zimmerman et al. (Upper Saddle River, NJ: Pearson Prentice Hall, 2005), 381.

26. Paul Messersmith-Glavin, "Between Social Ecology and Deep Ecology: Gary Snyder's Ecological Philosophy," *Perspective on Anarchist Theory*, 2010, http://www.anarchist-studies.org/node/496.

27. Ibid.

28. Ibid.

29. Gary Snyder, *The Practice of the Wild* (San Francisco, CA: North Point Press, 1990), 181.

30. Mick Smith, "Wild-life: Anarchy, Ecology, and Ethics," *Environmental Politics* 16, no. 3 (June 2007): 479 (emphasis in original); Marshall, *Demanding the Impossible*, 684.

31. Smith, "Wild-life," 479.

32. Ibid., 480.

33. Ibid. (emphasis in original).

34. Fredy Perlman, *Against His-story, Against Leviathan* (Detroit, MI: Black and Red, 1983).

35. Derrick Jensen, *Endgame, Volume 1: The Problem of Civilization* (New York: Seven Stories Press, 2006).

36. John Zerzan, ed., *Against Civilization: Readings and Reflections* (Port Townsend, WA: Feral House, 2005).

37. John Zerzan, *Future Primitive and Other Essays* (Brooklyn, NY: Autonomedia, 1994), 16.

38. Smith, "Wild-life," 472.

39. Elisa Aaltola, "Green Anarchy: Deep Ecology and Primitivism," in *Anarchism and Moral Philosophy*, ed. Benjamin Franks and Matthew Wilson (New York: Palgrave Macmillan, 2011), 177–78.

40. Jason McQuinn, "Why I Am Not a Primitivist," *Anarchy: A Journal of Desire Armed* (Summer 2001), http://www.postcivilized.net/2010/07/why-i-am-not-a-primitivist/.

41. Lawrence Jarach, "Why I Am Not an Anti-Primitivist," *Anarchy: A Journal of Desire Armed* (Summer 2009), http://www.anarchymag.org/node/1538; Clark, "What Is Social Ecology?", http://anarchistnews.org/node/11324

42. Marshall, *Demanding the Impossible*, 688.

43. Ibid.; Jarach, "Not an Anti-Primitivist."

44. Kingsley Widmer, "Eco-Anarchism, Unto Primitivism," *Social Anarchism* 18 (1993): 49.

45. Bookchin, "What Is Social Ecology?" 370.

46. McQuinn, "Not a Primitivist."

47. Murray Bookchin, *Post-Scarcity Anarchism* (Berkeley, CA: The Ramparts Press, 1971), 10.

48. Marshall, *Demanding the Impossible*, 683.

49. Ibid.

50. Derrick Jensen and George Draffan, *Welcome to the Machine: Science, Surveillance, and the Culture of Control* (White River Junction, VT: Chelsea Green Publishing, 2004).

51. Derrick Jensen, "Published," http://www.derrickjensen.org/published.html.

52. Marshall, *Demanding the Impossible*, 688.

53. Ibid., 687.

54. Zerzan, *Future Primitive*, 73.

55. Watson, "Against the Megamachine," 479–80.

56. Ibid., 481.

57. Michael Truscello, "Imperfect Necessity and the Mechanical Continuation of Everyday Life: A Post-Anarchist Politics of Technology," in *Post-Anarchism: A Reader*, ed. Duane Rousselle and Süreyyya Evren (London: Pluto Press, 2011), 250.

58. Ibid., 257 (emphasis in original).

59. Ibid.

60. Ibid.

61. Gordon, *Anarchy Alive!* 117.

62. Ibid., 110–11.

63. Ibid., 119.

64. Ibid., 127.

65. Ibid.

66. Brendan Story and Margie Lincita, "The Green Scare and Eco-prisoners: A Brief Synopsis," in *Let Freedom Ring: A Collection of Documents from the Movements to Free U.S. Political Prisoners*, ed. Matt Meyer (Oakland, CA: PM Press, 2008), 692.

67. Dave Foreman and Bill Haywood, eds., *Ecodefense: A Field Guide to Monkeywrenching*, 3rd ed. (Chico, CA: Abbzug Press, 1993), 8.

68. Ibid., 8–9.

69. Ibid., 9–10.

70. Ibid., 9.

71. James F. Jarboe, "Congressional Testimony: The Threat of Eco-Terrorism," Federal Bureau of Investigation, February 12, 2002, http://www .fbi.gov/news/testimony/the-threat-of-eco-terrorism.

72. Ibid.; Henry Schuster, "Domestic Terror: Who's Most Dangerous?" CNN.com, August 24, 2005, http://www.cnn.com/2005/US/08/24/schuster .column.

73. Robert Mueller III, "Statement Before the Senate Select Committee on Intelligence," Federal Bureau of Investigation, January 11, 2007, http://www .fbi.gov/news/testimony/global-threats-to-the-u.s.-and-the-fbis-response.

74. Story and Lincita, "The Green Scare," 698.

75. CrimethInc. Workers' Collective, "Analysis of Green Scare Repression: For Those Who Came In Late," in *Let Freedom Ring: A Collection of Documents from the Movements to Free U.S. Political Prisoners*, ed. Matt Meyer (Oakland, CA: PM Press, 2008), 708.

76. Larry Hendricks, "Ecoterror Suspect Called 'Mastermind,' " *Arizona Daily Sun*, December 17, 2005, A1.

77. Jarboe, "Congressional Testimony."

78. Thomas C. Shevory, "Monkeywrenching: Practice in Search of a Theory," in *Environmental Crime and Criminality: Theoretical and Practical Issues*, ed. Sally M. Edwards, Terry D. Edwards, and Charles B. Fields (New York: Garland Publishing, 2006), 190–95.

79. Quoted in MotherJones.com, "Talkback: Ecoterrorists or Earth's Defenders?" *Mother Jones*, February 14, 2002, http://motherjones.com/politics/ 2002/02/talkback-ecoterrorists-or-earths-defenders.

80. N. B. Woolf, "HR 5429 Takes Aim at Animal Rights Terrorism," *National Animal Interest Alliance*, 2000, http://www.naiaonline.org/body/ articles/archives/cunning.htm.

81. Jim Burns, "Legislation Would Combat Eco-Terrorism," CNS News, June 13, 2001, http://www.cnsnews.com/node/19720.

82. Judith Lewis, "Earth to ELF: Come In, Please," *LA Weekly*, December 22, 2005, http://www.laweekly.com/2005-12-22/news/earth-to-elf-come-in-please/.

83. Brian Denson and James Long, "Eco-Terrorism Sweeps the American West," *The Oregonian*, September 26, 1999, http://www.furcommission.com/resource/perspectdenson1.htm.

84. Earth First! "Free's Statement at His Sentencing," *EarthFirst! Journal* (August–September 2001).

85. Various Authors, "Articles on Animal and Earth Liberation Struggles from 'Green Anarchist,' " The Anarchist Library, 2003, http://theanarchistlibrary.org/HTML/Various_Authors__Articles_on_Animal_and_Earth_Liberation_Struggles_from__Green_Anarchist.html.

86. See generally Randall Amster, "Perspectives on Ecoterrorism: Catalysts, Conflations, and Casualties," *Contemporary Justice Review* 9, no. 3 (September 2006): 287–301.

87. Various Authors, "Articles on Animal and Earth Liberation Struggles.' "

88. CrimethInc. Workers' Collective, "Green Scare Repression," 712.

89. Messersmith-Glavin, "Gary Snyder's Ecological Philosophy."

90. De Cleyre, "Direct Action."

91. Goldman, *Anarchism and Other Essays*, 68; Peter Kropotkin, *Fields, Factories and Workshops* (New Brunswick, NJ: Transaction, 1993), 160–61; Rocker, *Anarchism and Anarcho-Syndicalism*, 7.

92. Murray Bookchin, *The Ecology of Freedom: The Emergence and Dissolution of Hierarchy* (Montreal: Black Rose Books, 1991), 335.

93. Ibid.

94. Watson, "Against the Megamachine," 491.

95. Purchase, *Anarchism & Environmental Survival*, 154.

96. Tina Lynn Evans, "Understanding the Political Economy of Enforced Dependency in the Globalized World: A Springboard for Sustainability-Oriented Action," Feasta: The Foundation for the Economics of Sustainability, 2011, http://www.feasta.org/documents/enforced_dependency/contents.html.

97. Michael N. Nagler, "Crisis or Opportunity? A Gandhian Answer to Financial Collapse," *New Clear Vision*, August 15, 2011, http://www.newclearvision.com/2011/08/15/crisis-or-opportunity/.

98. Starhawk, *Webs of Power*, 38, 238.

99. See Food Not Bombs, http://www.foodnotbombs.net/; The Really, Really Free Market, http://www.reallyreallyfree.org/; Earth Activist Training, http://www.earthactivisttraining.org/; Gordon, *Anarchy Alive!* 137; and Errol Schweizer, "Free the Land! The Victory Gardens Project," Green Anarchy, n.d., http://greenanarchy.webs.com/victorygardenproject.htm.

100. Graham Purchase, *Anarchism and Ecology* (Montreal: Black Rose Books, 1997), 26.

101. Ibid.

102. Ibid.

103. John Clark, "Bridging the Unbridgeable Chasm: On Bookchin's Critique of the Anarchist Tradition," *Perspectives on Anarchist Theory*, 2009, http://www.anarchist-studies.org/node/231.

104. Purchase, *Anarchism and Ecology*, 77; Purchase, *Anarchism & Environmental Survival*, 147.

105. Watson, "Against the Megamachine," 492.

106. Bookchin, *Post-Scarcity Anarchism*, 69.

107. John P. Clark, *The Anarchist Moment: Reflections on Culture, Nature, and Power* (Montreal: Black Rose Books, 1984), 160.

108. Messersmith-Glavin, "Gary Snyder's Ecological Philosophy."

109. Chernus, *American Nonviolence*.

110. Messersmith-Glavin, "Gary Snyder's Ecological Philosophy."

111. Peter Gelderloos, "More Wood for the Fire: Capitalist Solutions for Global Warming," *CounterPunch*, February 1, 2010, http://www .counterpunch.org/gelderloos02012010.html.

112. Ibid.

113. Ibid.

114. Brian Tokar, *Toward Climate Justice: Perspectives on the Climate Crisis and Social Change* (Porsgrunn, Norway: Communalism Press, 2010), 95.

115. Ibid.

116. Ibid., 119, 124.

117. Ibid., 120–23.

118. Ibid., 98.

Chapter 5

1. Kropotkin, *Fugitive Writings*, 142.

2. Howard H. Harriott, "Defensible Anarchy?" *International Philosophical Quarterly* 33, no. 3 (1993): 338.

3. Kropotkin, *Mutual Aid*, 92; Kropotkin, *Fugitive Writings*, 139.

4. Friends of the RNC 8, "About," http://rnc8.org/about/.

5. Quoted in Shantz, *Constructive Anarchy*, 9.

6. Stephen Condit, *Anarchist Studies: Two Inquiries into the Ideal and Material Purposes of Philosophical Anarchism* (Finland, Joensuu: University of Joensuu, 1987), 56.

7. Murray Bookchin, "Social Anarchism or Lifestyle Anarchism: An Unbridgeable Chasm," *Anarchy Archives*, 1995, http://dwardmac.pitzer.edu/ Anarchist_Archives/bookchin/soclife.html.

8. Ibid.

9. L. Susan Brown, *The Politics of Individualism: Liberalism, Liberal Feminism, and Anarchism*, 2nd ed. (Montreal: Black Rose Books, 2002), 2, 12.

10. Kropotkin, *Fugitive Writings*, 152.

11. Larry Tifft and Dennis Sullivan, *The Struggle to Be Human: Crime, Criminology, and Anarchism* (Orkney, UK: Cienfuegos Press, 1980), 146.

12. Read, *Anarchy and Order*, 145.

13. Peter Kropotkin, *Ethics: Origin and Development* (New York: Benjamin Blom, 1968), 61.

14. Ibid., 50.

15. Ibid., 51–59.

16. May, "Post-Structuralist Political Theory," 171.

17. Zerzan, *Future Primitive*, 34.

18. Kropotkin, *Fugitive Writings*, 144–45.

19. Ibid., 141.

20. Michael Taylor, *The Possibility of Cooperation: Studies in Rationality and Social Change* (New York: Cambridge, 1987), 168.

21. Ibid., 169.

22. Zygmunt Bauman, *Postmodern Ethics* (Cambridge, MA: Blackwell, 1993), 31.

23. Kropotkin, *Kropotkin's Revolutionary Pamphlets*, 197.

24. L. Susan Brown, "Beyond Feminism: Anarchism and Human Freedom," in *Reinventing Anarchy, Again*, ed. Howard J. Ehrlich (San Francisco, CA: AK Press, 1996), 150; Kropotkin, *Fugitive Writings*, 141.

25. Kathy E. Ferguson, "Toward a New Anarchism," *Contemporary Crises* 7 (January 1983): 41.

26. Peggy Kornegger, "Anarchism: The Feminist Connection," in *Reinventing Anarchy, Again*, ed. Howard J. Ehrlich (San Francisco, CA: AK Press, 1996), 158; Kropotkin, *Mutual Aid*, 22.

27. Teoman Gee, "Antiindividualistic Individuality: A Concept," *Alpine Anarchist Productions*, January 2003, 15 (emphasis in original).

28. Ibid., 7 (emphasis in original).

29. Morris, "Anthropology and Anarchism," 41.

30. Horrox, *A Living Revolution*, 4.

31. Kropotkin, *Kropotkin's Revolutionary Pamphlets*, 201.

32. Ibid., 210.

33. Ibid., 214.

34. Randall Amster, "Chasing Rainbows? Utopian Pragmatics and the Search for Anarchist Communities," *Anarchist Studies* 9, no. 1 (March 2001): 29–52; Randall Amster, "Restoring (Dis)order: Sanctions, Resolutions, and 'Social Control' in Anarchist Communities," *Contemporary Justice Review* 6, no. 1 (March 2003): 9–23.

35. Ward, *Anarchy in Action*, 126.

36. Emily Gaarder, "Addressing Violence against Women: Alternatives to State-Based Law and Punishment," in *Contemporary Anarchist Studies: An Introductory Anthology of Anarchy in the Academy*, ed. Randall Amster et al. (New York: Routledge, 2009), 54.

37. Tifft and Sullivan, *Crime, Criminology, and Anarchism*, 3.

38. Ibid., 7, 39–40.

39. Ibid., 47, 178.

40. Ibid., 146.

41. Alexei Borovoi, "Anarchism and Law," *Friends of Malatesta*, n.d., 2.

42. Ibid., 4.

43. Giovanni Baldelli, *Social Anarchism* (New York: Aldine-Atherton, 1971), 150–51.

44. Tifft and Sullivan, *Crime, Criminology, and Anarchism*, 44.

45. Ibid., 72.

46. Harold Barclay, *Culture and Anarchism* (London: Freedom Press, 1997), 154 (emphases in original).

47. Ibid., 153–55.

48. Borovoi, "Anarchism and Law," 8.

49. Tifft and Sullivan, *Crime, Criminology, and Anarchism*, 74.

50. Jeff Ferrell, "Against the Law: Anarchist Criminology," *Social Anarchism* 25 (1998), http://library.nothingness.org/articles/SA/en/display _printable/127.

51. Dennis Sullivan and Larry Tifft, *Restorative Justice: Healing the Foundations of Our Everyday Lives* (Monsey, NY: Willow Tree Press, 2001), 160.

52. Ibid., 119.

53. Ibid., 143.

54. Henry David Thoreau, *Civil Disobedience*, 1849, http://www.vcu.edu/engweb/transcendentalism/authors/thoreau/civil/.

55. Robert Paul Wolff, *In Defense of Anarchism* (New York: Harper and Row, 1970), 29, 42.

56. Tifft and Sullivan, *Crime, Criminology, and Anarchism*, 58.

57. Sullivan and Tifft, *Restorative Justice*, 10.

58. Kropotkin, *Kropotkin's Revolutionary Pamphlets*, 218, 235.

59. Ibid., 235; Kropotkin, *Other Writings*, 238.

60. Graham Purchase, "Evolution and Revolution," *Jura Media*, 1996, 107.

61. Donald Black, *The Behavior of Law* (New York: Academic Press, 1976), 129.

62. Barclay, *People Without Government*, 97.

63. Larry L. Tifft, "The Coming Redefinitions of Crime: An Anarchist Perspective," *Social Problems* 26, no. 4 (April 1979): 394, 399.

64. Ward, *Anarchy in Action*, 134.

65. Barclay, *People Without Government*, 24–27.

66. Black, *The Behavior of Law*, 126–27.

67. Purchase, "Evolution and Revolution," 84–88.

68. Michael Taylor, *Community, Anarchy and Liberty* (New York: Cambridge, 1982), 83–85.

69. Barclay, *People Without Government*, 24.

70. Purchase, "Evolution and Revolution," 84–88.

71. Barclay, *People Without Government*, 135.

72. Purchase, "Evolution and Revolution," 84, 106.

73. Tifft, "Redefinitions of Crime," 397–98.

74. Barclay, *People Without Government*, 48.

75. Ibid., 48–62.

76. Black, *The Behavior of Law*, 128–29.

77. Purchase, "Evolution and Revolution," 86–87.

78. Baldelli, *Social Anarchism*, 75.

79. Ibid., 86–88.

80. Bookchin, *The Ecology of Freedom*, 43, 55.

81. Black, *The Behavior of Law*, 137.

82. Bakunin, *God and the State*, 33.

83. Ward, *Anarchy in Action*, 28–41; see generally Michael I. Niman, *People of the Rainbow: A Nomadic Utopia* (Knoxville, TN: University of Tennessee Press, 1997).

84. Kropotkin, *Mutual Aid*, 133.

85. Shantz, *Constructive Anarchy*, 159.

86. Ibid., 160.

87. Caroline Estes, "Consensus," in *Reinventing Anarchy, Again*, ed. Howard J. Ehrlich (San Francisco, CA: AK Press, 1996), 369.

88. Tifft, "Redefinitions of Crime," 399.

89. Harriott, "Defensible Anarchy?" 335.

90. Christiania, "Information about Christiania," http://www.christiania. org/; Wikipedia, "Freetown Christiania," http://en.wikipedia.org/wiki/ Freetown_Christiania.

91. Jacques Blum, "Christiania—A Freetown: Slum, Alternative Culture or Social Experiment?" *Working Papers of the National Museum of Denmark*, 1977, 23, 37, 44, 49.

92. Seán M. Sheehan, *Anarchism* (London: Reaktion Books, 2003), 117.

93. Ibid., 118–19.

94. Horrox, *A Living Revolution*, 7.

95. Ibid., 18.

96. Ibid., 63, 76.

97. Ibid., 108–9 (emphasis in original).

98. Bey, *T.A.Z.*, 101 (emphasis in original).

99. Shantz, *Constructive Anarchy*, 150.

100. Ibid.

101. Old Market Autonomous Zone, "Recent Updates," http://a-zone.org/.

102. Ibid.

103. Mondragon Bookstore and Coffeehouse, "Home," http://mondragon.ca/.

104. Mondragon Bookstore and Coffeehouse, *Policy Handbook*, 7th draft, May 2011, http://mondragon.ca/wp-content/uploads/2011/05/PolicyHandbook -May-20111.pdf.

105. Paul Burrows, "Participatory Economics in Theory & Practice," *Z Net*, December 22, 2007, http://www.zcommunications.org/participatory-economics -in-theory-and-practice-by-paul-burrows.

106. ABC No Rio, "About," http://www.abcnorio.org/about/about.html.

107. Ibid.

108. Ibid.

109. ABC No Rio, "Affiliated Projects," http://www.abcnorio.org/affiliated/ affiliated_projects.html.

110. The Iron Rail, "Iron Rail History," http://ironrail.org/about/history/.

111. Ibid.

112. Ibid.

113. Ibid.

114. The Iron Rail, "Policies & Points of Unity," http://ironrail.org/policies/.

115. Anarchist Black Cross Federation, "What Is the ABCF?" http://www .abcf.net/abcf.asp?page=whats2.

116. Anarchist Black Cross Federation, "Four Basic Foundation Principles of Federation," http://www.abcf.net/abcf.asp?page=const2.

117. See generally Randall Amster, "Anarchist Pedagogies for Peace," *Peace Review* 14, no. 4 (December 2002): 433–39.

118. Joel Spring, *A Primer of Libertarian Education* (Montreal: Black Rose Books, 1998), 10.

119. Howard J. Ehrlich, Carol Ehrlich, David DeLeon, and Glenda Morris, "Questions and Answers about Anarchism," in *Reinventing Anarchy, Again*, ed. Howard J. Ehrlich (San Francisco, CA: AK Press, 1996), 15.

120. Ivan Illich, *Deschooling Society* (New York: Harrow Books, 1972), 46.

121. Ibid., 49–50.

122. Ibid., 54.

123. Larry J. Fisk, "Shaping Visionaries: Nurturing Peace through Education," in *Patterns of Conflict, Paths to Peace*, ed. Larry J. Fisk and John L. Schellenberg (New York: Broadview Press, 2000), 177, 184.

124. Ibid., 162.

125. Ibid., 177.

126. Ibid., 180–81.

127. Illich, *Deschooling Society*, 75–76, 81.

128. Ibid., 104.

129. Cf. Foer, "Protest Too Much," 22.

130. Ward, *Anarchy in Action*, 80 (emphases in original).

131. Bakunin, *God and the State*, 40.

132. Ibid., 41–42.

133. Francisco Ferrer, *The Origin and Ideals of the Modern School*, trans. Joseph McCabe (London: Watts and Co., 1913), http://dwardmac.pitzer.edu/ anarchist_archives/bright/ferrer/origin.html.

134. Quoted in Emma Goldman, "Francisco Ferrer and the Modern School," in *Anarchism and Other Essays*, 2nd ed. (New York: Mother Earth Publishing, 1911), 151–72, http://dwardmac.pitzer.edu/Anarchist_Archives/goldman/aando/ferrer.html.

135. Ward, *Anarchy in Action*, 81.

136. Leonard I. Krimerman and Lewis Perry, eds., *Patterns of Anarchy: A Collection of Writings on the Anarchist Tradition* (New York: Anchor Books, 1966), 310; Paulo Freire, *Pedagogy of the Oppressed* (New York: Continuum, 1970) (emphasis in original).

137. Paul Goodman, "Anarchism and the Ideal University," in *Patterns of Anarchy: A Collection of Writings on the Anarchist Tradition*, ed. Leonard I. Krimerman and Lewis Perry (New York: Anchor Books, 1966), 453–54 (emphasis in original).

138. Herbert Read, "Art as the Basis of Libertarian Education," in *Patterns of Anarchy: A Collection of Writings on the Anarchist Tradition*, ed. Leonard I. Krimerman and Lewis Perry (New York: Anchor Books, 1966), 408–410.

139. Tolstoy, *Government Is Violence*, 10.

140. Krimerman and Perry, *Patterns of Anarchy*, 449.

141. Ward, *Anarchy in Action*, 87 (emphasis in original).

142. P. M., *bolo'bolo*, 122–23.

143. Ibid., 123.

144. Free Skool, "About Free Skools," http://freeskool.org/.

145. Judith Suissa, *Anarchism and Education: A Philosophical Perspective* (Oakland, CA: PM Press, 2010), 92.

146. William T. Armaline, "Thoughts on Anarchist Pedagogy and Epistemology," in *Contemporary Anarchist Studies: An Introductory Anthology of Anarchy in the Academy*, ed. Randall Amster et al. (New York: Routledge, 2009), 139.

147. Paul Routledge, "Toward a Relational Ethics of Struggle: Embodiment, Affinity, and Affect," in *Contemporary Anarchist Studies: An Introductory Anthology of Anarchy in the Academy*, ed. Randall Amster et al. (New York: Routledge, 2009), 89.

148. Jamie Heckert, "Listening, Caring, Becoming: Anarchism as an Ethics of Direct Relationships," in *Anarchism and Moral Philosophy*, ed. Benjamin Franks and Matthew Wilson (New York: Palgrave Macmillan, 2011), 199.

149. Ibid., 189–90.

150. Landauer, *Revolution and Other Writings*, 214.

151. Heckert, "Listening, Caring, Becoming," 201.

152. Horrox, *A Living Revolution*, 30.

Chapter 6

1. Barclay, *People Without Government*, 42–54.

2. For example, Frank Fernández, *Cuban Anarchism: The History of a Movement*, trans. Charles Bufe (Tucson, AZ: See Sharp Press, 2001); Colin M.

MacLachlan, *Anarchism and the Mexican Revolution: The Political Trials of Ricardo Flores Magón in the United States* (Los Angeles: University of California Press, 1991); Marshall, *Demanding the Impossible*, 504–18.

3. Marshall, *Demanding the Impossible*, 519–35.

4. James C. Scott, *The Art of Not Being Governed: An Anarchist History of Upland Southeast Asia* (New Haven, CT: Yale University Press, 2009), ix.

5. Mbah and Igariwey, *African Anarchism*, 47, 52.

6. For example, Mohammed Bamyeh, "Anarchist, Liberal, and Authoritarian Enlightenments: Notes from the Arab Spring," *Jadaliyya*, July 30, 2011, http://www.jadaliyya.com/pages/index/2268/anarchist-liberal-and-authoritarian-enlightenments; Horrox, *A Living Revolution*; Uri Gordon, "Right of Reply: Anarchy in the Holy Land!" *Jerusalem Post*, June 12, 2007, http://www.jpost.com/Opinion/Op-EdContributors/Article.aspx?id=64651; Gordon, *Anarchy Alive!*

7. Sebastian Kalicha and Gabriel Kuhn, eds., *Von Jakarta bis Johannesburg: Anarchismus Weltweit* (Münster, Germany: Unrast-Verlag, 2010).

8. Noam Chomsky, *The Chomsky Reader*, ed. James Peck (New York: Pantheon Books, 1987), 321.

9. Ibid. (emphasis in original).

10. Ibid., 322.

11. John Clark, "Anarchism and the Present World Crisis," in *Reinventing Anarchy, Again*, ed. Howard J. Ehrlich (Oakland, CA: AK Press, 1996), 85.

12. Richard Falk, "Anarchism Without Anarchism: Searching for Progressive Politics in the Early 21st Century," *Citizen Pilgrimage*, November 26, 2010, http://richardfalk.wordpress.com/2010/11/26/anarchism-without-anarchism-searching-for-progressive-politics/.

13. Andrej Grubacic, "The Irresistible Charm of Global Anarchism," *The Defenestrator*, March 7, 2010, http://www.defenestrator.org/node/1765.

14. Falk, "Anarchism Without Anarchism."

15. Ibid.

16. Clark, "Anarchism and the Present World Crisis," 86.

17. Prichard, "Anarchism and World Politics," 377, 380.

18. Alex Prichard, "Deepening Anarchism: International Relations and the Anarchist Ideal," *Anarchist Studies* 18, no. 2 (2010): 30, 35.

19. Ibid., 49.

20. Grubacic, "The Irresistible Charm."

21. Clark, "Anarchism and the Present World Crisis," 94.

22. Ibid., 98.

23. Ibid., 94.

24. Workers Solidarity Movement, "Anarchism, Internationalism & the Euro Zone Crisis," *Anarchist News*, July 10, 2011, http://anarchistnews.org/?q=node/14998.

25. Richard Falk, "Is the State a Monster? Pro and Contra Nietzsche," *Z Net*, June 18, 2011, http://www.zcommunications.org/is-the-state-a-monster-pro-and-contra-nietzsche-by-richard-falk.

26. Ibid.
27. Sartwell, *Against the State*, 8–9.
28. Workers Solidarity Movement, "Anarchism, Internationalism."
29. Schmidt and van der Walt, *Black Flame*, 297.
30. MacLachlan, *Anarchism and the Mexican Revolution*, 132.
31. See Uri Gordon, "Israeli Anarchism: Statist Dilemmas and the Dynamics of Joint Struggle," *Anarchist Studies* 15, no. 1 (2007): 10–11.
32. Falk, "Is the State a Monster?"
33. Sartwell, *Against the State*, 9.
34. Schmidt and van der Walt, *Black Flame*, 310.
35. Gordon, "Israeli Anarchism," 12.
36. Shantz, *Constructive Anarchy*, 114.
37. Ibid.
38. Clark, "Anarchism and the Present World Crisis," 99.
39. Richard J. F. Day, *Gramsci Is Dead: Anarchist Currents in the Newest Social Movements* (London: Pluto Press, 2005), 38 (emphasis in original).
40. David Graeber, "Anarchism, Academia, and the Avant-Garde," in *Contemporary Anarchist Studies: An Introductory Anthology of Anarchy in the Academy*, ed. Randall Amster et al. (New York: Routledge, 2009), 105.
41. Day, *Gramsci Is Dead*, 203–4.
42. Ibid., 204.
43. Tadzio Mueller, "Empowering Anarchy: Power, Hegemony and Anarchist Strategy," in *Post-Anarchism: A Reader*, ed. Duane Rousselle and Süreyyya Evren (London: Pluto Press, 2011), 89.
44. Peoples' Global Action, "Organisational Principles," http://www.nadir .org/nadir/initiativ/agp/cocha/principles.htm.
45. Peoples' Global Action, "Hallmarks of Peoples' Global Action," http:// nadir.org/nadir/initiativ/agp/free/pga/hallm.htm.
46. Graeber, *Direct Action*, xii.
47. Ibid., 227.
48. Milstein, *Anarchism and Its Aspirations*, 117–18.
49. Guérin, *Anarchism*, 67.
50. Michael Bakunin, "An Internationalist Federalism," in *No Gods, No Masters: An Anthology of Anarchism*, ed. Daniel Guérin (Oakland, CA: AK Press, 2005), 167.
51. Ibid., 169.
52. Mueller, "Empowering Anarchy," 90.
53. Shantz, *Constructive Anarchy*, 115.
54. Falk, "Anarchism Without Anarchism."
55. Day, *Gramsci Is Dead*, 186, 189.
56. Jeffrey S. Juris, "Anarchism, or the Cultural Logic of Networking," in *Contemporary Anarchist Studies: An Introductory Anthology of Anarchy in the Academy*, ed. Randall Amster et al. (New York: Routledge, 2009), 213.
57. Ibid., 214.

58. Ibid., 215 (emphasis in original).

59. Ibid., 214.

60. Geert Lovink, "Inside Networked Movements: Interview with Jeffrey Juris," *Institute of Network Cultures*, n.d., http://networkcultures.org/wpmu/geert/inside-networked-movements-interview-with-jeffrey-juris/.

61. Ibid. See generally Jeffrey S. Juris, *Networking Futures: The Movements against Corporate Globalization* (Durham, NC: Duke University Press Books, 2008).

62. Graeber, *Direct Action*, xvii.

63. Guérin, *Anarchism*, 69.

64. James Guillaume, "Ideas on Social Organization," in *No Gods, No Masters: An Anthology of Anarchism*, ed. Daniel Guérin (Oakland, CA: AK Press, 2005), 266.

65. Bamyeh, "Notes from the Arab Spring."

66. Ibid.

67. Ibid.

68. For example, Abdul-Ahad et al., "Rescue the Arab Spring."

69. Nathan Schneider, "Mubarak Fears Chaos," *Waging Nonviolence*, February 4, 2011, http://wagingnonviolence.org/2011/02/mubarak-fears-chaos/.

70. Jake Olzen, "A Modest (Anarchist) Proposal for Egypt," *Waging Nonviolence*, February 14, 2011, http://wagingnonviolence.org/2011/02/a-modest-anarchist-proposal-for-egypt/.

71. Ibid.

72. Beyond Resistance, "Egypt Unrest: Interview with an Egyptian Anarchist," Beyond Resistance, February 5, 2011, http://beyondresistance.wordpress.com/2011/02/05/egypt-unrest-interview-with-an-egyptian-anarchist/.

73. Linda Herrera, " 'V for Vendetta': The Other Face of Egypt's Youth Movement," *Jadaliyya*, May 30, 2011, http://www.jadaliyya.com/pages/index/1723/v-for-vendetta_the-other-face-of-egypts-youth-move.

74. Jason Brownlee, "Egypt's Incomplete Revolution: The Challenge of Post-Mubarak Authoritarianism," *Jadaliyya*, July 5, 2011, http://www.jadaliyya.com/pages/index/2059/egypts-incomplete-revolution_the-challenge-of-post.

75. Asher, "Anarchist Resistance in Israel," *Anarchia*, July 27, 2006, http://anarchia.wordpress.com/2006/07/27/anarchist-resistance-in-israel/.

76. Uri Gordon, "Against the Wall: Anarchist Mobilization in the Israeli-Palestinian Conflict," *Peace & Change* 35, no. 3 (July 2010): 413.

77. Ibid., 415.

78. Ibid., 420.

79. Anarchists Against the Wall, "About AATW," http://awalls.org/about_aatw.

80. Ibid.

81. Amira Hass, "Shin Bet Puts Israeli 'Anarchists' in Crosshairs," *Haaretz*, December 27, 2010, http://www.haaretz.com/print-edition/features/shin-bet-puts-israeli-anarchists-in-crosshairs-1.333140.

82. Gordon, "Right of Reply."

83. Gordon, *Anarchy Alive!* 148–49.

84. Ibid., 139.

85. Ibid., 153.

86. Ibid., 154–56.

87. Gordon, "Against the Wall," 422–24.

88. Gordon, *Anarchy Alive!* 158–59.

89. Horrox, *A Living Revolution*, 118.

90. Bill Templer, "From Mutual Struggle to Mutual Aid: Moving beyond the Statist Impasse in Israel/Palestine," *Borderlands* 2, no. 3 (2003), http://www.borderlands.net.au/vol2no3_2003/templer_impasse.htm (citations omitted).

91. Ibid. (emphasis in original).

92. James Herod, "Palestine: The No-State Solution," February 2009, http://www.jamesherod.info/index.php?sec=paper&id=63&print=y&PHPSESSID=874c500f14218d34d24d0df6f0992eff.

93. Randall Amster, "The No-State Solution: Can the Israel-Palestine Conflict Provide a Path to Peace?" *New Clear Vision*, June 25, 2011, http://www.newclearvision.com/2011/06/25/the-no-state-solution/.

94. Ibid.

Chapter 7

1. Marco Giugni, "How Social Movements Matter: Past Research, Present Problems, Future Developments," in *How Social Movements Matter*, ed. Marco Giugni, Doug McAdam, and Charles Tilly (Minneapolis, MN: University of Minnesota Press, 1999), xxii.

2. Ibid., xxix.

3. Baldelli, *Social Anarchism*, 188.

4. Rocker, *Anarchism and Anarcho-Syndicalism*, 14.

5. Milstein, *Anarchism and Its Aspirations*, 121.

6. Krimerman and Perry, eds., *Patterns of Anarchy*, 554.

7. Dupuis-Déri, "The Black Blocs," 69.

8. Howard J. Ehrlich, "Anarchism and Formal Organizations," in *Reinventing Anarchy, Again*, ed. Howard J. Ehrlich (San Francisco, CA: AK Press, 1996), 59.

9. Giugni, "How Social Movements Matter," xxx–xxxi.

10. Heckert, "Listening, Caring, Becoming," 190.

11. Day, *Gramsci Is Dead*, 45; Heckert, "Listening, Caring, Becoming," 190; Killing King Abacus, "Some Notes on Insurrectionary Anarchism," *KKA Publications*, 2001, http://www.batko.se/en_issue2_ch6.php.

12. See generally Marco Giugni, Doug McAdam, and Charles Tilly, eds., *How Social Movements Matter* (Minneapolis, MN: University of Minnesota Press, 1999).

13. Lynd and Grubacic, *Wobblies & Zapatistas*, 90.

14. Howard S. Becker, *Sociological Work: Method and Substance* (Chicago: Aldine, 1970), 62.

15. Abbey, "Theory of Anarchy," 26.

16. Koch, "Poststructuralism," 344.

17. Sartwell, *Against the State*, 115.

18. John D. McCarthy and Mayer N. Zald, "Resource Mobilization and Social Movements: A Partial Theory," *American Journal of Sociology* 82 (1977): 1227.

19. See Tom Knoche, "Organizing Communities," in *Reinventing Anarchy, Again*, ed. Howard J. Ehrlich (San Francisco, CA: AK Press, 1996), 350–67; Dave, "The Intersections of Anarchism and Community Organizing," *NEFAC*, November 9, 2002, http://nefac.net/node/92.

20. Joel Olson, "The Problem with Infoshops and Insurrection: US Anarchism, Movement Building, and the Racial Order," in *Contemporary Anarchist Studies: An Introductory Anthology of Anarchism in the Academy*, ed. Randall Amster et al. (New York: Routledge, 2009), 40–41.

21. Charles Tilly, *Social Movements: 1768–2004* (Boulder, CO: Paradigm Publishers, 2004), 6–7.

22. Charles Tilly, "From Interactions to Outcomes in Social Movements," in *How Social Movements Matter*, ed. Marco Giugni, Doug McAdam, and Charles Tilly (Minneapolis, MN: University of Minnesota Press, 1999), 267.

23. Ibid., 261.

24. Ibid., 263.

25. Ibid., 270.

26. Giugni, "How Social Movements Matter," xvii.

27. William A. Gamson, "Reflections on *The Strategy of Social Protest*," *Sociological Forum* 4, no. 1 (1989): 458–59, 466.

28. Joel Olson, "The Freshness of Fanaticism: The Abolitionist Defense of Zealotry," *Perspectives on Politics* 5, no. 4 (December 2007): 688 (emphasis in original).

29. Martin Luther King, Jr., "Letter from a Birmingham Jail," April 16, 1963, http://www.africa.upenn.edu/Articles_Gen/Letter_Birmingham.html.

30. Gamson, "Reflections," 458, 464.

31. Ibid., 464.

32. Ibid., 466.

33. See Amory Starr, Luis A. Fernandez, Randall Amster, Lesley J. Wood, and Manuel J. Caro, "The Impact of State Surveillance on Political Assembly and Association: A Socio-Legal Analysis," *Qualitative Sociology* 31 (2008): 251–70.

34. Tilly, *Social Movements*, 8.

35. Giugni, "How Social Movements Matter," xxi.

36. See generally Fernandez, *Policing Dissent*.

37. Uri Gordon, "Dark Tidings: Anarchist Politics in the Age of Collapse," in *Contemporary Anarchist Studies: An Introductory Anthology of Anarchy in the Academy*, ed. Randall Amster et al. (New York: Routledge, 2009), 253.

38. See generally Starhawk, *Webs of Power*.

39. Baldelli, *Social Anarchism*, 169.
40. Ward, *Anarchy in Action*, 135.
41. Baldelli, *Social Anarchism*, 177.
42. George Plekhanov, "Anarchist Tactics: A Pageant of Futility, Obstruction, and Decadence?" in *Patterns of Anarchy: A Collection of Writings on the Anarchist Tradition*, ed. Leonard I. Krimerman and Lewis Perry (New York: Anchor Books, 1966), 499.
43. Ward, *Anarchy in Action*, 143.
44. Olson, "The Problem with Infoshops," 35.
45. Ibid., 37.
46. Ibid.
47. Brown, "Beyond Feminism," 150, 154.
48. Ibid., 153 (emphases in original).
49. Charles Tilly, "From Interactions to Outcomes," 258–59.
50. See Jamie Heckert and Richard Cleminson, eds., *Anarchism & Sexuality: Ethics, Relationships and Power* (New York: Routledge, 2011); Liat Ben-Moshe, Dave Hill, Anthony J. Nocella II, and Bill Templer, "*Dis-abling* Capitalism and an Anarchism of 'Radical Equality' in Resistance to Ideologies of Normalcy," in *Contemporary Anarchist Studies: An Introductory Anthology of Anarchism in the Academy*, ed. Randall Amster et al. (New York: Routledge, 2009), 116.
51. Stevphen Shukaitis, "Infrapolitics and the Nomadic Educational Machine," in *Contemporary Anarchist Studies: An Introductory Anthology of Anarchism in the Academy*, ed. Randall Amster et al. (New York: Routledge, 2009), 170.
52. For example, Randall Amster, *Lost in Space: The Criminalization, Globalization, and Urban Ecology of Homelessness* (New York: LFB Scholarly, 2008); Jeff Ferrell, *Empire of Scrounge: Inside the Urban Underground of Dumpster Diving, Trash Picking, and Street Scavenging* (New York: New York University Press, 2006).
53. See, for example, Elaine Leeder, "Let Our Mothers Show the Way," in *Reinventing Anarchy, Again*, ed. Howard J. Ehrlich (San Francisco, CA: AK Press, 1996), 142–48; Tomas Moniz and Jeremy Adam Smith, eds., *Rad Dad: Dispatches from the Frontiers of Fatherhood* (Oakland, CA: PM Press, 2011); Vikki Law, "Creating Space for Kids in Our Movements," *Left Turn*, August 11, 2011, http://www.leftturn.org/creating-space-kids-our-movements; Heckert, "Listening, Caring, Becoming."
54. Marshall, *Demanding the Impossible*, 702.
55. Niman, *People of the Rainbow*.
56. Barclay, *People Without Government*, 150.

Conclusion

1. Chomsky, *Chomsky on Anarchism*, 178.
2. Ward, *Anarchism*, 96–98.
3. Gordon, "Anarchism: The A Word."
4. Marshall, *Demanding the Impossible*, 703.

5. Gordon, "Dark Tidings," 257.

6. Amster et al., *Contemporary Anarchist Studies*, 247.

7. Ibid., 5.

8. Zerzan, *Future Primitive*, 45–46.

9. Kornegger, "Anarchism: The Feminist Connection," 166–67 (emphasis in original).

10. Amster et al., *Contemporary Anarchist Studies*, 247.

11. Starhawk, *Webs of Power*, 252, 255.

12. Ibid., 237–41.

13. Peter Gelderloos, "An Anarchist Solution to Global Warming," *Infoshop News*, September 16, 2010, http://news.infoshop.org/article.php?story=20100 915231738789.

14. Ibid.

15. Marshall, *Demanding the Impossible*, 704.

16. Sartwell, *Against the State*, 99–115.

17. Honeywell, *The British Anarchist Tradition*, 187.

18. Black, *The Behavior of Law*, 137.

19. P. M., *bolo'bolo*, 78.

20. Milstein, *Anarchism and Its Aspirations*, 69.

21. Ibid., 68.

22. Ibid., 67; Kornegger, "Anarchism: The Feminist Connection," 158; Shantz, *Constructive Anarchy*, 183.

23. Chomsky, *Chomsky on Anarchism*, 190.

24. Ibid., 222.

25. Zerzan, *Future Primitive*, 73.

26. Purchase, "Anarchism and Ecology," 19.

27. David L. Hall, "Irony and Anarchy: The Utopian Sensibility," *Alternative Futures: The Journal of Utopian Studies* 2, no. 2 (Spring 1979): 18, 22.

28. Day, *Gramsci Is Dead*, 205.

29. Gordon, *Anarchy Alive!* 134.

30. Bey, *T.A.Z.*, 44–45.

31. Gordon, "Dark Tidings," 249.

32. Ibid.

33. Gordon, *Anarchy Alive!* 136.

34. Bey, *T.A.Z.*, 131; Gordon, *Anarchy Alive!* 138.

35. Gordon, "Dark Tidings," 257.

36. See generally Peter Seyferth, "Anarchism and Utopia," in *Contemporary Anarchist Studies: An Introductory Anthology of Anarchism in the Academy*, ed. Randall Amster et al. (New York: Routledge, 2009), 280–89.

37. Pat Murphy, *The City, Not Long After* (New York: Doubleday, 1989), 161.

38. Starhawk, *The Fifth Sacred Thing* (New York: Bantam, 1993), i.

39. Kim Stanley Robinson, ed., *Future Primitive: The New Ecotopias* (New York: TOR, 1994), 9.

40. Ibid., 9–11.

Bibliography

Aaltola, Elisa. "Green Anarchy: Deep Ecology and Primitivism." In *Anarchism and Moral Philosophy*, edited by Benjamin Franks and Matthew Wilson, 161–85. New York: Palgrave Macmillan, 2011.

Abbey, Edward. "Theory of Anarchy." In *One Life at a Time, Please*. New York: Macmillan, 1988.

Abdul-Ahad, Ghaith, Jack Shenker, Nour Ali, Martin Chulov, and Ian Black. "The Fight to Rescue the Arab Spring." *The Guardian*, July 15, 2011. http://www.guardian.co.uk/world/2011/jul/15/arab-spring-rescue-renewed-protesters.

Amster, Randall. "Anarchism as Moral Theory: Praxis, Property, and the Postmodern." *Anarchist Studies* 6, no. 2 (October 1998): 97–112.

Amster, Randall. "Anarchist Pedagogies for Peace." *Peace Review* 14, no. 4 (December 2002): 433–39.

Amster, Randall. "Anarchy, Utopia, and the State of Things to Come." In *Contemporary Anarchist Studies: An Introductory Anthology of Anarchy in the Academy*, edited by Randall Amster et al., 290–301. New York: Routledge, 2009.

Amster, Randall. "Chasing Rainbows? Utopian Pragmatics and the Search for Anarchist Communities." *Anarchist Studies* 9, no. 1 (March 2001): 29–52.

Amster, Randall. *Lost in Space: The Criminalization, Globalization, and Urban Ecology of Homelessness*. New York: LFB Scholarly, 2008.

Amster, Randall. "The No-State Solution: Can the Israel-Palestine Conflict Provide a Path to Peace?" *New Clear Vision*, June 25, 2011. http://www.newclearvision.com/2011/06/25/the-no-state-solution/.

Amster, Randall. "Perspectives on Ecoterrorism: Catalysts, Conflations, and Casualties." *Contemporary Justice Review* 9, no. 3 (September 2006): 287–301.

Amster, Randall. "Restoring (Dis)order: Sanctions, Resolutions, and 'Social Control' in Anarchist Communities." *Contemporary Justice Review* 6, no. 1 (March 2003): 9–23.

Amster, Randall, Abraham DeLeon, Luis A. Fernandez, Anthony J. Nocella II, and Deric Shannon, eds. *Contemporary Anarchist Studies: An Introductory Anthology of Anarchy in the Academy.* New York: Routledge, 2009.

Antliff, Alan, ed. *Only "A" Beginning: An Anarchist Anthology.* Vancouver, BC: Arsenal Pulp Press, 2004.

Armaline, William T. "Thoughts on Anarchist Pedagogy and Epistemology." In *Contemporary Anarchist Studies: An Introductory Anthology of Anarchy in the Academy,* edited by Randall Amster et al., 136–46. New York: Routledge, 2009.

Asher. "Anarchist Resistance in Israel." *Anarchia,* July 27, 2006. http://anarchia .wordpress.com/2006/07/27/anarchist-resistance-in-israel/.

Associated Press. "European Anarchists Grow More Violent, Coordinated." *USA Today,* December 28, 2010. http://www.usatoday.com/news/world/ 2010-12-28-european-anarchists_N.htm.

Bakunin, Michael. *God and the State.* New York: Dover Publications, 1970.

Bakunin, Michael. "An Internationalist Federalism." In *No Gods, No Masters: An Anthology of Anarchism,* edited by Daniel Guérin, 166–69. Oakland, CA: AK Press, 2005.

Baldelli, Giovanni. *Social Anarchism.* New York: Aldine-Atherton, 1971.

Bamyeh, Mohammed. "Anarchist, Liberal, and Authoritarian Enlightenments: Notes from the Arab Spring." *Jadaliyya,* July 30, 2011. http://www .jadaliyya.com/pages/index/2268/anarchist-liberal-and-authoritarian -enlightenments.

Barclay, Harold. *Culture and Anarchism.* London: Freedom Press, 1997.

Barclay, Harold. *People Without Government: An Anthropology of Anarchy.* Seattle, WA: Left Bank Books, 1990.

Bari, Judi. "Earth First! and the FBI." In *States of Confinement: Policing, Detention, and Prisons,* edited by Joy James, 322–31. New York: Palgrave Macmillan, 2000.

Bauman, Zygmunt. *Postmodern Ethics.* Cambridge, MA: Blackwell, 1993.

Becker, Howard S. *Sociological Work: Method and Substance.* Chicago: Aldine, 1970.

Ben-Moshe, Liat, Dave Hill, Anthony J. Nocella II, and Bill Templer. "*Dis-abling* Capitalism and an Anarchism of 'Radical Equality' in Resistance to Ideologies of Normalcy." In *Contemporary Anarchist Studies: An Introductory Anthology of Anarchism in the Academy,* edited by Randall Amster et al., 113–22. New York: Routledge, 2009.

Berkman, Alexander. "What Is Communist Anarchism?" *The Anarchist Library* (1929). http://theanarchistlibrary.org/HTML/Alexander_Berkman_What _Is_Communist_Anarchism_.html.

Bey, Hakim. *T.A.Z.: The Temporary Autonomous Zone, Ontological Anarchy, Poetic Terrorism*. Brooklyn, NY: Autonomedia, 1991.

Beyond Resistance. "Egypt Unrest: Interview with an Egyptian Anarchist." Beyond Resistance, February 5, 2011. http://beyondresistance.wordpress.com/2011/02/05/egypt-unrest-interview-with-an-egyptian-anarchist/.

Black, Donald. *The Behavior of Law*. New York: Academic Press, 1976.

Blum, Jacques. "Christiania—A Freetown: Slum, Alternative Culture or Social Experiment?" *Working Papers of the National Museum of Denmark*, 1977.

Bookchin, Murray. *The Ecology of Freedom: The Emergence and Dissolution of Hierarchy*. Montreal: Black Rose Books, 1982.

Bookchin, Murray. *Post-Scarcity Anarchism*. Berkeley, CA: The Ramparts Press, 1971.

Bookchin, Murray. "Social Anarchism or Lifestyle Anarchism: An Unbridgeable Chasm." *Anarchy Archives*, 1995. http://dwardmac.pitzer.edu/Anarchist_Archives/bookchin/soclife.html.

Bookchin, Murray. "What Is Social Ecology?" In *Environmental Philosophy: From Animal Rights to Radical Ecology*, 2nd ed., edited by Michael E. Zimmerman et al., 354–73. Englewood Cliffs, NJ: Prentice Hall, 1993.

Borovoi, Alexei. "Anarchism and Law." *Friends of Malatesta*, n.d.

Brown, L. Susan. "Beyond Feminism: Anarchism and Human Freedom." In *Reinventing Anarchy, Again*, edited by Howard J. Ehrlich, 149–55. San Francisco, CA: AK Press, 1996.

Brown, L. Susan. *The Politics of Individualism: Liberalism, Liberal Feminism, and Anarchism*, 2nd ed. Montreal: Black Rose Books, 2002.

Brownlee, Jason. "Egypt's Incomplete Revolution: The Challenge of Post-Mubarak Authoritarianism." *Jadaliyya*, July 5, 2011. http://www.jadaliyya.com/pages/index/2059/egypts-incomplete-revolution_the-challenge-of-post.

Bufe, Chaz. "Anarchism: What It Is & What It Isn't." Tucson, AZ: See Sharp Press, 2003. http://www.seesharppress.com/anarchismwhatis.html.

Burns, Jim. "Legislation Would Combat Eco-Terrorism." CNS News, June 13, 2001. http://www.cnsnews.com/node/19720.

Burrows, Paul. "Participatory Economics in Theory & Practice." *Z Net*, December 22, 2007. http://www.zcommunications.org/participatory-economics-in-theory-and-practice-by-paul-burrows.

Carter, Alan. "Saving Nature and Feeding People." *Environmental Ethics* 26, no. 4 (2004): 339–60.

Carter, April. "Anarchism and Violence." In *Anarchism (Nomos XIX)*, edited by J. Roland Pennock and John W. Chapman, 320–40. New York: New York University Press, 1978.

Chan, Andy. "Anarchists, Violence and Social Change: Perspectives from Today's Grassroots." *Anarchist Studies* 3, no. 1 (Spring 1999): 45–68.

Chernus, Ira. *American Nonviolence: The History of an Idea*. Maryknoll, NY: Orbis Books, 2004. http://spot.colorado.edu/~chernus/NonviolenceBook/.

Chomsky, Noam. *Chomsky on Anarchism*. Edited by Barry Pateman. Oakland, CA: AK Press, 2005.

Chomsky, Noam. *The Chomsky Reader*. Edited by James Peck. New York: Pantheon Books, 1987.

Churchill, Ward. *Pacifism as Pathology: Reflections on the Role of Armed Struggle in North America*. Winnipeg, MB: Arbeiter Ring, 1998.

Clark, John. "Anarchism and the Present World Crisis." In *Reinventing Anarchy, Again*, edited by Howard J. Ehrlich, 85–103. Oakland, CA: AK Press, 1996.

Clark, John. "Bridging the Unbridgeable Chasm: On Bookchin's Critique of the Anarchist Tradition." *Perspectives on Anarchist Theory*, 2009. http://www.anarchist-studies.org/node/231.

Clark, John. "Political Ecology: Introduction." In *Environmental Philosophy: From Animal Rights to Radical Ecology*, 4th ed., edited by Michael E. Zimmerman et al., 361–89. Upper Saddle River, NJ: Pearson Prentice Hall, 2005.

Clark, John. "What Is Social Ecology?" In *Renewing the Earth: The Promise of Social Ecology*, edited by John Clark, 5–11. London: Green Print, 1990.

Clark, John P. *The Anarchist Moment: Reflections on Culture, Nature, and Power*. Montreal: Black Rose Books, 1984.

Clark, John P., and Camille Martin, eds. *Anarchy, Geography, Modernity: The Radical Social Thought of Elisée Reclus*. New York: Lexington Books, 2004.

Condit, Stephen. *Anarchist Studies: Two Inquiries into the Ideal and Material Purposes of Philosophical Anarchism*. Finland: University of Joensuu, 1987.

Cornell, Andrew. "Anarchism and the Movement for a New Society: Direct Action and Prefigurative Community in the 1970s and 80s." *Perspectives on Anarchist Theory*, 2009. http://www.anarchiststudies.org/node/292.

CrimethInc. "Fighting for Our Lives: An Anarchist Primer," n.d. http://crimethinc.com/tools/ffol.html.

CrimethInc. *Recipes for Disaster: An Anarchist Cookbook*. Olympia, WA: CrimethInc. Ex-Workers' Collective, 2004.

CrimethInc. Ex-Workers' Collective. "Analysis of Green Scare Repression: For Those Who Came In Late." In *Let Freedom Ring: A Collection of Documents from the Movements to Free U.S. Political Prisoners*, edited by Matt Meyer, 699–713. Oakland, CA: PM Press, 2008.

Crowder, George. *Classical Anarchism: The Political Thought of Godwin, Proudhon, Bakunin, and Kropotkin*. Oxford, UK: Clarendon Press, 1991.

Curious George Brigade. "The End of Arrogance: Decentralization and Anarchist Organizing." *Infoshop News*, August 8, 2002. http://news.infoshop.org/article.php?story=02/08/08/4834233.

Dave. "The Intersections of Anarchism and Community Organizing." *NEFAC*, November 9, 2002. http://nefac.net/node/92.

Day, Richard J. F. *Gramsci Is Dead: Anarchist Currents in the Newest Social Movements*. London: Pluto Press, 2005.

Day, Richard J. F. "Hegemony, Affinity and the Newest Social Movements: At the End of the 00s." In *Post-Anarchism: A Reader*, edited by Duane Rousselle and Süreyyya Evren, 95–116. London: Pluto Press, 2011.

De Cleyre, Voltairine. "Direct Action." *Anarchy Archives* (1912). http://dwardmac.pitzer.edu/Anarchist_Archives/bright/cleyre/direct.html.

De Ligt, Bart. *The Conquest of Violence: An Essay on War and Revolution*. London: Pluto Press, 1989.

Denson, Brian, and James Long. "Eco-Terrorism Sweeps the American West." *The Oregonian*, September 26, 1999. http://www.furcommission.com/resource/perspectdenson1.htm.

Devall, Bill, and George Sessions. *Deep Ecology: Living as if Nature Mattered*. Salt Lake City, UT: Peregrine Smith Books, 1985.

Dodge, Chris. "Anarchism 101." *Utne Reader*, May–June 2001.

Dunt, Ian. "Police Call for Information on Anarchists," Politics.co.uk, July 31, 2011, http://www.politics.co.uk/news/2011/07/31/police-call-for-information-on -anarchists.

Dupuis-Déri, Francis. "The Black Blocs Ten Years after Seattle." *Journal for the Study of Radicalism* 4, no. 2 (2010): 45–82.

Earth First! "Free's Statement at His Sentencing." *EarthFirst! Journal* (August– September 2001).

Ehrlich, Howard J. "Anarchism and Formal Organizations." In *Reinventing Anarchy, Again*, edited by Howard J. Ehrlich, 56–68. San Francisco, CA: AK Press, 1996.

Ehrlich, Howard J. "How to Get from Here to There: Building Revolutionary Transfer Culture." In *Reinventing Anarchy, Again*, edited by Howard J. Ehrlich, 331–49. San Francisco, CA: AK Press, 1996.

Ehrlich, Howard J., Carol Ehrlich, David DeLeon, and Glenda Morris. "Questions and Answers about Anarchism." In *Reinventing Anarchy, Again*, edited by Howard J. Ehrlich, 4–18. San Francisco, CA: AK Press, 1996.

Estes, Caroline. "Consensus." In *Reinventing Anarchy, Again*, edited by Howard J. Ehrlich, 368–74. San Francisco, CA: AK Press, 1996.

Evans, Tina Lynn. "Understanding the Political Economy of Enforced Dependency in the Globalized World: A Springboard for Sustainability-Oriented Action." Feasta: The Foundation for the Economics of Sustainability, 2011. http://www.feasta.org/documents/enforced_dependency/contents.html.

Evren, Süreyyya. "Introduction: How New Anarchism Changed the World (of Opposition) after Seattle and Gave Birth to Post-Anarchism." In *Post-Anarchism: A Reader*, edited by Duane Rousselle and Süreyyya Evren, 1–19. London: Pluto Press, 2011.

Falk, Richard. "Anarchism without Anarchism: Searching for Progressive Politics in the Early 21st Century." *Citizen Pilgrimage*, November 26, 2010.

http://richardfalk.wordpress.com/2010/11/26/anarchism-without-anarchism-searching-for-progressive-politics/.

Falk, Richard. "Is the State a Monster? Pro and Contra Nietzsche." *Z Net*, June 18, 2011. http://www.zcommunications.org/is-the-state-a-monster-pro-and-contra-nietzsche-by-richard-falk.

Faris, Stephan. "Who Are the Anarchists behind the Rome Embassy Bombs?" *Time*, December 24, 2010. http://www.time.com/time/world/article/0,8599,2039647,00.html.

Farrell, Bryan. "Vandalism, a Dead-End Tactic at Toronto G20 Demonstrations." *Waging Nonviolence*, June 28, 2010. http://wagingnonviolence.org/2010/06/vandalism-a-dead-end-tactic-at-toronto-g20-demonstrations/.

Fattal, Josh. "Was Gandhi an Anarchist?" *Peace Power: Berkeley's Journal of Principled Nonviolence and Conflict Transformation* 2, no.1 (Winter 2006): 4–5.

Ferguson, Kathy E. "Toward a New Anarchism." *Contemporary Crises* 7 (January 1983): 39–57.

Fernández, Frank. *Cuban Anarchism: The History of a Movement.* Translated by Charles Bufe. Tucson, AZ: See Sharp Press, 2001.

Fernandez, Luis A. *Policing Dissent: Social Control and the Anti-Globalization Movement.* Brunswick, NJ: Rutgers University Press, 2008.

Ferrell, Jeff. "Against the Law: Anarchist Criminology." *Social Anarchism* 25 (1998): 5–15. http://library.nothingness.org/articles/SA/en/display_printable/127.

Ferrell, Jeff. *Empire of Scrounge: Inside the Urban Underground of Dumpster Diving, Trash Picking, and Street Scavenging.* New York: New York University Press, 2006.

Ferrell, Jeff. *Tearing Down the Streets: Adventures in Urban Anarchy.* New York: Palgrave, 2001.

Ferrer, Francisco. *The Origin and Ideals of the Modern School.* Translated by Joseph McCabe. London: Watts and Co., 1913. http://dwardmac.pitzer.edu/anarchist_archives/bright/ferrer/origin.html.

Fisk, Larry J. "Shaping Visionaries: Nurturing Peace through Education." In *Patterns of Conflict, Paths to Peace*, edited by Larry J. Fisk and John L. Schellenberg, 159–94. New York: Broadview Press, 2000.

Flood, Andrew. "Anarchism and the Environmental Movement." *Struggle* (April 1995). http://struggle.ws/talks/envir_anarchism.html.

Foer, Franklin. "Protest Too Much." *New Republic*, May 1, 2000. http://greenspun.com/bboard/q-and-a-fetch-msg.tcl?msg_id=0033Wy.

Foreman, Dave, and Bill Haywood, eds. *Ecodefense: A Field Guide to Monkeywrenching*, 3rd ed. Chico, CA: Abbzug Press, 1993.

Foster, John Bellamy, Brett Clark, and Richard York. *The Ecological Rift: Capitalism's War on the Earth*. New York: Monthly Review Press, 2010.

Freire, Paulo. *Pedagogy of the Oppressed.* New York: Continuum, 1970.

Gaarder, Emily. "Addressing Violence against Women: Alternatives to State-Based Law and Punishment." In *Contemporary Anarchist Studies: An Introductory Anthology of Anarchy in the Academy*, edited by Randall Amster et al., 46–56. New York: Routledge, 2009.

Gabbatt, Adam. "Student Protests: After the March." *The Guardian*, November 11, 2010. http://www.guardian.co.uk/commentisfree/2010/nov/11/student-protests-tuition-fees-london.

Gamson, William A. "Reflections on *The Strategy of Social Protest*." *Sociological Forum* 4, no. 1 (1989): 455–67.

Gandhi, Mohandas. Benares Hindu University Speech. Benares, India, February 4, 1916. http://www.emersonkent.com/speeches/benares_hindu_university_speech.htm.

Gee, Teoman. "Antiindividualistic Individuality: A Concept." *Alpine Anarchist Productions*, January 2003.

Gee, Teoman. "Militancy beyond Black Blocs: An Essay." *Alpine Anarchist Productions*, December 2001.

Gee, Teoman. " 'New Anarchism': Some Thoughts." *Alpine Anarchist Productions*, January 2003.

Gelderloos, Peter. "An Anarchist Solution to Global Warming." *Infoshop News*, September 16, 2010. http://news.infoshop.org/article.php?story=20100915231738789.

Gelderloos, Peter. *How Nonviolence Protects the State*. Cambridge, MA: South End Press, 2007.

Gelderloos, Peter. "More Wood for the Fire: Capitalist Solutions for Global Warming." *CounterPunch*, February 1, 2010. http://www.counterpunch.org/gelderloos02012010.html.

Giugni, Marco. "How Social Movements Matter: Past Research, Present Problems, Future Developments." In *How Social Movements Matter*, edited by Marco Giugni, Doug McAdam, and Charles Tilly, xiii–xxxiii. Minneapolis, MN: University of Minnesota Press, 1999.

Giugni, Marco, Doug McAdam, and Charles Tilly, eds. *How Social Movements Matter*. Minneapolis, MN: University of Minnesota Press, 1999.

Goldman, Emma. *Anarchism and Other Essays*. Port Washington, NY: Kennikat Press, 1969.

Goldman, Emma. "Francisco Ferrer and the Modern School." In *Anarchism and Other Essays*, 2nd cd., 151 72. New York: Mother Earth Publishing, 1911. http://dwardmac.pitzer.edu/Anarchist_Archives/goldman/aando/ferrer.html.

Goldman, Emma. "My Further Disillusionment with Russia." 1924. http://www.panarchy.org/goldman/russia.1924.html.

Goldman, Emma. *Red Emma Speaks: An Emma Goldman Reader*. Edited by Alix Kates Shulman. Atlantic Highlands, NJ: Humanities Press, 1996.

Goodman, Paul. "Anarchism and the Ideal University." In *Patterns of Anarchy: A Collection of Writings on the Anarchist Tradition*, edited by Leonard I. Krimerman and Lewis Perry, 449–56. New York: Anchor Books, 1966.

Gordon, Uri. "Against the Wall: Anarchist Mobilization in the Israeli-Palestinian Conflict." *Peace & Change* 35, no. 3 (July 2010): 412–33.

Gordon, Uri. "Anarchism: The A Word." *New Internationalist*, June 1, 2011. http://www.newint.org/features/2011/06/01/anarchism-explained.

Gordon, Uri. *Anarchy Alive! Anti-Authoritarian Politics from Practice to Theory*. Ann Arbor, MI: Pluto Press, 2008.

Gordon, Uri. "Dark Tidings: Anarchist Politics in the Age of Collapse." In *Contemporary Anarchist Studies: An Introductory Anthology of Anarchy in the Academy*, edited by Randall Amster et al., 249–58. New York: Routledge, 2009.

Gordon, Uri. "Israeli Anarchism: Statist Dilemmas and the Dynamics of Joint Struggle." *Anarchist Studies* 15, no. 1 (2007): 7–30.

Gordon, Uri. "Right of Reply: Anarchy in the Holy Land!" *Jerusalem Post*, June 12, 2007. http://www.jpost.com/Opinion/Op-EdContributors/Article.aspx?id=64651.

Graeber, David. "Anarchism, Academia, and the Avant-Garde." In *Contemporary Anarchist Studies: An Introductory Anthology of Anarchy in the Academy*, edited by Randall Amster et al., 103–112. New York: Routledge, 2009.

Graeber, David. *Direct Action: An Ethnography*. Oakland, CA: AK Press, 2009.

Graeber, David. "The New Anarchists." *New Left Review* 13 (January–February 2002). http://www.newleftreview.org/A2368.

Graeber, David. "Occupy and Anarchism's Gift of Democracy." *The Guardian*, November 15, 2011. http://www.guardian.co.uk/commentisfree/cifamerica/2011/nov/15/occupy-anarchism-gift-democracy.

Graeber, David. "Revolution in Reverse." *Infoshop News*, October 16, 2007. http://news.infoshop.org/article.php?story=2007graeber-revolution-reverse.

Graeber, David, and Andrej Grubacic. "Anarchism, or the Revolutionary Movement of the 21st Century." *Irvine Radical Infoshop*, n.d. http://irvineinfoshop.wordpress.com.

Green Anarchist International Association (GAIA). "The Ecoanarchist Manifesto." June 2008. http://www.anarchy.no/eam.html.

Greenwald, Abe. "The Return of Anarchism." *Commentary*, March 2011. http://www.commentarymagazine.com/article/the-return-of-anarchism/.

Grubacic, Andrej. "The Irresistible Charm of Global Anarchism." *The Defenestrator*, March 7, 2010. http://www.defenestrator.org/node/1765.

Guérin, Daniel. *Anarchism: From Theory to Practice*. Translated by Mary Klopper. New York: Monthly Review Press, 1970.

Guérin, Daniel, ed. *No Gods, No Masters: An Anthology of Anarchism*. Oakland, CA: AK Press, 2005.

Guillaume, James. "Ideas on Social Organization." In *No Gods, No Masters: An Anthology of Anarchism*, edited by Daniel Guérin, 247–67. Oakland, CA: AK Press, 2005.

Hall, David L. "Irony and Anarchy: The Utopian Sensibility." *Alternative Futures: The Journal of Utopian Studies* 2, no. 2 (Spring 1979): 3–24.

Harriott, Howard H. "Defensible Anarchy?" *International Philosophical Quarterly* 33, no. 3 (1993): 319–39.

Harrold, Max. "New Police Unit Targeting Anarchists Comes Under Fire." *Vancouver Sun*, July 16, 2011. http://www.vancouversun.com/ news/police+unit+targeting+anarchists+comes+under+fire/5112795/ story.html.

Hass, Amira. "Shin Bet Puts Israeli 'Anarchists' in Crosshairs." *Haaretz*, December 27, 2010. http://www.haaretz.com/print-edition/features/shin -bet-puts-israeli-anarchists-in-crosshairs-1.333140.

Hathaway, William T. "Anarchists for Peace." *Dissident Voice*, February 2, 2011. http://dissidentvoice.org/2011/02/anarchists-for-peace/.

Heckert, Jamie. "Listening, Caring, Becoming: Anarchism as an Ethics of Direct Relationships." In *Anarchism and Moral Philosophy*, edited by Benjamin Franks and Matthew Wilson, 186–207. New York: Palgrave Macmillan, 2011.

Heckert, Jamie, and Richard Cleminson, eds. *Anarchism & Sexuality: Ethics, Relationships and Power*. New York: Routledge, 2011.

Hendricks, Larry. "Ecoterror Suspect Called 'Mastermind.' " *Arizona Daily Sun*, December 17, 2005, A1.

Herod, James. "Palestine: The No-State Solution." February 2009. http://www .jamesherod.info/index.php?sec=paper&id=63&print=y&PHPSESSID=874 c500f14218d34d24d0df6f0992eff.

Herrera, Linda. " 'V for Vendetta': The Other Face of Egypt's Youth Movement." *Jadaliyya*, May 30, 2011. http://www.jadaliyya.com/pages/ index/1723/v-for-vendetta_the-other-face-of-egypts-youth-move.

Hogan, James P. *Voyage from Yesteryear*. New York: Doubleday, 1982.

Honeywell, Carissa. *The British Anarchist Tradition: Herbert Read, Alex Comfort, and Colin Ward*. London: Continuum, 2011.

Horrox, James. *A Living Revolution: Anarchism in the Kibbutz Movement*. Oakland, CA: AK Press, 2009.

Illich, Ivan. *Deschooling Society*. New York: Harrow Books, 1972.

Jarach, Lawrence. "Why I Am Not an Anti-Primitivist." *Anarchy: A Journal of Desire Armed* (Summer 2009). http://anarchistnews.org/node/11324.

Jarboe, James F. "Congressional Testimony: The Threat of Eco-Terrorism." Federal Bureau of Investigation, February 12, 2002. http://www.fbi.gov/ news/testimony/the-threat-of-eco-terrorism.

Jensen, Derrick. "Actions Speak Louder Than Words." *The Earth First! Journal* (September/October 1998). http://www.derrickjensen.org/work/ published/essays-interviews/actions-speak-louder-than-words/.

Jensen, Derrick. *Endgame, Volume 1: The Problem of Civilization*. New York: Seven Stories Press, 2006.

Jensen, Derrick, and George Draffan. *Welcome to the Machine: Science, Surveillance, and the Culture of Control*. White River Junction, VT: Chelsea Green Publishing, 2004.

Juris, Jeffrey S. "Anarchism, or the Cultural Logic of Networking." In *Contemporary Anarchist Studies: An Introductory Anthology of Anarchy in the Academy*, edited by Randall Amster et al., 213–23. New York: Routledge, 2009.

Juris, Jeffrey S. *Networking Futures: The Movements against Corporate Globalization*. Durham, NC: Duke University Press Books, 2008.

Kalicha, Sebastian, and Gabriel Kuhn, eds. *Von Jakarta bis Johannesburg: Anarchismus Weltweit*. Münster, Germany: Unrast-Verlag, 2010.

Kaulbars, Mike. "Diversity of Tactics: The Noise before Defeat." *News Junkie Post*, July 26, 2010. http://newsjunkiepost.com/2010/07/26/diversity-of -tactics-the-noise-before-defeat/.

Kemmerer, Lisa. "Anarchy: Foundations in Faith." In *Contemporary Anarchist Studies: An Introductory Anthology of Anarchism in the Academy*, edited by Randall Amster et al., 200–212. New York: Routledge, 2009.

Kennedy, Scott. "Violence and Anarchists: The Two Don't Go Together." *Santa Cruz Sentinel*, January 16, 2011. http://www.santacruzsentinel.com/ opinion/ci_17109835.

Killing King Abacus. "Some Notes on Insurrectionary Anarchism." *KKA Publications*, 2001. http://www.batko.se/en_issue2_ch6.php.

King, Martin Luther, Jr. "Beyond Vietnam: A Time to Break the Silence." Riverside Church, New York, New York, April 4, 1967. http://www .americanrhetoric.com/speeches/mlkatimetobreaksilence.htm.

King, Martin Luther, Jr. "Letter from a Birmingham Jail." April 16, 1963. http:// www.africa.upenn.edu/Articles_Gen/Letter_Birmingham.html.

Klein, Ezra. "You're Creating a Vision of the Sort of Society You Want to Have in Miniature." *Washington Post*, October 3, 2011. http://www.washington post.com/blogs/ezra-klien/post/youre-creating-a-vision-of-the-sort-of-society -you-want-to-have-in-miniature/2011/08/25/gIQAXug7HL_blog.html.

Knoche, Tom. "Organizing Communities." In *Reinventing Anarchy, Again*, edited by Howard J. Ehrlich, 350–67. San Francisco, CA: AK Press, 1996.

Koch, Andrew M. "Poststructuralism and the Epistemological Basis of Anarchism." *Philosophy of the Social Sciences* 23, no. 3 (September 1993): 327–49.

Kornegger, Peggy. "Anarchism: The Feminist Connection." In *Reinventing Anarchy, Again*, edited by Howard J. Ehrlich, 156–68. San Francisco, CA: AK Press, 1996.

Kovel, Joel. *The Enemy of Nature: The End of Capitalism or the End of the World?* 2nd ed. London: Zed Books, 2007.

Krimerman, Leonard I., and Lewis Perry, eds. *Patterns of Anarchy: A Collection of Writings on the Anarchist Tradition*. New York: Anchor Books, 1966.

Kropotkin, Peter. *The Conquest of Bread*. Edited by Charles Weigl. London: Taylor & Francis, 2006.

Kropotkin, Peter. *The Conquest of Bread and Other Writings*. Edited by Marshall Shatz. Cambridge, UK: Cambridge University Press, 1995.

Kropotkin, Peter. *Ethics: Origin and Development*. New York: Benjamin Blom, 1968.

Kropotkin, Peter. *Fields, Factories and Workshops*. New Brunswick, NJ: Transaction, 1993.

Kropotkin, Peter. *Fugitive Writings*. Edited by George Woodcock. New York: Black Rose Books, 1993.

Kropotkin, Peter. *Kropotkin's Revolutionary Pamphlets*. Edited by Roger N. Baldwin. New York: Benjamin Blom, 1968.

Kropotkin, Peter. *Mutual Aid: A Factor of Evolution*. Edited by Paul Avrich. New York: New York University Press, 1972.

Kuhn, Gabriel, ed. *Neuer Anarchismus in den U.S.: Seattle und die Folgen*. Münster, Germany: Unrast-Verlag, 2008.

La Ganga, Maria L. "Oakland Officials Praise Response to Violence after BART Shooting Verdict." *Los Angeles Times*, July 10, 2010. http://articles.latimes.com/2010/jul/10/local/la-me-0710-oakland-20100710.

Landauer, Gustav. *Revolution and Other Writings: A Political Reader*. Edited and translated by Gabriel Kuhn. Oakland, CA: PM Press, 2010.

Law, Vikki. "Creating Space for Kids in Our Movements." *Left Turn*, August 11, 2011. http://www.leftturn.org/creating-space-kids-our-movements.

Leeder, Elaine. "Let Our Mothers Show the Way." In *Reinventing Anarchy, Again*, edited by Howard J. Ehrlich, 142–48. San Francisco, CA: AK Press, 1996.

Le Guin, Ursula K. *The Dispossessed: An Ambiguous Utopia*. New York: Harper and Row, 1974.

Lewis, Judith. "Earth to ELF: Come In, Please." *LA Weekly*, December 22, 2005. http://www.laweekly.com/2005-12-22/news/earth-to-elf-come-in-please/.

Libertäre Aktion Winterthur (Anarchist Action). "No Solidarity with 'Anarchist' Letter Bombers." *Anarkismo*, January 6, 2011. http://www.anarkismo.net/article/18439.

Libertarian Socialist Organization. "You Can't Blow Up a Social Relationship—The Anarchist Case against Terrorism." Anarres Book Collective, 1979. http://libcom.org/book/export/html/122.

Lovell, Jarret S. *Crimes of Dissent: Civil Disobedience, Criminal Justice and the Politics of Conscience*. New York: New York University Press, 2009.

Lovink, Geert. "Inside Networked Movements: Interview with Jeffrey Juris." *Institute of Network Cultures*, n.d. http://networkcultures.org/wpmu/geert/inside-networked-movements-interview-with-jeffrey-juris/.

Lynd, Staughton, and Andrej Grubacic. *Wobblies & Zapatistas: Conversations on Anarchism, Marxism and Radical History*. Oakland, CA: PM Press, 2008.

MacLachlan, Colin M. *Anarchism and the Mexican Revolution: The Political Trials of Ricardo Flores Magón in the United States*. Los Angeles: University of California Press, 1991.

Malatesta, Errico. "Anarchism and Violence." *Zabalaza Books*, n.d. http://zinelibrary.info/files/Anarchism_and_Violence.pdf.

Malatesta, Errico. "The Anarchist Revolution." *Anarchy Archives* (c. 1925). http://dwardmac.pitzer.edu/anarchist_archives/malatesta/tar.html.

Marshall, Peter. *Demanding the Impossible: A History of Anarchism.* New York: Harper Perennial, 2008.

May, Todd. *The Political Philosophy of Poststructuralist Anarchism.* University Park, PA: The Pennsylvania State University Press, 1994.

May, Todd. "Is Post-Structuralist Political Theory Anarchist?" *Philosophy and Social Criticism* 15, no. 2 (1989): 167–82.

Mbah, Sam, and I. E. Igariwey. *African Anarchism: The History of a Movement.* Tucson, AZ: See Sharp Press, 1997.

McCarthy, John D., and Mayer N. Zald. "Resource Mobilization and Social Movements: A Partial Theory." *American Journal of Sociology* 82 (1977): 1212–41.

McQuinn, Jason. "Why I Am Not a Primitivist." *Anarchy: A Journal of Desire Armed* (Summer 2001). http://www.postcivilized.net/2010/07/why-i-am -not-a-primitivist/.

Messersmith-Glavin, Paul. "Between Social Ecology and Deep Ecology: Gary Snyder's Ecological Philosophy." *Perspective on Anarchist Theory*, 2010. http://www.anarchist-studies.org/node/496.

Milstein, Cindy. *Anarchism and Its Aspirations.* Oakland, CA: AK Press, 2010.

Mondragon Bookstore and Coffeehouse. *Policy Handbook*, 7th draft. May 2011. http://mondragon.ca/wp-content/uploads/2011/05/Policy Handbook-May-20111.pdf.

Moniz, Tomas, and Jeremy Adam Smith, eds. *Rad Dad: Dispatches from the Frontiers of Fatherhood.* Oakland, CA: PM Press, 2011.

Morris, Brian. "Anthropology and Anarchism." *Anarchy: A Journal of Desire Armed* (Spring/Summer 1998): 35–41.

Morris, Brian. *Ecology and Anarchism.* Malvern, UK: Images Publishing, 1996.

MotherJones.com. "Talkback: Ecoterrorists or Earth's Defenders?" *Mother Jones*, February 14, 2002. http://motherjones.com/politics/2002/02/ talkback-ecoterrorists-or-earths-defenders.

Mueller, Robert, III. "Statement Before the Senate Select Committee on Intelligence." Federal Bureau of Investigation, January 11, 2007. http:// www.fbi.gov/news/testimony/global-threats-to-the-u.s.-and-the-fbis -response.

Mueller, Tadzio. "Empowering Anarchy: Power, Hegemony and Anarchist Strategy." In *Post-Anarchism: A Reader*, edited by Duane Rousselle and Süreyyya Evren, 75–94. London: Pluto Press, 2011.

Murphy, Pat. *The City, Not Long After.* New York: Doubleday, 1989.

Murthy, Srinivasa. *Mahatma Gandhi and Leo Tolstoy Letters.* Long Beach, CA: Long Beach Publications, 1987.

Nagler, Michael N. "Crisis or Opportunity? A Gandhian Answer to Financial Collapse." *New Clear Vision*, August 15, 2011. http://www.newclear vision.com/2011/08/15/crisis-or-opportunity/.

Niman, Michael I. *People of the Rainbow: A Nomadic Utopia.* Knoxville, TN: University of Tennessee Press, 1997.

Olson, Joel. "The Freshness of Fanaticism: The Abolitionist Defense of Zealotry." *Perspectives on Politics* 5, no. 4 (December 2007): 685–701.

Olson, Joel. "The Problem with Infoshops and Insurrection: US Anarchism, Movement Building, and the Racial Order." In *Contemporary Anarchist Studies: An Introductory Anthology of Anarchism in the Academy*, edited by Randall Amster et al., 35–45. New York: Routledge, 2009.

Olzen, Jake. "A Modest (Anarchist) Proposal for Egypt." *Waging Nonviolence*, February 14, 2011. http://wagingnonviolence.org/2011/02/a-modest-anarchist-proposal-for-egypt/.

Orton, David. "My Path to Left Biocentrism, Part V: Deep Ecology and Anarchism." *Green Web Bulletin* 72 (2001). http://home.ca.inter.net/~greenweb/GW72-Path.html.

Parel, Anthony. *Gandhi, Freedom, and Self-Rule.* Lanham, MD: Lexington Books, 2000.

Perlman, Fredy. *Against His-story, Against Leviathan.* Detroit, MI: Black and Red, 1983.

Piercy, Marge. *Woman on the Edge of Time.* New York: Fawcett, 1976.

Plekhanov, George. "Anarchist Tactics: A Pageant of Futility, Obstruction, and Decadence?" In *Patterns of Anarchy: A Collection of Writings on the Anarchist Tradition*, edited by Leonard I. Krimerman and Lewis Perry, 495–99. New York: Anchor Books, 1966.

P. M. *bolo'bolo.* Brooklyn, NY: Semiotext(e), 1995.

Prichard, Alex. "Deepening Anarchism: International Relations and the Anarchist Ideal." *Anarchist Studies* 18, no. 2 (2010): 29–57.

Prichard, Alex. "Introduction: Anarchism and World Politics." *Millennium: Journal of International Studies* 39, no. 2 (2010): 373–80.

Purchase, Graham. *Anarchism and Ecology.* Montreal: Black Rose Books, 1997.

Purchase, Graham. "Anarchism and Ecology: The Historical Relationship." *Jura Media*, 1998.

Purchase, Graham. *Anarchism & Environmental Survival.* Tucson, AZ: See Sharp Press, 1994.

Purchase, Graham. "Evolution and Revolution." *Jura Media*, 1996.

Read, Herbert. *Anarchy and Order: Essays in Politics.* Boston, MA: Beacon Press, 1954.

Read, Herbert. "Art as the Basis of Libertarian Education." In *Patterns of Anarchy: A Collection of Writings on the Anarchist Tradition*, edited by Leonard I. Krimerman and Lewis Perry, 406–12. New York: Anchor Books, 1966.

Reclus, Elisée. *Evolution and Revolution*, 7th ed. London: W. Reeves, 1891. http://dwardmac.pitzer.edu/anarchist_archives/coldoffthepresses/evandrev.html.

Robinson, Kim Stanley, ed. *Future Primitive: The New Ecotopias*. New York: TOR, 1994.

Robinson, Sean. "The Elusive Face of Anarchism." *The News Tribune*, July 10, 2011. http://www.thenewstribune.com/2011/07/10/1739559/the-elusive -face-of-anarchism.html.

Rocker, Rudolf. *Anarchism and Anarcho-Syndicalism*. London: Freedom Press, 2001.

Rosebraugh, Craig. "Hit 'Em Where It Hurts." *The Anarchist Library*, Summer 2003. http://theanarchistlibrary.org/HTML/Craig_Rosebraugh_Hit_Em _Where_it_Hurts.html.

Rousseau, Jean-Jacques. *The Social Contract and the Discourses*. London: Everyman's Library, 1973.

Rousselle, Duane, and Süreyyya Evren, eds. *Post-Anarchism: A Reader*. London: Pluto Press, 2011.

Routledge, Paul. "Toward a Relational Ethics of Struggle: Embodiment, Affinity, and Affect." In *Contemporary Anarchist Studies: An Introductory Anthology of Anarchy in the Academy*, edited by Randall Amster et al., 82–92. New York: Routledge, 2009.

Russell, Eric Frank. *The Great Explosion*. New York: Dodd, Mead, and Co. 1962.

Sartwell, Crispin. *Against the State: An Introduction to Anarchist Political Theory*. Albany, NY: SUNY Press, 2008.

Schmidt, Michael, and Lucien van der Walt. *Black Flame: The Revolutionary Class Politics of Anarchism and Syndicalism*. Oakland, CA: AK Press, 2009.

Schneider, Nathan. "Mubarak Fears Chaos." *Waging Nonviolence*, February 4, 2011. http://wagingnonviolence.org/2011/02/mubarak-fears-chaos/.

Schuster, Henry. "Domestic Terror: Who's Most Dangerous?" CNN.com, August 24, 2005. http://www.cnn.com/2005/US/08/24/schuster.column.

Schweizer, Errol. "Free the Land! The Victory Gardens Project." Green Anarchy: For a Free Society in Harmony with Nature, n.d. http://greenanarchy. webs.com/victorygardenproject.htm.

Scott, James C. *The Art of Not Being Governed: An Anarchist History of Upland Southeast Asia*. New Haven, CT: Yale University Press, 2009.

Seyferth, Peter. "Anarchism and Utopia." In *Contemporary Anarchist Studies: An Introductory Anthology of Anarchism in the Academy*, edited by Randall Amster et al., 280–89. New York: Routledge, 2009.

Shantz, Jeff. *Constructive Anarchy: Building Infrastructures of Resistance*. Burlington, VT: Ashgate, 2010.

Sheehan, Seán M. *Anarchism*. London: Reaktion Books, 2003.

Shevory, Thomas C. "Monkeywrenching: Practice in Search of a Theory." In *Environmental Crime and Criminality: Theoretical and Practical Issues*, edited by Sally M. Edwards, Terry D. Edwards, and Charles B. Fields, 183–204. New York: Garland Publishing, 2006.

Shiva, Vandana. *Earth Democracy: Justice, Sustainability, and Peace.* Cambridge, MA: South End Press, 2005.

Shukaitis, Stevphen. "Infrapolitics and the Nomadic Educational Machine." In *Contemporary Anarchist Studies: An Introductory Anthology of Anarchism in the Academy,* edited by Randall Amster et al., 166–74. New York: Routledge, 2009.

Smith, Mick. "Wild-life: Anarchy, Ecology, and Ethics." *Environmental Politics* 16, no. 3 (June 2007): 470–87.

Snyder, Gary. *The Practice of the Wild.* San Francisco, CA: North Point Press, 1990.

Sparrow, Rob. "Anarchist Politics and Direct Action." *Spunk Library*, n.d. http://www.spunk.org/texts/intro/sp001641.html.

Spring, Joel. *A Primer of Libertarian Education.* Montreal: Black Rose Books, 1998.

Starhawk. *The Fifth Sacred Thing.* New York: Bantam, 1993.

Starhawk. *Webs of Power: Notes from the Global Uprising.* Gabriola Island, BC: New Society Publishers, 2002.

Starr, Amory, Luis A. Fernandez, Randall Amster, Lesley J. Wood, and Manuel J. Caro. "The Impact of State Surveillance on Political Assembly and Association: A Socio-Legal Analysis." *Qualitative Sociology* 31 (2008): 251–70.

Story, Brendan, and Margie Lincita. "The Green Scare and Eco-prisoners: A Brief Synopsis." In *Let Freedom Ring: A Collection of Documents from the Movements to Free U.S. Political Prisoners,* edited by Matt Meyer, 692–98. Oakland, CA: PM Press, 2008.

Suissa, Judith. *Anarchism and Education: A Philosophical Perspective.* Oakland, CA: PM Press, 2010.

Sullivan, Dennis, and Larry Tifft. Restorative Justice: Healing the Foundations of Our Everyday Lives. Monsey, NY: Willow Tree Press, 2001.

Taylor, Michael. *Community, Anarchy and Liberty.* New York: Cambridge, 1982.

Taylor, Michael. *The Possibility of Cooperation: Studies in Rationality and Social Change.* New York: Cambridge, 1987.

Templer, Bill. "From Mutual Struggle to Mutual Aid: Moving beyond the Statist Impasse in Israel/Palestine." *Borderlands* 2, no. 3 (2003). http://www.borderlands.net.au/vol2no3_2003/templer_impasse.htm.

The Anarchist Studies Network. "What Anarchism Really Means." *The Guardian,* November 18, 2010. http://www.guardian.co.uk/commentisfree/2010/nov/18/anarchism-direct-action-student-protests.

Thomas, Janet. *The Battle in Seattle: The Story Behind and Beyond the WTO* Demonstrations. Golden, CO: Fulcrum Publishing, 2000.

Thoreau, Henry David. *Civil Disobedience.* 1849. http://www.vcu.edu/engweb/transcendentalism/authors/thoreau/civil/.

Tifft, Larry L. "The Coming Redefinitions of Crime: An Anarchist Perspective." *Social Problems* 26, no. 4 (April 1979): 392–402.

Tifft, Larry, and Dennis Sullivan. *The Struggle to Be Human: Crime, Criminology, and Anarchism*. Orkney, UK: Cienfuegos Press, 1980.

Tilly, Charles. "From Interactions to Outcomes in Social Movements." In *How Social Movements Matter*, edited by Marco Giugni, Doug McAdam, and Charles Tilly, 253–70. Minneapolis, MN: University of Minnesota Press, 1999.

Tilly, Charles. *Social Movements: 1768–2004*. Boulder, CO: Paradigm Publishers, 2004.

Tokar, Brian. *Toward Climate Justice: Perspectives on the Climate Crisis and Social Change*. Porsgrunn, Norway: Communalism Press, 2010.

Tolstoy, Leo. *Government Is Violence: Essays on Anarchism and Pacifism*. Edited by David Stephens. London: Phoenix Press, 1990.

Truscello, Michael. "Imperfect Necessity and the Mechanical Continuation of Everyday Life: A Post-Anarchist Politics of Technology." In *Post-Anarchism: A Reader*, edited by Duane Rousselle and Süreyyya Evren, 250–59. London: Pluto Press, 2011.

Turner, Royce Logan. "Anarchism—A Political Philosophy for the Age?" *Contemporary Review*. n.d.

Various Authors. "Articles on Animal and Earth Liberation Struggles from 'Green Anarchist.'" The Anarchist Library, 2003. http://the anarchistlibrary.org/HTML/Various_Authors_Articles_on_Animal_and _Earth_Liberation_Struggles_from_Green_Anarchist.html.

Ward, Colin. *Anarchism: A Very Short Introduction*. Oxford, UK: Oxford University Press, 2004.

Ward, Colin. *Anarchy in Action*. New York: Harper Torchbooks, 1973.

Watson, David. "Against the Megamachine: Empire and the Earth." In *Environmental Philosophy: From Animal Rights to Radical Ecology*, 4th ed., edited by Michael E. Zimmerman et al., 479–95. Upper Saddle River, NJ: Pearson Prentice Hall, 2005.

Wenzer, Kenneth C. "Godwin's Place in the Anarchist Tradition—A Bicentennial Tribute." *Social Anarchism: A Journal of Theory and Practice* 20 (2006). http://www.socialanarchism.org/mod/magazine/display/27/index.php.

Widmer, Kingsley. "Eco-Anarchism, Unto Primitivism." *Social Anarchism* 18 (1993): 44–52.

Williams, Zach. "O.W.S. Through the Lens of Anarchy." *Downtown Express*, November 23, 2011. http://www.downtownexpress.com/?p=4864.

Winston, Ali. "Anarchists, the FBI and the Aftermath of the Oscar Grant Murder Trial." *KALW News*, January 26, 2011. http://kalwnews.org/audio/2011/ 01/26/anarchists-fbi-and-aftermath-oscar-grant-murder-trial_811029.html.

Wolff, Robert Paul. *In Defense of Anarchism*. New York: Harper and Row, 1970.

Woodcock, George. *Anarchism: A History of Libertarian Ideas and Movements.* New York: Meridian Books, 1962.

Woolf, N. B. "HR 5429 Takes Aim at Animal Rights Terrorism." *National Animal Interest Alliance*, 2000. http://www.naiaonline.org/body/articles/archives/cunning.htm.

Workers Solidarity Movement. "Anarchism, Internationalism & the Euro Zone Crisis." *Anarchist News*, July 10, 2011. http://anarchistnews.org/?q=node/14998.

Zerzan, John, ed. *Against Civilization: Readings and Reflections.* Port Townsend, WA: Feral House, 2005.

Zerzan, John. *Future Primitive and Other Essays.* Brooklyn, NY: Autonomedia, 1994.

Zinn, Howard. "Introduction: The Art of Revolution." In *Anarchy and Order: Essays in Politics*, by Herbert Read, ix–xxii. Boston, MA: Beacon Press, 1954.

Index

About the Author

RANDALL AMSTER holds a JD from Brooklyn Law School and a PhD in Justice Studies from Arizona State University. He teaches Peace Studies and is the graduate chair of humanities at Prescott College; he also serves as the executive director of the Peace and Justice Studies Association. He publishes widely in areas including anarchism, ecology, non-violence, war and peace, social movements, homelessness, immigration, and sustainable communities. Dr. Amster is a member of the editorial advisory boards for the *Contemporary Justice Review* and the *Journal of Sustainability Education*, and is a regular contributor to numerous publications including *Truthout* and the *Huffington Post*; he is also the founder and editor of the news and commentary Web site *New Clear Vision*.